Cecil B Hartley

**Hunting sports in the West,**

Comprising Adventures of the Most Celebrated Hunters and Trappers

Cecil B Hartley

**Hunting sports in the West,**
*Comprising Adventures of the Most Celebrated Hunters and Trappers*

ISBN/EAN: 9783337178000

Printed in Europe, USA, Canada, Australia, Japan

Cover: Foto ©Andreas Hilbeck / pixelio.de

More available books at **www.hansebooks.com**

# HUNTING SPORTS

IN THE

# WEST,

COMPRISING

ADVENTURES OF THE MOST CELEBRATED

HUNTERS AND TRAPPERS.

BY
CECIL B. HARTLEY.

PHILADELPHIA:
PUBLISHED BY BRADLEY & CO.,
No. 66 NORTH FOURTH STREET.
1865.

# PREFACE.

THIS collection of stories is designed to exhibit the western hunters and trappers in their true character. The narratives are all matters of fact and not of fancy, and they have been selected from a great mass of a similar character, on a principle of choice, which the compiler believes will be approved by his readers; the principle, namely, of displaying all the different phases of the western hunter's perilous and adventurous life, as far as was practicable in so small a space.

The reader, it is believed, will find in the volume a sufficient amount of novelty and variety, to repay him for the time spent in perusing its pages; and he will, probably, on closing it, come to the same conclusion which the compiler arrived at long since, namely, that hunting adventures with bears, panthers, wild cats, and other animals of a similar description, are, on the whole, enjoyed much better as one reads them in a book, by a quiet fireside, than as one who goes through them in the forest or field. Tastes, however, differ on this point.

Books of this class are peculiarly fascinating to a large class of readers, especially young persons, who are always delighted with the narratives which abound in wild adventures, thrilling incidents, and hairbreadth escapes. Such narratives, besides being very entertaining, are not without a certain share of positive utility. They display to advantage certain characteristics which are not unworthy of study and imitation, such as patience and perseverance under great difficulties; coolness, and presence of mind in the midst of threatening dangers, endurance of fatigue, hunger, thirst, and cold, without murmuring; and that hardy spirit of enterprise, which has led to some of the noblest undertakings recorded in the history of our country.

The early pioneers of the West were all hunters. They acquired in the pursuit of the bear, the panther, and the bison, those habits of courage, coolness, presence of mind, and indifference to danger, which made them such formidable enemies to the Indians, and such efficient defenders of the infant settlements, which are now large towns and cities.

Boone, the Wetzels, Kenton, Hughs, Clarke, and a thousand other heroes of the West, all commenced their career of victory and glory in the character of hunters;

and they showed themselves worthy of the hardy school in which they were educated. Hunting is useful, not only for the taking of game and the killing of animals of prey, but for the excellent physical education which it confers, and the useful, moral, and intellectual traits which it developes.

# CONTENTS.

|  | PAGE |
|---|---|
| Grand Circular Hunt | 13 |
| Forest Life—Play | 21 |
| Forest Life—Peril | 34 |
| The Prairie | 39 |
| Great Pine Swamp | 47 |
| Hunting on the Arkansaw | 59 |
| Hunting in Arkansas | 82 |
| Hunting Bears and Panthers | 103 |
| A Kentuckian's Account of a Panther Fight | 118 |
| Angling for Bass | 119 |
| Hunting on the Ozark Mountains | 124 |
| Bear and Panther Hunting | 152 |
| Drives | 194 |
| Hunting Adventures of Ichabod Merritt | 200 |
| Perilous Adventures of Mr. Ross Cox | 205 |
| Hunting on the Columbia River | 223 |
| Shooting Wild Turkeys | 230 |
| Hunting the Cougar | 235 |
| The Traveler and the Pole-Cat | 245 |
| Deer Hunting | 251 |

## CONTENTS.

|  | PAGE |
|---|---|
| Scipio and the Bear | 260 |
| Hunting the Grizzly Bear | 266 |
| Hunting the Grizzly Bear in his Den | 273 |
| Curious Method of Hunting the Deer | 281 |
| Bear Hunting Adventure of Ichabod Merritt | 282 |
| Ugly Adventure with a Bear | 284 |
| Adventures in the Backwoods | 285 |
| Hunting a Black Bear in his Den | 295 |
| Adventures of an English Sportsman on the Prairies | 298 |
| Bear Hunting in Arkansas | 309 |
| Colonel David Crockett's Encounter with a Bear | 319 |

# HUNTING SPORTS OF THE WEST.

### GRAND CIRCULAR HUNT.

THE spirit of the Hunters of Kentucky, says the Hesperian, is not not yet extinct.

Rapid as has been the advance of population in the West, and the progress of what is called refined life, during the last quarter of a century—evident as is the aversion or indifference to manly sports, among the great body of the descendants and successors of the Pioneers —much as silks and broadcloths have superseded "factory" and "home-made," and delicate canes and cushioned curricles have taken the place of rifles and the good old horseback exercises; yet one's eyes are now and then gladdened with the sight of a real hunting-shirt upon the back of a true Anakim of the ancient stock, and one's ears occasionally delighted with accounts of attempts to revive and keep up the manly old sports of our fathers.

The following is an account of a regular old fashioned Circular Hunt, which took place in Kentucky, several years since. The readers of Dr. Livingstone's travels, will recognize in it a resemblance to certain hunting sports which he mentions:

We rose in the morning at an early hour, to make

preparation for the sports of the day. The major, who was to be the Grand Master of the Hunt, selected his best rifles, and we went to work moulding bullets. The notes of preparation were sounded in every direction, the negroes laughed, the dogs barked, the horses neighed, and all was bustle and confusion. All the arrangements had been made the previous night, and every man must be at his post by sunrise. The circle was to be three miles in diameter; and all the neighbors within a half-day's ride, were to assist at the ceremony. The centre of the circle was within sight of the major's farm. Here was a large pond or lake, which, being frozen over, had been chosen by universal consent, for the place of meeting. As our starting point was at a considerable distance, the major gave directions for the house to be closed, the windows to be barred and protected from any danger from the infuriated animals; then bidding the females keep close in their asylum, and leaving one of the negroes with a rifle to guard it, we started off. Little Willie, the major's eldest son, a boy of about twelve years of age, after hard entreaty, was permitted to accompany us, under the care of one of the negroes. A small rifle, suitable to his age and strength, was furnished, and he marched before us, proud of his permission, and boasting of his intended glorious warfare on the smaller game.

We reached the appointed place, and exactly at the hour commenced our advance. The hunters were placed at a distance of about fifty yards apart, in order that nothing of consequence might escape. Little Willie kept close to his father at first, but getting bolder as we proceeded, he wandered off ahead, keeping his guardian negro, who was rather old, puffing, and blowing, and scolding at his temerity: "You young rascal," said the privileged old man, "why you no keep along wid me and de rest of the gemmen? Shouldn't wonder if a big 'coon or somethin' or 'noder cocht hole ob you dracly." The young gentleman turned up his nose at his monitor, and shouldering his rifle proudly, shot off into a thicket, while the old man started in full chase, venting his spleen on the branches that impeded him. As the forest in which we were stationed was very thickly covered with brush and elm timber, our progress was very slow. Major Wiley and myself kept as much together as possible. From all parts of the forest we could hear the sharp crack of the rifles, or the louder reports of the shotguns, which were carried by the younger portions of the community, to the great terror of squirrels and turkeys, and other small game.

Occasionally a deer, wounded by the shot of some of the hunters, would appear flying swiftly among the trees, and over logs, disregarding everything in its flight, and, as it met the formidable line, would speed swiftly back again towards the open place, until it fell from the loss of blood. The howling of the dogs was heard continually from every quarter, as, far in advance of their masters, in the language of the country, they "treed" some animal, and were giving notice of their success. Game was plenty; foxes and wolves were started from their caves in every direction. The major, who was an excellent shot, was very successful, frequently bringing down his mark on the full run. For my part, I generally squatted behind a log, being a novice, and took aim when anything was at bay.

Old Pompey and little Willie had been absent from the company for more than an hour, but the major, who was well acquainted with the daring spirit of the boy, was perfectly unconcerned. The only danger he feared was, that he might be injured by some straggling shot from some of the hunters.

We had stopped near some fallen timber, to examine a hollow in a large oak, in which the major supposed a bear might have retreated, when a startling shriek from a thicket, about three hundred yards in advance, arrested our attention. A crack of a rifle was then heard, and another scream, accompanied with a fierce growling. We started off at a run in the direction of the sounds, which seemed to increase as we came near. The major, who was a tall, powerful man, made his way through the brush, as if there were only so many corn-stalks to impede him. There was an open space in the thicket, with a large tree in the centre. The first thing we saw on entering it, was little Willie loading his rifle, and trembling and screaming at the same time. A little beyond him was a terrible scene. Old Pompey was lying prostrate on the ground, bleeding profusely, and an immense panther crouching upon his body, the claws of one of his paws firmly fastened in his side, while with the other, he was keeping a dog at bay, growling furiously, and shaking his immense tail, as I have seen a cat when interrupted in his sport with an unfortunate mouse.

Poor Pompey lay perfectly still, and was only saved by the well-timed exertions of his dog, from being instantly torn to pieces. At our approach the panther crouched still closer to the body of his victim, seemingly meditating another leap. The major's rifle was instantly leveled, but he was fearful that he might strike the negro, and hesitated. Fortunately, at that instant, a fierce attack of the dog behind, incommoded the panther so much that he thought it best to retreat. With one bound he reached the foot of the tree, and was soon high up among the branches. As he sat crouching in the fork, showing his white teeth, and snapping his eyes until they seemed to emit sparks of fire, the major again raised his piece—there was a sharp, quick report, and the animal sprang from the tree with convulsive energy, and fell dead upon the ground. The ball had struck immediately between his eyes.

We ran and raised Pompey from the ground, and examined his wounds. "Oh, massa Wiley, me dead for sartain," sobbed the poor fellow; "pooh-hoo-hoo." But he was much more frightened than hurt. Though considerably torn in his thigh and side, none of his wounds were dangerous. It seemed that Willie, who as usual was ahead of his keeper, had got into the thicket, and seeing the panther among the branches of the tree, was taking aim for a sure shot, when Pompey broke through the bushes, and seeing the panther, uttered a terrific scream that disconcerted the hunter and caused him to miss his aim. Simultaneously with the report, the panther leaped upon the negro, and bore him to the ground. Little Willie, frightened almost to death, commenced reloading his gun and screaming for assistance. It happened very fortunately for both, that we were so near.

Some others of the company now came up, to whom the major consigned Pompey and his young charge to conduct home, while we again pursued our course.

It had been settled that, when the line of the hunt had reached a certain point, for fear of danger, all firing should cease. We were now within sight of the lake. Its surface, which was white with snow, was crowded with the frightened animals, huddled together in a group, or rushing backward and forward, endeavoring to find a point in the line through which to make their escape. But the hunters were so numerous that there was not, at this time, an opening of a yard wide to be discovered. It was now about 11 o'clock, the sun was shining very brightly; and as the animals flew about the surface of the ice, the snow, tossed up by their feet, sparkled like diamonds. It was a glorious sight to see the line gradually forming upon the edge of the lake—the barrels of their rifles reflecting the sunbeams, and almost all arrayed in hunting-shirts, with knives fastened to their belts. There were at least two hundred and fifty animals, of all kinds, assembled within the enclosure—wolves, foxes, deer, bears, and wild cats in abundance. A few of the best hunters were selected to destroy the game. The dogs were called in and fastened, and they proceeded to the work of death. Taking stations as near as possible to the group in the centre, the firing commenced. Every shot told, and as the animals fell, the hills around reverberated with the shouts of the joyous hunters. At length the frightened beasts grew furious; they flew around in all directions, but the line was too formidable for them to break through it, and, wherever they attempted to escape, they were met by the shouts and more terrible knives of the party.

Among the deer was one particularly large and powerful. His antlers appeared at their points, to be at least nine feet apart. His color was a dark red, with only a single white star on his forehead. He made several attempts to escape, but for a while was unsuccessful. His eyes flashed with rage. He pawed the ice, until the spot where he stood was entirely free from snow. He shook his antlered head at the hunters, and appeared several times on the point of attempting to break through the thickest portion of the line. Finally, after coursing around the circle several times, at the top of his speed, he made directly towards the line. Their cries were unavailing; nothing seemed now to have power to drive him back. With a tremendous leap, he passed over the heads of the hunters—cleared every obstacle—and was, in an instant, lost to sight in the depths of the forest. This gallant exploit was received with a tremendous cheer; and I firmly believe that not a hunter in the crowd would willingly have harmed him, had he presented the fairest mark for his rifle. Had it been a man, he would have been sent to Congress.

Now came the most exciting part of the hunt. The unerring guns of the marksmen had thinned the group considerably; and those that remained no longer continued in the centre, but kept running about the ice, at a loss how to act. The heat of the sun and the weight of the animals had considerably weakened the ice. Suddenly, as a volley was poured into the crowd, they all gathered again in the centre of the lake. There was a sharp report of the yielding ice—a crash followed—and the whole body of frightened beasts were soused promiscuously together into the water. Such a struggling, and fighting, and screaming, and fluttering, I could never have conceived of. The deer made desperate efforts to escape: throwing their breasts against the edges of the ice, and endeavoring to obtain a hold upon the slippery surface for their feet. The wolves howled, the foxes barked, and the wild cats fastened their claws into the backs of the deer, and leaped from thence upon the firm ice. I was highly amused at the efforts of a bear—the only one that remained. Blowing and snorting furiously, he floundered about, and threw his paws in every direction; now trying to mount, like the more active cats, upon the backs of the deer, then throwing his huge paws lovingly round the neck of the smaller animals, with his whole weight, and popping them under. He finally succeeded in mounting upon the ice, and, stopping an instant, uttered a tremendous growl, shook the water from his shaggy sides, and started off at a dog-trot. But danger was in poor bruin's front as well as his rear. A shot entered his brain before he had advanced ten paces, and he rolled over on his back, moaned a few times, then breathed his last.

When the last of the terrified victims was despatched, the hunters began the work of skinning and scalping. The shore was lined with the bodies of the slain. Parties went out and collected those that fell during the progress of the hunt; and when all were in, they were counted; seven bears, eleven panthers, and foxes, deer, and wolves, innumerable, were the result of the day's sport. Major Wiley, as master of the ceremonies, divided the spoils among the hunters, and all retired to their homes satisfied and contented with their operations.

## FOREST LIFE--PLAY.*

BETWEEN the St. Lawrence and Lake Champlain, lies a broad tract of country, covered with dense forests abounding with deer, and pierced by lakes and streams, which, beautiful in themselves, are still more attractive to many from their store of trout. Hills, dales, wood, water, leafy trees, herbage, are enough for some people; others cannot be happy amid them, without their rod and gun.

It was to this latter class that the party belonged, who, one fine morning, found themselves in this lovely district, bent on having a holiday; guns, dogs, fishing-rods, tents, all were there for a month's scramble in the forest. Part of their equipment consisted of two boats, one for themselves, the other for their baggage, which was to be sent forward in advance, in order that tents might be pitched for the night, wherever the little company might choose to rest, or linger for a shot. The boats used for this purpose, are small and very light; for "rapids," that is, cataracts in miniature, interrupt many of the American rivers; and when the voyagers come to one of these, the

* "Wild Scenes in North America."—HAMMOND.

boatman pops his craft on his back, and trots off with it to smooth water.

Sailing quietly up the river, the tents were pitched, the first night, on the shores of Round Lake, a fine sheet of water about twelve miles in circumference, and surrounded by hills; tall over-hanging trees shading their encampment, which looked westward over the lake. The accommodation within was primitive enough; their beds being made of green spruce, and fir boughs, while a bundle of the same, bound into a fagot, served for a pillow.

While enjoying the evening breeze, in front of their tents, a long wake in the water, evidently caused by some moving body, attracted their notice. Two of the party set off to make out what it was; and finding it was a deer swimming across, they turned it in the direction of the camp. It bounded ashore close to the tent, sprang right through the group assembled there, and dashed into the thicket behind. A shout greeted his advent among the hunters; given with such hearty goodwill, that in his fright, he leaped, bleating, a dozen feet into the air, and plunged wildly on, crossed the little isle with great jumps, the last being into the water at the other side.

Next morning the boatmen were sent onward with the tents and baggage, while their masters made the tour of this lovely little lake. Near its upper part is a deep indentation, bordered by a luxuriant meadow of Nature's own making, where the wild herbage, and water-lilies that skirt its margin, afford a plentiful pasture for the deer. They were enjoying it to their heart's content: browsing away at grass and flowers; (that must be some-

THE DEER'S LEAP.

thing like bread and butter; the grass, plain bread, the flowers, ornamental and savory butter;) in utter ignorance, poor animals! of the evil designs entertained against them by those two-legged visitors who were so placidly watching them round the corner. The light skiffs were noiselessly paddled to within a short distance of them, and then, coming full into sight, away bounded four-legs in a fright.

These boats may always be paddled very close to the deer, by a clever fellow, who will take care to place himself so that the wind shall not blow *from* him to the animal, otherwise the keen scent of the deer would instantly make him aware of his dangerous neighbor, to whom he would forthwith say good-bye, with more haste than ceremony.

Camping again, on an island in the Upper Saranac, as the sun went down, the fish were jumping about so temptingly, in the quiet lake, that the boat was rowed out to troll for the large dark trout. These lake trout are not nearly so handsome as their cousins of the stream and river; but what is wanting in beauty, they make up in size, and in the sport which they consequently afford the angler, who needs be a skilful hand, to land his fish after having hooked him.

One of these large gentlemen was soon struck, and then began an exciting struggle. Fish, finding he was caught, made off in a hurry to the middle of the lake, bending the rod like a bow in his hasty flight. But Angler was thoroughly up to him. Holding hard on by the butt, he gave him a hundred and fifty feet of line, and by the time he had used that up, Fish began to feel tired, though not so much so as to prevent him holding back with all the dogged determination of a mule, when an insinuating effort was made to draw him to the boat. The intimation that he was wanted, was, however, one that he found it impossible to resist. Then he tried a furious rush forwards, and leaping fairly out of the water, seemed to try to shake his jaw free from the hook, dashing as fiercely down towards the bottom, when he found it of no use. The reel sang again, as it whirled round with his efforts to release himself; but it was of no use, the skilful hand at the other end of the line, constantly and irresistibly urging him towards the boat. At last he rose gasping to the surface, and was drawn within twenty feet of his persecutors; when catching a sight of them, gave strength to his previously passive terrors, and away he darted through the water, a hundred and fifty feet out. But fish against man has small chance, spite of all his twistings and windings, and the end of it was, that he was handed by means of the landing net, into the boat, a splendid ten pound trout! Beautiful and tempting looked he in the clear water; but oh, ten times more beautiful and tempting looked he on the breakfast table next morning! A pleased and happy, nay, conceited man, was his captor.

Pursuing their course, hunting, fishing, story-telling, up Bog River, the lower chain of ponds, surrounded by well wooded hills, was approached; the river here becoming broad and shallow, with meadows stretching away on either side. Here the oars were shipped, and the boatmen paddled along, sitting in the stern of the boats, in each of whose bows stood a marksman, with rifle in hand, for deer, who fed quietly on the borders of the winding stream, were now their game. Each one who failed to bring down his game, was to give place to some one else to try his hand, and so on throughout their number, till they had secured a deer.

As they stole noiselessly along the ins and outs of the crooked river, a deer was suddenly seen to start from among the reeds, and go dashing and snorting across the shallow water, almost close to the head of the boat. Bang, went one gun after him, sending him at rather a brisker pace up hill among the brushwood. Crack went number two: the only effect being to make him take rather longer jumps as he bounded, snorting with terror, into the woods, leaving his pursuers gaping and staring after him: he had evidently the best of it.

The first boat being discomfitted, now gave way to the second, which speedily came in sight of another deer, daintily cropping lilies on the river side. Paddling noiselessly to within a few rods of him, long and anxiously did the sportsman take aim, but before he could draw the trigger, the deer looked up nervously, lowered his long ears, and after one second's disgusted gaze at his enemy, made for the shore at the top of his speed. *Ping*, went a rifle bullet after him, but at random, and the usual result of a random shot ensued; the deer was none the worse, only stimulated by the report into a more railway pace up the bank, where he disappeared among the brushwood. All this was very bad. Two deer, three shots, and venison as far off as ever.

It was now the third sportsman's turn. Gliding quietly along till the boat was within fifteen rods of a deer, tranquilly browsing his pasture, up went the rifle, one moment's pause, and then the sharp report rang out, and wakened the echoes of the shore and surrounding hills. This time mischief was done; the animal sprang into the air, and bounded up the steep as though unhurt, instantly disappearing among the brushwood. There he was speedily found, a noble fellow with branching antlers, but stone dead, the ball having passed clean through him.

Enough for one day; and beside, not loving killing for mere killing's sake, they had determined to shoot no more deer than were needful to keep the spit turning during their forest life.

They were right glad to rest on their rustic beds that night, after the hot fatiguing day. Their van-guard, too, had not been without his share of fatigue; having, in addition to the same long journey, some parts of which he had had to traverse three times over, killed two deer, whose flesh he had cut up into thin slips, and was drying it for future provender, in the smoke of a wood fire, kindled in a bark hut for the purpose. This mode of preparing meat, is called "jerking" it. In very hot countries, it is dried in the sun, the long thin slips, from three to six yards long, being hung in festoons on the branches of some neighboring tree.

On the river, just above the traveller's camp, was a dam constructed of large logs, and slenderer ones laid cross-wise, on which brushwood and earth were placed, so as to make all tight. Entangled in this, a fine young deer was found dead. The poor creature's foot had slipped between the logs; struggling to free himself the leg was broken, and then he must have perished of pain and hunger, a worse death than that from the hunter's rifle.

Going down stream in the morning, the trout were abundant but shy. Hooks and baits were dangled before them in the most tempting manner, but not a single mouthful would any trout among them take. Tired of this, a line, with a weight attached, was let down quietly among them, with a number of bare hooks tied to it. A sudden jerk, and one of the largest was hooked by the tail, and, together with some half dozen more, actually dragged out of the water in this way, tail foremost! A novel mode of catching fish, undoubtedly.

Hitherto the hunters had made no use of their dogs. Game was so abundant that they were not needed. One coursing match, however, was had with them that ended pleasantly enough for the deer. The dogs, doubtless, thought differently of it.

The deer was upon a small island in the lake by which the hunters were camped; and having stationed their boats so as to prevent his reaching the shore, if he took to the water, the dogs were sent to the island. In less than five minutes the stillness was broken by the sudden and fierce cry of the dogs, who had just started their game. Away they went in full cry after him, making the hills and woods ring again as he swept along, doubling and winding, with them still at his heels. Presently he made his appearance close to the hunters; who, caring more for the excitement of the chase than the capture of the deer, received him with such a volley of shouts and halloos, as fairly frightened him back again into the woods, whence he had broken cover. From that shelter, however, the dogs soon chased him into the water; only to be driven back again to dry land. A second attempt to take water was again frustrated, and he retreated, baffled, to the thickets. Thrice was he coursed round the island, the hunters facing him wherever he attempted to escape. At last he plunged desperately into the lake, and swam towards the shore three-quarters of a mile off, his tormentors contriving again to disappoint his design, and compel him to land on a little shrub-covered island, not more than half an acre in size, and that stood at about the distance of half a mile down the lake. When he neared this he sprang on the shore, frantically looking on all sides for some hiding-place, or means of escape. None was to be had; whichever way he turned, there was one of the hunters ahead of him, shouting and driving him nearly mad. This way and that rushed the poor beast in vain, till in despair he took up his post among the bushes, that covered a knoll in the middle of the island; and there, after tossing his head up and down, as he looked from one to another of his enemies, he waited for what might come. He at length quietly lay down. Fortunately for him the hunters had had all they wanted, a coursing match; and, satisfied with his performance, they rowed away, leaving him to recover at leisure from his exertions. Once rid of them, he swam to the main land, and speedily disappeared among his own forests.

Let us see the hunters going to dinner, before we leave them. There are pieces of moose, (a very clumsy kind of deer peculiar to northern countries, and in northern Europe called the elk,) and bear's meat, spitted on long sticks before a roasting fire. Further, there are fresh trout from the lake, whether caught by the head or tail does not matter; the jerked venison that we have heard of, and savoury salt pork; all of which, when ready for dishing, are placed on slices of birch-bark fresh peeled from the trees. While for drinkables, there are tea, and excellent spring water, into which people with whom cold water disagrees, (there are such queer folks in the world,) may pop the least possible dose of brandy. Those who, for once and away, cannot contrive to make a dinner on such materials, are recommended to keep out of the woods!

In this lake country, deer are sometimes hunted by candlelight. A box open in front, and large enough to hold several candles, is placed on a post about four feet high in the bows of the boat. The marksman sits on a low seat close behind this; and then, rowing noiselessly in the dark to where the deer are feeding by the edges of the stream, a full blaze is thrown upon the animal, while the hunter, who is quiet in the shadow, takes aim quietly, and "does" for him.

But deer, and moose, and bears, are not the only "game" to be found in American forests. In some of them, that comical little pig, the peccary, may be met with; and a fierce little beast he is too. His teeth are as sharp as knives; and woe be to man or beast who comes within their reach; for it is "no surrender" with the peccary. The creatures go about in droves of from ten to fifty; will attack anything, or anybody that comes in their way, no matter how well armed; and, as they make a point of fighting it out to the last, till there is not one piggy of their number left, people who are acquainted with their manners and habits generally prefer letting them alone.

Their mode of "camping" at night is particularly droll. Selecting a large hollow tree, overthrown by some storm of wind, the whole drove will get into it, one after the other, *backwards*, so that the last stands guard, with his snout to the entrance. And it is when they have betaken themselves to their lodgings for the night, that the settler, (to whose crops they are terribly destructive,) has his almost sole chance of destroying them.

When he finds one of these hollow trees, he soon ascertains whether or not the peccaries have chosen it for their sleeping-place. If they have, he waits with as much patience as he can, for a regular dull, dark, drizzling day; for in such weather the peccaries, disliking either a wet jacket, or wet feet, or both, do not stir abroad, but remain in the retirement of their hollow tree trunk. On such a day, therefore, the settler, armed with his rifle, takes his stand at day-dawn, directly opposite to what we may call the peccary's front door; concealing himself cautiously among the neighboring bushes. Presently there is light enough to see the nose and sharp eyes of the sentinel peccary. Covering him with his rifle, the trigger is pulled; and with the ball in his brain, over head and heels tumbles poor piggy-wiggy, and there is an end of him. Wakened by the explosion, another pops himself into the opening to see what is the matter; but a second bullet finishes him in like manner. A third, fourth, even more, it is said, may be shot in this way, if the man is only careful enough not to stir the bushes among which he is hidden. If he do, there is an end of the game; out jumps the beast in the door-way, with all the rest at his heels, and together they make a grand charge at the sportsman, who finds a tree, or a light pair of heels, his best defence against these fierce and fearless animals.

A bear hunt in Texas, which is one of the places where peccaries are found, was one day brought to a very amusing termination by these small pests. The bear, trying to climb a tree, as the hunters came up to him, was surrounded by the dogs, who held him on every side in such a manner as to render it difficult to get a shot at him, for fear of wounding them. Bruin was accordingly pitching them right and left, when all at once a drove of peccaries dashed, grunting, upon the whole group. The dogs, cut and slashed by their villanous sharp teeth, slank off howling to their masters. The poor bear found himself in worse hands even than before; and, roaring with pain, rolled about, striking out at random in all directions with his huge paws, at these new assailants: while from the hunters themselves, half angry, half laughing, rose a general cry of "Peccaries! run, run!" And sticking spurs into their horses, they bounded off through the cane brake, only too glad to leave the peccaries and the bear to fight it out between themselves.

## FOREST LIFE--PERIL.

The huge forests of America and Canada are slowly yielding to the axe of the backwoodsman. From morning to night, his broad keen blade glitters in its relentless descent, and the bright flashing chips fly, till down thunders one monarch of the woods after another, whose only revenge on his destroyer, is the leaving of a tormenting stump. Those stumps, dotted here and there among his cleared land, are dreadfully in the way of the plowman, till time or gunpowder, completes their destruction, and enables him to achieve that pride of his heart, a straight furrow.

But if the axe were the only means of turning the woodlands into cornfields and pastures, or into what may some day become so, the process would go on much more slowly than it does. Fire plays no unimportant part in the destruction of the woods; and its fierceness, and the extent of its ravages, are such as none can conceive, save those who have witnessed them. Lightning strikes a dry tree, and kindles up a blaze; or, perhaps, the heaped-up cuttings and brushwood, left by the "lumberer" or backwoodsman, are set on fire, either accidentally, (possibly by a spark from the odious tobacco-pipe, which we can scarcely forgive, even in that comfortless place,) or purposely, to get rid of the rubbish; and the conflagration runs on for miles, consuming, not trees only, and the frightened wild inhabitants of the forest, but, in its unchecked fury, licking up the tender crops, and the homestead itself, of the struggling emigrant, who is too happy if he and his little ones can only escape with their lives. Fire is the best remedy for fires of this kind. That sounds odd enough. In the city, if we catch fire, we run post haste for the "engine," and should think any one mad who prescribed fire instead of water. But the meaning of it is, that the most effectual way of checking the flames in these forest and bush fires is, to set fire to the grass and brushwood, sufficiently in advance of the great fire that is to be extinguished, to allow them to be burnt out, before the wave of flame comes up to the place. If this can be managed,—it requires much care and adroitness,—the original fire, of course, goes out for want of fuel, and there is an end of it. But too frequently the intensity of the conflagration baffles all attempts to stop it. In the hot season, dead trees, broken branches, and decaying underwood, are dry as tinder; the resin and pitch, in such trees as the fir, give unconquerable fury to the flames, while the violent wind, which is the natural result of a vast body of intense heat, fans the whole into still stronger combustion. A fire of this kind that took place in one of the English possessions in North America, in 1825, burnt on for the astounding distance of a hundred and forty miles, and on both sides of a large river. On one bank alone, a breadth of more than sixty miles was ravaged by it.

It appears that for several days previously the woods had been on fire; but this being no infrequent thing, did not produce any alarm. Suddenly, however, a storm of wind arose, accompanied by so extraordinary a sound, like distant thunder, proceeding from the depths of the forests, as made the inhabitants of the district fear that there was something worse than the mere ordinary burning of the woods. The sky also became obscured with the rolling smoke, and speedily the surrounding woods flashed out into flames, whose long forky tongues licked and twined in all directions, around the tall boles of the forest trees, and even leaped high into air, thirty or forty yards above their tops. Two towns were almost immediately involved in the fire, many of whose inhabitants were suffocated or burnt to death, and others dreadfully injured. Those who escaped death, had no time to save any of their property; but, hurrying to the banks of the river, sought in canoes, on rafts, logs of timber, or indeed anything that could float, to make their escape from the horrid death that threatened them on shore. Nor, stripped of everything, were they safe even there; since the violence of the tempest whirled aloft burning logs, fragments of houses, and even trees, and dashed them, flaming, into the water. Of how many of the backwoodsmen perished in the forest, where they had made their homes, no account could be taken; but it is supposed that, altogether, at least five hundred human beings lost their lives in this dreadful fire.

One poor lumberer, (a backwoodsman is so named from his occupation of felling timber or *lumber*, as it is called,) had just built his "shanty" or log-hut, and was beginning to cut timber when the fire broke out. He was told of it by some of his men who had passed through the wood to bring provisions to the little camp, but thought nothing of it, till one of them, leaving the shanty for a minute, came back hastily with news that the fire was a bad one, and within a mile of the hut. They instantly looked out, and as far as they could see, there was nothing but fire, waving high above the forest, and whose roar, like that of a gigantic furnace, was broken in upon, from time to time, by the crash of falling trees.

Not a moment was to be lost. Without staying to save an article, they ran to a small stream a little way off. Some of them thought this would be a sufficient check to the flames, and so contented themselves with crossing it, and going a short distance down its opposite bank, to a spot which they had formerly cleared. The lumberer, however, felt sure, that such a fire as that now raging behind them, would soon leap the comparatively narrow thread of water, and, as safety was on neither bank, he adopted the bold plan of taking refuge *in* the stream itself. Wading into it, therefore, shoulder high, he took up his post underneath a hanging bank, and awaited his fate.

The flames advanced, consuming all before them, and filling the sky with a lurid glare. Their hot breath was almost stifling to the poor trembling wretch in the river. Another minute, and the trees overhead were a-light, and he, forced for safety, to plunge his head under the water, holding it there as long as he could for suffocation, and then taking breath for a moment. When he was able once more to stand erect, the flame was still raging onward before him. Behind, where it had passed, blackened boles were still blazing; mere stumps, with all their branches burnt off, and soon to die out for want of fresh fuel. The poor man dared not, for some hours, leave his watery fortress, but at last made good his escape from the ruined neighborhood. His log-hut and everything in it was of course destroyed; but happily for him, some of the provisions lying in a cellar, escaped injury; otherwise, after escaping fire, he might have died of starvation, before he could get away. His companions were lost in the burning forest.

The lumberer himself told the story of his wonderful escape to Major Strickland, who relates it in the man's own words in his account of his own life as a settler in Canada.

Mr. Charles Murray, in his travels in North America, describes this setting fire to the woods as being done on purpose by Indians, in order to drive himself and his companions from their hunting grounds. In whatever direction they turned for sport, a light was certain to be applied to the dry grass, and then all was in a blaze. On more than one occasion, not only was his sport spoiled, but his life endangered by this practice. One day he had to take to the water, to escape from the flames, which they had kindled in the wood for his particular accommodation. Another time, seeing him cross the prairie to a wood where it was supposed deer might be found, they fired the grass in several places, and in such a direction that the wind, which was rather high, might carry the flames his way. Mr. Murray soon perceived that he could not outrun the fire, and therefore adopted the plan of which we have spoken, curing fire by means of fire. He set the grass near him alight, and then, when it was burnt out, took up his post in the centre of the bare space thus created. He had the satisfaction of seeing that the Indians' fire could not pass its circumference for want of fuel, but skirting it, seized grass, and brushwood, and timber, and so carried the conflagration onwards, leaving him safe, though half suffocated.

The next day he went out in a different direction, where there had not been any fire. But his Indian friends were ready for him. As evening drew on, slight columns of smoke were seen spiring out of the wood; and presently the flames burst forth, the old dry timber crushing down, and sending up a shower of sparks. The flames crept here, along the brushwood, and leaped up there, as they folded themselves round some resinous tree; while huge clouds of smoke, black and lurid, as they shifted about, canopied the magnificent scene.

The Indians had the best of it, for they fairly burnt out Mr. Murray and his sporting friends.

## THE PRAIRIE.

The ponderous buffalo is the "game" of the north American plains or prairies; in some of which it still abounds, notwithstanding the incredible destruction which necessity, or mere wantonness, has wrought among these beasts. Some idea of the killing that goes on among herds of buffalo may be formed from a knowledge of the circumstance of a hundred thousand prepared skins—buffalo robes they are called—being every year brought into

Canada and the United States, where they are much used as a defence from the extreme winter cold of those countries. This is, in addition to any number that may be killed to provide the same covering for the Indians themselves, who are as fond of it as their white neighbors are. The buffalo is to them great gain; they eat him, wear him, and trade him away for the various articles of use and luxury which their uncivilized wandering life fails to provide for them, but the taste for which it by no means extinguishes.

A traveller camping out in the prairies, heard one night a noise like distant thunder, but so prolonged that he was certain it could not be that. Puzzled to account for it, as it came nearer and nearer, he listened with his ear close to the ground, and at length became aware that it was the heavy tread of a herd of buffaloes on one of their usual migrations on the plains; and a momentary gleam of moonlight showed him the prairie, black over with thousands upon thousands of these huge beasts. How to escape their headlong rush became a subject of no little anxiety, as camp and all, placed in their immediate track, was in danger of being borne away by the torrent. Hastening to his comrades, he roused them up; and by dint of repeated volleys from their muskets, aided by the united screeches and yells of the whole party, they succeeded in frightening the monsters into a different path to that which led directly over their encampment, and thus escaped the chance of being crushed to death. The herd, under this double salute, divided into two; one-half thundering off to the plains, while the other tramped through the adjacent river, where their splashing and dashing, as they crossed the water, was heard for hours. Such are the numbers in which these great creatures roam about their native prairies.

It is said that the buffalo is not naturally a fierce animal; but its looks are against it. Its huge head, and rough beard and mane, are not unlike those of a lion, only much larger in proportion to the size of its body. When urged to its speed these are tossed about in what appears to be a most threatening manner; but the poor beast does not mean mischief, unless his pursuers drive him to it; and then, woe betide all that come in his way!

The Indians sometimes manage to slaughter even the largest herds of buffaloes, in what may be called a wholesale way. In order to make it intelligible, some description of the nature of these prairies is needful. They are, as has been said, vast undulating plains, studded here and there with clumps of park-like timber; but these plains are occasionally broken up by great clefts or cañons, which go suddenly, and almost sheer down for many hundred feet. Mr. Kendall, in his account of the Santa Fé expedition, relates that he and his party were traversing one of these plains, in which no break of the surface could be perceived far as the eye could reach, when all at once they found themselves on the brink of one of these tremendous chasms. Its almost perpendicular depth beneath their feet was near three hundred yards, and it was from three to five hundred yards wide. A slender stream, now hidden by some huge rock, now bubbling again into view, coursed along the bottom, wearing its channel into fantastic shapes. The depth, and dark abrupt character of this rent in the earth, made them almost sick as they looked down into it; the more so, perhaps, that there was no way of continuing their journey but by crossing it. Had they been made of india-rubber, they might have rolled themselves up into balls and bowled down to the bottom, with the utmost ease; but even that would have left them with the difficulty of getting up the other side, as apparently insuperable as ever. However, cross it they must; and as, the day previous, they had seen numerous foot-marks of Indians, horses, and buffaloes leading in this direction, it was evident that they had managed to pass it, and if they could, so might others. It was dangerous, but that could not be helped; so the steadiest and best behaved horses and mules were first induced to begin the perilous descent, those who were less to be trusted bringing up the rear. There was one advantage attending their steep downward course, and that was, that, once in for it, and there was no turning back. Onward they were obliged to go; and amid clattering stones, loosened by their tread, and that leaped and bounded down before them, they at last reached in safety the very bottom of this dreary ravine.

Here they rested for a while, as was evident their predecessors the Indians had done; various traces of whose camp were scattered about. The track upwards and out of the cleft was presently discovered; and winding along the ravine till it was reached, afforded ample opportunity for noticing the remarkable and fantastic effects of the rushing waters that coursed throughout it. Pillars, forts, battlements, turrets, by turns presented themselves, till

INDIANS HUNTING BUFFALOES.

the traveler might have imagined himself wandering among the ruins of some deserted city.

Getting down was bad; getting up again was worse. Guns, baggage, and horse furniture had to be carried in the hand, while the animals scrambled up as they could. One of them struck against a piece of rock that stuck out upon the path, and was hurled down by the shock a distance of near twenty feet, falling right upon his back. Of course he was given up for lost; but, thank you, Dobbin had no idea of that. He just got up again, gave himself a shake, and then trying it a second time, marched up as steadily as any of them. The passage of this ravine took them five or six hours; by the middle of the afternoon they had accomplished it, and were restored to the upper world. Continuing their route on the plain, they found that by the time they had left the chasm a few hundred yards behind them, not the slightest trace of its existence was to be seen.

It is into chasms such as these that the mounted Indians, spurring their half-wild horses to their utmost speed, drive the immense herds of buffaloes, when they come upon them in a situation suitable for this purpose. Urged onward by the yells and rapid hoof-trampling behind them, headlong, and tumbling over each other go the huge terror-stricken brutes, a dark avalanche of beast-life, bounding from crag to crag in the rugged descent, till, at the very bottom of the cañon, lies a writhing, swelling heap of carcases, a rich spoil for their savage pursuers to gloat over.

The bow and arrow is a formidable weapon for the destruction of buffalo, in the hands of an Indian. Some of the Pawnees will launch their arrows with such force as to drive them almost up to the feathered end in the animal's body. Nay, it is said that they are sometimes shot clean through him, and left quivering in the ground beyond.

The ordinary way of shooting the buffalo by civilized sportsmen, is either by hunting him or by stalking. The former is accomplished on horseback, bringing him down at a long shot. The latter is done on foot, creeping along from bush to bush, hiding here, and dodging there, keeping in such a direction that the wind may not blow the scent of the hunter to his game, in stealing upon him unawares. But there is no object of the chase that takes so much killing as the poor buffalo. His enormous frame offers so wide a range of others than fatal marks for a bullet, that the chances are, save in skillful hands, that the wretched animal may be riddled before he falls. A well-placed shot behind the shoulder, will soon bring down even his vast bulk; and it should not be forgotten that though we may, and must kill these creatures, it is our duty to do so with as little suffering to them as possible. A bungling sportsman deserves to rank with a butcher; and not even with him, if he is expert at his business.

Hunting buffalo is not the only business of the Indians of the prairie. The wild horse that scours those boundless plains forms a still more exciting chase. No popping at him with rifles, or twanging bow-strings at him; he must be taken alive and uninjured. And my lord is not always so easily caught as his pursuers would wish. If a troop of horses is seen, the mode employed is that of forming a wide circle round them by mounted Indians, who gradually draw nearer and nearer to each other, driving the horses before them, till their prey is within reach of the lasso. The lasso is a long cord with a noose at one end, which the Indians throw with wonderful precision. This is skillfully thrown round the necks of those who are thought best worth taking; and the Indians, riding off with their struggling, prancing captives, soon succeed in making them understand the value of obedience. They may kick, and plunge, and rear, and caper, as they think proper; but it is all of no use. Between a powerful bit, tremendous spurs, and a rider who sticks to his steed like wax, the noble animal is effectually subdued, and henceforth must follow the bidding of another, instead of his own.

If there be but a solitary horse, or the hunters are few, of course there is just a race for it, generally ending in favor of the hunter; who, it must be said, occasionally receives a handsome kick or two from his captive.

## GREAT PINE SWAMP.*

I LEFT Philadelphia, at four in the morning, by the coach, with no other accoutrements than I knew to be

* Of all hunters, Audubon is the most interesting. He hunted with a noble purpose; he saw with the eye, and described with the pen of an artist. This account of the Swamp is extracted from his Ornithological Biography.

absolutely necessary for the jaunt which I intended to make. These consisted of a wooden box, containing a small stock of linen, drawing paper, my journal, colors, and pencils, together with twenty-five pounds of shot, some flints, the due quantum of cash, my gun, *Tear-jacket*, and a heart as true to nature as ever.

Our coaches are none of the best, nor do they move with the velocity of those of some other countries. It was eight, and a dark night, when I reached Mauch Chunk, now so celebrated in the Union, for its rich coal mines, and eighty-eight miles distant from Philadelphia. I had passed through a very diversified country, part of which was highly cultivated, while the rest was yet in a state of nature, and consequently much more agreeable to me. On alighting, I was shown to the travelers' room, and, on asking for the landlord, saw, coming towards me, a fine-looking young man, to whom I made known my wishes. He spoke kindly, and offered to lodge and board me at a much lower rate than travelers who go there for the very simple pleasure of being dragged on the railway. In a word, I was fixed in four minutes, and that most comfortably.

No sooner had the approach of day been announced by the cocks of the little village, than I marched out with my gun and note-book, to judge for myself of the wealth of the country. After traversing much ground, and crossing many steep hills, I returned, if not wearied, at least much disappointed at the extraordinary scarcity of birds. So I bargained to be carried in a cart, to the central parts of Great Pine Swamp, and, although a heavy storm was rising, ordered my conductor to proceed.

We winded round many a mountain, and at last crossed the highest. The weather had become tremendous, and we were thoroughly drenched, but my resolution being fixed, the boy was obliged to continue his driving. Having already traveled about fifteen miles or so, we left the turnpike, and struck up a narrow and bad road, that seemed merely cut out to enable the people of the Swamp to receive the necessary supplies from the village which I had left. Some mistakes were made, and and it was almost dark, when a post directed us to the habitation of a Mr. Jediah Irish, to whom I had been recommended. We now rattled down a steep declivity, edged on one side by almost perpendicular rocks, and on the other, by a noisy stream, which seemed grumbling at the approach of strangers. The ground was so overgrown by laurels, and tall pines of different kinds, that the whole presented only a mass of darkness.

At length we got to the house, the door of which was already opened, the sight of strangers being nothing uncommon in our woods, even in the most remote parts. On entering, I was presented with a chair, while my conductor was shown the way to the stable, and on expressing a wish that I should be permitted to remain in the house for some weeks, I was gratified by receiving the sanction of the good woman to my proposal, although her husband was then from home. As I immediately fell a-talking about the nature of the country, and inquired if the birds were numerous in the neighborhood, Mrs. Irish, more *au fait* to household affairs than ornithology, sent for a nephew of her husband's, who soon made his appearance, and in whose favor I became at once prepossessed. He conversed like an educated person, saw that I was comfortably disposed of, and finally bade me good-night, in such a tone as made me quite happy.

The storm had rolled away before the first beams of the morning sun shone brightly on the wet foliage, displaying all its richness and beauty. My ears were greeted by the notes, always sweet and mellow, of the Wood Thrush and other songsters. Before I had gone many steps, the woods echoed to the report of my gun, and I picked from among the leaves a lovely Sylvia, long sought for, but until then, sought for in vain. I needed no more, and standing still for awhile, I was soon convinced that the Great Pine Swamp harbored many other objects as valuable to me.

The young man joined me, bearing his rifle, and offered to accompany me through the woods, all of which he well knew. But I was anxious to transfer to paper the form and beauty of the little bird I had in my hand; and requesting him to break a twig of blooming laurel, we returned to the house, speaking of nothing else than the picturesque beauty of the country around.

A few days passed, during which I became acquainted with my hostess and her sweet children, and made occasional rambles, but spent the greater portion of my time in drawing. One morning, as I stood near the window of my room, I remarked a tall and powerful man alight from his horse, loose the girth of the saddle, raise the latter with one hand, pass the bridle over the head of the animal with the other, and move towards the house, while the horse betook himself to the little brook to drink. I heard some movements in the room below, and again the same tall person walked towards the mills and stores, a few hundred yards off from the house. In America, business is the first object in view at all times, and right it is that it should be so. Soon after, my hostess entered my room, accompanied by a fine-looking woodsman, to whom, as Mr. Jediah Irish, I was introduced. Reader, to describe to you the qualities of that excellent man were vain; you should know him as I do, to estimate the value of such men in our sequestered forests. He not only made me welcome, but promised all his assistance in forwarding my views.

The long walks and long talks we have had together, I never can forget, or the many beautiful birds which we pursued, shot, and admired. The juicy venison, excellent bear flesh, and delightful trout, that daily formed my food, methinks I can still enjoy. And then, what pleasure I had in listening to him as he read his favorite poems of Burns, while my pencil was occupied in smoothing and softening the drawing of the bird before me! Was not this enough to recall to my mind the early impressions that had been made upon it, by the description of the golden age, which I here found realized?

The Lehigh about this place, forms numerous short turns between the mountains, and affords frequent falls, as well as below the falls deep pools, which render this stream a most valuable one for mills of any kind. Not many years before this date, my host was chosen by the agent of the Lehigh Coal Company, as their mill-wright, and manager for cutting down the fine trees which covered the mountains around. He was young, robust, active, industrious, and persevering. He marched to the spot where his abode now is, with some workmen, and by dint of hard labor, first cleared the road mentioned above, and reached the river at the centre of a bend, where he fixed on erecting various mills. The pass here is so narrow, that it looks as if formed by the bursting asunder of the mountain, both sides ascending abruptly, so that the place where the settlement was made, is in many parts difficult of access, and the road, when newly cut, was only sufficient to permit men and horses to come to the spot where Jediah and his men were at work. So great, in fact, were the difficulties of access, that, as he told me, pointing to a spot about 150 feet above us, they, for many months slipped from it their barrelled provisions, assisted by ropes, to their camp below. But no sooner was the first saw-mill erected, than the axe-men began their devastations. Trees, one after another were, and are yet constantly heard falling during the days; and in calm nights, the greedy mills told the sad tale, that in a century the noble forests around should exist no more. Many mills were erected, many dams raised, in defiance of the impetuous Lehigh. One full third of the trees have already been culled, turned into boards, and floated as far as Philadelphia.

In such an undertaking, the cutting of the trees is not all. They have afterwards to be hauled to the edge of the mountains bordering the river, launched into the stream, and led to the mills over many shallows and difficult places. Whilst I was in the Great Pine Swamp, I frequently visited one of the principal places for the launching of logs. To see them tumbling from such a height, touching here and there the rough angle of a projecting rock, bouncing from it with the elasticity of a foot-ball, and at last falling with awful crash into the river, forms a sight interesting in the highest degree, but impossible for me to describe. Shall I tell you that I have seen masses of these logs heaped above each other to the number of five thousand? I may so tell you, for such I have seen. My friend Irish assured me that at some seasons, these piles consisted of a much greater number, the river becoming in those places completely choked up.

When *freshets* (or floods) take place, then is the time chosen for forwarding the logs to the different mills. This is called a *frolic*. Jediah Irish, who is generally the leader, proceeds to the upper leap with his men, each provided with a strong wooden handspike, and a short-handled axe. They all take to the water, be it summer or winter, like so many Newfoundland spaniels. The logs are gradually detached, and, after a time, are seen floating down the dancing stream, here striking against a rock and whirling many times round, there suddenly checked in dozens by a shallow, over which they have to be forced with the handspikes. Now they arrive at the edge of a dam, and are again pushed over. Certain numbers are left in each dam, and when the party has arrived at the last, which lies just where my friend Irish's camp was first formed, the drenched leader and his men, about sixty in number, make their way home, find there a healthful repast, and spend the evening and a portion of the night in dancing and frolicking, in their own simple manner, in the most perfect amity, seldom troubling themselves with the idea of the labor prepared for them on the morrow.

That morrow now come, one sounds a horn from the door of the store-house, at the call of which each returns to his work. The sawyers, the millers, the rafters, and raftsmen are all immediately busy. The mills are all going, and the logs, which a few months before were the supporters of broad and leafy tops, are now in the act of being split asunder. The boards are then launched into the stream, and rafts are formed of them for market.

During the summer and autumnal months, the Lehigh, a small river of itself, soon becomes extremely shallow, and to float the rafts would prove impossible, had not art managed to provide a supply of water for this express purpose. At the breast of the lower dam is a curiously constructed lock, which is opened at the approach of the rafts. They pass through this lock with the rapidity of lightning, propelled by the water that had been accumulated in the dam, and which is of itself generally sufficient to float them to Mauch Chunk, after which, entering regular canals, they find no other impediments, but are conveyed to their ultimate destination.

Before population had greatly advanced in this part of Pennsylvania, game of all descriptions found within that range was extremely abundant. The Elk itself did not disdain to browse on the shoulders of the mountains, near the Lehigh. Bears and the Common Deer must have been plentiful, as, at the moment when I write, many of both kinds are seen and killed by the resident hunters. The Wild Turkey, the Pheasant, and the Grouse, are also tolerably abundant; and as to Trout in

the streams—Ah, reader, if you are an angler, go there, and try for yourself. For my part, I can only say, that I have been made weary with pulling up from the rivulets the sparkling fish, allured by the struggles of the common grasshopper.

A comical affair happened with the bears, which I will relate. A party of my friend Irish's raftsmen, returning from Mauch Chunk, one afternoon, through sundry short cuts over the mountains, at the season when the huckleberries are ripe and plentiful, were suddenly apprised of the proximity of some of these animals, by their snuffing the air. No sooner was this perceived than, to the astonishment of the party, not fewer than eight bears, I was told, made their appearance. Each man, being provided with his short-handled axe, faced about and willingly came to the scratch; but the assailed soon proved the assailants, and with claw and tooth drove off the men in a twinkling. Down they all rushed from the mountain; the noise spread quickly; rifles were soon procured and shouldered; but when the spot was reached, no bears were to be found; night forced the hunters back to their homes, and a laugh concluded the affair.

I spent six weeks in the Great Pine Forest—Swamp it cannot be called—where I made many a drawing. Wishing to leave Pennsylvania, and to follow the migratory flocks of our birds to the south, I bade adieu to the excellent wife and rosy children of my friend, and to his kind nephew. Jediah Irish, shouldering his heavy rifle, accompanied me, and trudging directly across the mountains, we arrived at Mauch Chunk, in good time for dinner. Shall I ever have the pleasure of seeing that good, that generous man again?

At Mauch Chunk, where we both spent the night, Mr. White, the civil engineer, visited me, and looked at the drawings which I had made in the Great Pine Forest. The news he gave me of my sons, then in Kentucky, made me still more anxious to move in their direction, and, long before day-break, I shook hands with the good man of the forest, and found myself moving towards the capital of Pennsylvania, having, as my sole companion, a sharp frosty breeze. Left to my thoughts, I felt amazed that such a place as the Great Pine Forest should be so little known to the Philadelphians, scarcely any of whom could direct me towards it. How much is it to be regretted, thought I, that the many young gentlemen who are there, so much at a loss how to employ their leisure days, should not visit these wild retreats, valuable as they are to the student of nature! How differently would they feel, if, instead of spending weeks in smoothing a useless bow, and walking out in full dress, intent on displaying the make of their legs, to some rendezvous where they may enjoy their wines, they were to occupy themselves in contemplating the rich profusion which nature has poured around them, or even in procuring some desired specimen for their *Peale's Museum*, once so valuable and so finely arrranged! But alas! no: they are none of them aware of the richness of the Great Pine Swamp, nor are they likely to share the hospitality to be found there.

Night came on, as I was thinking of such things, and I was turned out of the coach into the streets of the fair city, just as the clock struck ten. I cannot say that my bones were much rested, but not a moment was to be lost. So I desired a porter to take up my little luggage, and leading him towards the nearest wharf, I found myself, soon after, gliding across the Delaware, towards my former lodgings in the Jerseys. The lights were shining from the parallel streets as I crossed them, all was tranquil and serene, until there came the increasing sound of the Baltimore steamer, which, for some reason unknown to me, was that evening later than usual in its arrival. My luggage was landed and carried home by means of a bribe. The people had all retired to rest, but my voice was instantly recognized, and an entrance was afforded to me.

## HUNTING ON THE ARKANSAW.

One of the most entertaining narrators of hunting adventures, is Frederick Gerstaccker, a German traveler, who came to this country several years since, apparently for the sole purpose of hunting in the far west. He worked at various employments to raise money, and when he had obtained a supply, would shoulder his rifle, go into the woods and hunt. His book, "Wild Sports in the Far West," is exceedingly entertaining. We make some extracts from it; commencing at a point where, having been employed on a steamboat, he had quarreled with the captain and got set on shore, on the banks of the Arkansaw river. His narrative proceeds thus:

All around me was a solitary wilderness; the river behind me, the ground frozen hard, and covered with a thin sheet of snow, a cold north wind blowing through the leafless branches. I felt in my pocket for my fire apparatus, it was all wet; not a single grain of powder in my powder-horn, and only one barrel loaded. I thought it would never do to discharge my gun for the sake of lighting a fire, and remain unarmed in the wilderness. I cleared away the snow from under a tree, lay down, and tried to sleep; but the wind was too sharp, the cold insupportable, and I was afraid of being frozen. Driven to extremity, I discharged my gun against the root of a tree lighted a match by the burning wadding, collected dry grass and wood, and in a minute or two had a glorious fire.

Although I heard the howls of several wolves, I did not mind them, but enjoyed a sound sleep. Certainly, on the following morning, I trudged on, rather out of spirits, with no powder, and a very hungry stomach.

I followed the direction of the river downwards, in hopes of finding a house. After I had gone some distance, I saw an old half-sunken canoe. I baled out the water with my cap, and found that she was still serviceable. My former intentions of visiting Texas, returned in full force; I decided on crossing to the other side, to look for a house, and procure food and powder, and resolved then to strike off in a south-west direction in search of the route to Texas.

I had hardly gained the opposite bank when I discovered a large flock of wild turkeys. I took aim, and pulled the trigger, forgetting that I had not loaded; they took to the trees on my approach, and I suffered the tortures of Tantalus at the sight; but there was no help for it, and I was obliged to pass on. As it always happens in such cases, I saw quantities of game this day.

Cold and cloudy descended the night, bringing with it the dreaded north wind; I was obliged to lie down without a fire. In order to avoid the bears and panthers, I had climbed up a tree, but the wind was too sharp to make such an airy perch endurable. At length I found a hollow tree, crept in, covered my feet with my game-bag, placed my gun on my left side, and, with my knife in my right hand, I passed one of the most uncomfortable nights of my life. I heard the howling of the wolves, and once the roar of a panther in the distance; but nothing came to disturb me, and the bright morning sun saw me early on the march, for my couch was not inviting enough to detain me. At length, what music to my ears! the crow of a cock and the bark of a dog announced the neighborhood of a farm. I soon perceived the thin, blue smoke of a chimney ascending into the beautiful clear sky, and, with a quickened pace, made towards it, hoping soon to refresh both body and soul.

The good people gave me such a hospitable reception, and placed so much on the table, that, notwithstanding my fearful appetite, there was a great deal more than I could eat. Fortunately, the farmer had a stock of gunpowder, and filled my powder-horn for a quarter of a dollar.

As I was about to depart, he asked if I would not like to join a shooting party; several of his neighbors were coming this morning to search a thicket not far from his house, where they expected to find a bear which had robbed him of many of his pigs. I did not long hesitate, cleaned my gun, loaded the left hand barrel with ball, and the right with buck-shot, and so was ready for anything. We had not long to wait, and all mounted on horseback. We soon arrived at the spot, and rode round and round it; it was the thickly overgrown bed of a former spring. Suddenly the dogs gave tongue, and immediately afterwards the bear started out of his hiding-place. Eager as we were, we could only follow him slowly, on account of the thick underwood; so we hobbled the horses' fore-legs, and pressed forward on foot.

One of the party soon proclaimed that, judging by the bark of the dogs, the bear must have climbed up a tree. Such proved to be the case, and we had hardly discovered him, when I and one of the farmers fired; both balls had taken effect, but a dull cry was the only consequence; two others of the party coming up, fired. He was mortally wounded, drew himself together, and hung by one paw from the tree; as I hit him on the paw with my buck-shot, he fell, and died under the bites of the dogs, who threw themselves furiously on him. His flesh was savory and tender, but he was not so fat as was expected. I remained the night with these kind people, and set off again on the following morning.

Without anything further worth noticing, I came, on the 15th of March, to the bank of the Great Red river, the boundary between the United States and Texas. A farmer who had a canoe, set me over the river, and following a well-trodden path on the other side, I came to a large slave plantation. The overseer, who directed the labors of the negroes, said, at first, that he had no room for me to sleep in; but as there was no other house far and wide where I could find shelter, he at last agreed, and I found a sumptuous supper and comfortable bed.

The land near the river was very swampy, and overgrown with thick canes, but the wood became more open and the ground dryer as I left the river. On the evening of the third day, I again slept at a plantation, and this was the last night I passed in a house for some time to come. The overseer lived in a block-house, and all around stood the smaller huts of the slaves, one for each family. During the hours of labor, he carried a heavy whip to keep the blacks in order; yet he did not seem to feel quite safe amongst these poor, ill-treated people, for he had a pair of pistols in his saddle holsters.

From these quarters I marched along fresh and in good spirits into the forest, which already began to look green. The birds sang so sweetly on the branches, that my heart was joyful and mournful at the same time; I longed in vain for a companion, with whom I could exchange thoughts. A shot echoed from the plantation, and innumerable wild geese rose from the cotton-fields behind me; with a deafening noise they formed their usual triangle, and flew all in the same direction.

Luckily for me, I had in my bag a couple of wild ducks that I had killed and roasted the day before. The forest was mortally dull, and the march began to grow rather tedious, for my rambles in the north were still fresh in my memory. I passed the night very pleasantly by a fire, while my hunger took the second duck into consideration.

Towards noon I came to the little river Sulphur-fork, which I was obliged to wade through, after many vain attempts to find a shallow place, the water coming up to my chest. I began to despair of getting any thing to eat, and, being thoroughly wet, I resolved to come soon to a halt, and dry myself by a fire, when all at once I saw about fifty deer, within shot, all quietly feeding, and taking no notice of me. For an instant I stood petrified; then every fibre in my body beat and trembled with delight. The suddenness of the sight had so excited me that I could not take aim, and I was obliged to wait to collect myself. It was a glorious sight, such a number of those noble animals together; I counted fifty-seven, and derived particular pleasure from the antics of two fawns, which made the most comical bounds, and came very near me without any suspicion. Regret to kill such a beautiful innocent creature withheld my hand for some time, but hunger was not to be cajoled,—I fired, and one of them fell without a cry. The effect of the report upon the herd was quite ludicrous,—each of the hitherto unsuspicious animals became an image of attention, then fled with immense bounds towards the thicket. As I did

GERSTAECKER SHOOTING A PANTHER.

not move they stopped again, and began to feed, but not without frequently raising their heads to listen. The impression which the fall of his playfellow had produced on the other fawn was very different. Far from flying, he came nearer, smelt the poor animal as if he thought it was play, setting his fore-foot several times on the body of his comrade as if to induce him to get up. I had the other barrel still loaded, but thought it would be like murder to injure a hair of the little creature.

As I stepped out from the bushes, the fawn stared at me with astonishment in his large clear eyes; probably he had never seen a man before. He then flew like the wind towards his dam, but stopping now and then as if he expected his comrade. I quickly made a fire on the spot to roast my game, putting the greater part of the back and the brisket on sticks before the fire with hollow bark underneath to catch the dripping for basting; and a delicious meal was very soon the result of this simple proceeding.

Next day, as I was going quietly along through forest and prairie, looking out right and left for game or amusement, I caught sight of something in a large oak. Fixing my eyes steadily on it, and coming closer, I recognized the glowing eyes of a panther crouched on a bough, and seemingly ready to spring. I gave him both barrels, one after the other, when he fell from the tree, and died with a fearful howl. He was a large handsome beast, of an ashy gray color, and measuring from seven to eight feet from the nose to the end of the tail.

It was well that I had venison in my game-bag, for the panther would have been a tough morsel. I dragged the rather heavy skin with me till the evening, and slept soundly on it for my trouble. A damp fog came on towards morning, which soon turned to fine penetrating rain, seeming to foretell a disagreeable day; but as I had enjoyed beautiful weather in general, I could not complain. The sky became quite dark, the rain fell heavier, and I was soon wet through. I left the panther skin where I had slept, so that I had no heavy burden to carry. I found my stomach beginning to loathe the quantity of animal food that was put into it, and to long for bread, but I was obliged to divert my thoughts from the subject, and the last remains of the venison were discreetly devoured. Meantime I had killed a turkey, so that at all events I had something in store.

My plan hitherto had been to push on to the nearest eastern settlement; but the road was too long and tedious, so I turned southwards, in order afterwards to proceed eastward towards Louisiana and the Red river. The constant rain made it impossible to light a fire this evening, and I passed a miserable night, for though I tried to make a shelter of pieces of bark, I could not manage it; however, the night came at last to an end, and cold, cross, and hungry as a lion, I went along with only a plucked turkey in my bag.

About noon my day's journey was brought to an unexpected end by a river that had overflowed its banks. The rain had ceased, so that, with better fortune than yesterday, I succeeded in making a fire, and my turkey, divided into four quarters, was soon in front of it. Now, comfortably stretched before my fire, I considered whether I should cross the river; I had no sort of business on the other side, and it seemed absurd to swim across for nothing—so I settled on quitting Texas, and returning to the United States. If I had a friend with me I could have gone on to the shores of the Pacific, but I had no mind to do it alone. When I had finished my repast, I got up and made my way in an E. S. E. direction.

As the rain had left off, I made up to-night for the wakefulness of the last; when I awoke, the fire had burnt out, and the sun was shining through the bursting buds of the trees. I had a good wash in a neighboring spring, and felt like a giant refreshed.

After taking my frugal breakfast, the remains of yesterday's meal, I drew more towards the east, in order the sooner to fall in with human beings, to eat bread, and taste salt. I had occasionally used gunpowder instead of salt, but my store of powder was not sufficient for such a luxury, and it was better to be without salt than without powder.

Gun on shoulder, I trudged slowly and surely on, over hill and dale, through prairies and forest streams, towards the sun-rising, taking sharp notice of all around. While thus proceeding, wrapped in my thoughts suddenly something rustled in a bush in front of me, and a bear started out and took to flight. My ball was soon in his interior; on being hit, he stopped and looked round at me in a fury. Expecting nothing less than an attack, I quietly cocked the other barrel; but his intentions of attacking me, seemed to pass off, and he crept into a thicket instead. I quickly loaded with ball, and followed him; as I approached, he retreated slowly, probably suffering from his wound; as soon as I got a clear view of his head, I fired again, but only grazed his skull. As I ran towards him, his fury increased, and he turned to meet me; on taking aim with my second barrel, at about thirty paces, it missed fire. With open jaws, and ears laid back, he rushed towards me; in this mortal danger I preserved my presence of mind. Dropping my gun, and drawing my knife, I sprang back a couple of paces, behind a small tree; at this moment, the bear was only a few feet from me. As he rose on his hind legs to embrace me, he was almost as tall as I, and his fiery eyes and long teeth had nothing very attractive; but he was not destined to know the taste of my flesh.

I was quite collected, feeling sure that one or the other must die. The moment he tried to grasp me, I thrust my long double-edged hunting knife into the yawning abyss of his jaws, and boring it into his brain, I brought him to the ground. I did not then know better, but I ought to have sprung back after wounding him, and then I should have escaped unhurt. As it was, he dragged away my coat in falling, and tore my arm slightly. I thanked God that it was no worse. There I sat on the sweet smelling heath, with my coat all in rags, and no other to put on. To assuage my sorrow, I cut a large steak from the bear, which tasted particularly good after my severe exertions. I carried away the skin. In the evening, I fell in with a herd of deer, but did not fire at them, as I was well provided with meat.

On the following evening, I heard a shot. The sound ran through me like an electric shock. There were, then, other people in this wilderness, and not very far off, for the shooter must be on the other side of the nearest hill. I turned rapidly in the direction whence the sound came, and had hardly gained the crest of the hill, when a romantic and variegated scene spread itself before my eyes.

It was an Indian camp, and all were occupied in pitching their tents, and preparing for the night. Here, were some cutting tent-poles with their tomahawks; there, women collecting firewood for cooking; men securing the horses by hobbling their forelegs; another skinning a deer. In short, it was life in the wilds in highest force. I should never have tired of looking at these noble muscular figures, their faces marked with various ochres, their heads adorned with feathers, and their bright-colored dresses.

I was not long allowed to remain a spectator, for the dogs barked and ran at me. Breaking off a green bough, I went with it to the camp. The Indians called off the dogs, and all eyes were now directed towards the stranger. Going up to a group of young men, who were stretching a deer-skin, I asked if any of them spoke English, and was directed to an elderly man, who was sitting smoking under a tree, and watching me. I told him that I was a traveler, that I wished to return to the banks of the Red river, and asked if I could pass the night in his camp. A considerable group of young men had, in the meantime, assembled round us. At length the old man asked, "Are white men so scarce that you come alone into the wilderness?" I replied that I had only come for the sake of shooting, and now wished to return. Instead of an answer, he silently gave me his pipe, out of which I took a few whiffs, and then handed it to one of the Indians standing near me. He did the same, and returned it to the chief. I now sat down beside him. He asked a great many questions, amongst others, how I had torn my coat so badly? Whereupon I related my affair with the bear. He smiled, and translated my account to the others, who also showed interest in my adventure.

The chief then told me that it was highly dangerous for any one unused to these encounters, to risk such a fight, and that it was necessary to spring quickly back after the thrust, the dying bear having sometimes succeeded in killing his enemy. He took particular notice of my double-barrelled gun and hunting-knife, and said that he had never before seen two barrels joined together. He spoke English better than I did, and, what was very agreeable, he spoke slowly.

The Indians belonged to the Choctaw tribe, and were come out of Arkansas in search of game. As night came on, fires were burning all around us, and the women, among whom were some beautiful figures, cooked the suppers, while the men quietly smoked their pipes. Finding the Indian fashion of staring at the fire, rather tedious, I made several attempts to engage the chief in conversation, but only received short answers, so that at last there was nothing left for it but to play the Indian, and maintain a dignified silence.

At length we retired to rest. I slept on a bear-skin beside the fire, in front of the chief's tent. Before sunrise, I was awakened by the noise and songs of the Indians who were preparing for a shooting excursion. I jumped up, and was getting ready to join them, but soon remembered that, with my ragged coat, I could not venture among the thorns; I should have been caught every moment. I showed it to one of the young men, he immediately ran off, and soon returned with a sort of coat, or rather hunting-shirt made out of a blanket. He made signs that he would sell it to me, and was delighted to receive a dollar for it, with the rags of my green coat into the bargain. For a second dollar, I obtained his embroidered belt, and was now quite set up again. Resolving to be quite an Indian for the time, I left my game bag in the camp.

We set off, sixteen in number, all on foot, some of the Indians with firearms, others with bows and arrows, with which they can hit their mark at a great distance. I attached myself to one of the young men with a bow and arrows, and, as we could not understand each other's language, we proceeded in silence. Each of us had provisions, which we ate as we went along. It may have been about noon when we saw a herd of deer. My companion went round to gain the wind of them, and shot a couple with his unerring arrows. Away flew the others in headlong fright, coming directly towards me, in such blind haste, that the leader of the herd, a fat buck of eleven, was little more than ten paces off, when he discovered me. My ball pierced his heart, and he fell without a cry. The rest flew in all directions.

We were obliged to return to the camp for horses to carry our booty. My companion started off in a straight line for the camp, which I should never have been able to find again. It was only a few miles distant, although I thought it must be at least half a day's journey behind us. On arriving at the camp, we each mounted on horseback, and rode off at a quick trot to the place where our game lay, which we found without difficulty, the Indian having marked several trees with his tomahawk as we returned. The last prize we came to was my buck, and on him we saw a wild-cat preparing to enjoy itself. The Indian rushed forward, and the cat, which did not perceive him till too late, flew up a tree, whence an arrow from the sure hand of my companion soon brought it to the ground. It was of a gray color, and larger than the domestic cat. When these animals are irritated they will attack men: my comrade carried off the skin.

We rode back with our booty to the camp, and were received with cheers. The party all returned one after the other, most of them with game, one with an immense bear that he had killed, the largest I had yet seen.

While cooking was going on, the young men danced and sang, the women taking no part in their amusements, but quietly continuing their occupations.

On the following morning the chief said that he had set a wolf-trap, and we went to see if anything had been caught. As there was plenty of food in the camp, we all went together, except three, who, having killed nothing yesterday, set off to try their luck again to-day. We took four large strong dogs with us, and followed the chief. With a triumphant smile, he showed me where he had set the trap, and near it a trace of blood; it was shown to the dogs, and they followed it up in full cry.

After running about a mile, they barked louder and

A WOLF WORRIED TO DEATH BY DOGS.

louder. We hurried on as fast as we could, and found the wolf at his last gasp under the furious attack of the dogs. They were immediately called off, and appeared to have suffered considerably, particularly one, whose ear the wolf, a great black beast, had bitten quite away.

These traps are set with a bait, but not fastened, for if the wolf is caught, and the trap should be immovable, he would bite off his own leg sooner than let himself be taken. So the trap is only fastened by a chain to an iron clog with four hooks; as soon as the wolf finds himself caught, he attempts to hurry away with the trap, but is detained every moment by the hooks catching in the roots and bushes; yet he manages to get clear again, and has been known to take the iron clog in his mouth—but the trap still remains a hinderance, and he is easily traced.

By this time I had enjoyed Indian life long enough, and wished myself back again in more civilized society; yet I remained another day with them, during which we shot at a mark with bows and arrows, and I caused many a smile among the Indians, as I shot a foot wide of the mark, which they seldom missed. We next threw tomahawks at a tree, and in this practice I was rather more successful.

On the following morning I resumed my journey to the east, provided with venison and coarse salt, and as I saw the last Indians disappear behind the trees, it seemed as if I was now for the first time alone in the forest; but I soon became reaccustomed to my former life, and slept again this night, as well as a man can sleep, on grass and fragrant moss.

Next day I came to the Sabine, seeking in vain for a ford; and as the river was considerably swelled, and seemed wider and deeper further south, there was nothing for it but a swim. I made a small raft, which I bound together with creepers, and securing my gun, game-bag, knife, tomahawk, and powder-horn on the top of it, I pushed it before me to the opposite bank.

On the 30th of January, as I arrived at the Great Red river, I saw a farm-house, and the crow of a cock broke on my ear as the music of the spheres. But the house was on the other side of the broad and swollen stream, which rolled along it's dirty red waves at a fearful rate. In vain I shouted and roared myself hoarse; a shot had no better effect. I had made up my mind to hide my gun and other things in the bush, and swim over, when a second shot roused the farmer's attention. He came to the bank, and seeing some one calling and beckoning on the opposite side, he cast off his canoe, and coming cross, was not a little astonishing at finding me alone.

I received a hearty welcome from his family, who were exceedingly amused at the appetite with which I made the bread disappear, and at my enjoyment of the coffee.

As I did not wish to remain here long, I soon came to an agreement with the farmer about the sale of his canoe; he let me have it for four dollars, throwing a smoked leg of venison, a roast turkey, and some loaves of maize bread into the bargain.

I was soon afloat in this hollowed trunk, drifting rapidly down the stream, which carried gigantic trees along with it. The light craft dashed forward like an arrow under the strokes of my paddle, so that, according to a reckoning made afterwards, I must have gone about 400 miles in five days. It was not till late in the night that I ran in among the reeds, and slept quietly in my own property.

On the day after my departure, I fell in with a number of planks; they had probably been washed away from some village on the banks. They had floated against a tree, that was stuck fast in the bed of the river. Intending to take them with me, in the hope of making something by their sale, I paddled to the tree, and, in attempting to secure the planks, I over-reached myself; the current carried away the canoe from under me, and in an instant I was in the water, holding on to the bough of the tree, and close to an alligator. Luckily, the beast was as much afraid of me as I of him, and he disappeared under the water. I quickly swung myself on the bough to reach my canoe, but too late, it was already in the full strength of the current, leaving me hanging on the waving bough, with canoe, gun, powder, and all that I possessed, a prey to the waves. I saw perfectly well, at once, that I must either regain my canoe, or perish miserably of starvation, so I let go the bough, and swam with all my might towards the fugitive. It cost a quarter of an hour's desperate exertion before I reached it, and then I had to push her to the bank, in order to get on board, for any attempt to do so in the middle of the stream, would have upset her. In regaining the canoe I had saved my life.

When my store of provisions was exhausted, I shot wild fowl, and got them cooked at the nearest plantation; for now, as I approached Louisiana, the land was more occupied.

Several hundred miles above its junction with the Mississippi, the Great Red river is blocked up by numbers of trees that have been carried down and become fixed, and although the United States government has caused a passage for steamers to be cut through them, yet I was advised not to attempt it with my canoe, because the current ran through it with such force, that the least obstacle I might encounter, would infallibly overset the canoe. I was therefore obliged to traverse two lakes, called Clear Lake, and Soda Lake, which are connected with the river above and below the Raft, as the collection of matted trees is called.

I saw a great number of alligators sunning themselves on the warm sands. I shot ten or twelve of them, but could never prevail on myself to touch them. They were from three to twelve feet long, and sometimes even eighteen feet. Not far from the mouth of the river, on the fifth day, just about dusk, seeing something white in the water ahead of me, I paddled to it, and laid hold of it, but drew my hand back with a shudder, and the blood ran cold in my veins; it was a corpse; the naked white back alone floated above the surface, head, arms, and legs hanging down; a wound several inches long, was visible on the left side, just under the ribs. I paddled hastily away in sickening disgust, and left the horrid object behind me.

On the following morning I entered the Mississippi, the excessively dirty "Father of Waters." The scenery assumed a more tropical character, and the long waving moss hanging from the gigantic trees, gave it a peculiarly strange aspect. After entering this magnificent river, I took on board fresh provender, not far from the junction, and directed my course towards that "New Orleans," now some 240 miles distant, about which I had heard so much. But on the second day, when I was still some hundred miles from it, a little above Baton Rouge, it came on to blow fresh, and the wind caused such a swell in the river, that I could no longer keep my little craft free of water, indeed it was not without great effort and difficulty that I was able to reach the shore.

There was a farm near the place where I landed, whose owner had a quantity of wood for sale, ready cut, and piled up for the use of steamers. A steamer bound for New Orleans, was in the act of wooding at the time. It would have been folly to have attempted to continue the voyage in such a swell in so frail a craft as mine, and as I found the farmer willing to buy her, we soon agreed as to terms. I transferred my effects to the steamer, and late on the same evening, arrived at New Orleans.

For the night I slept on board, but early the next morning went to a German tavern to refresh myself after all the hardships I had undergone, and to sleep in a regular bed. Oh, how comfortably I stretched myself on the soft mattress! I got up very early to have a look at the place, having no wish to show myself in the costume of a savage, when the streets were thronged. For nine months my hair had been uncut, and during five, no razor had approached my chin; then what, with my old woollen hunting-shirt, my embroidered belt, and the high waterproof boots, which had faithfully held out to the last, people would have thought me more like a scarecrow than a human being; my first visit was to a barber.

I had heard too much boasting and bragging about New Orleans, not to be disappointed in my expectations. I found it by no means so splendidly or so tastefully built as was asserted, and as I walked along the narrow streets my thoughts wandered to the far more agreeable Cincinnati. The only handsome building in New Orleans, and one without parallel, is the St. Charles' Hotel, which certainly is very magnificent.

It is no wonder that the air of New Orleans should be generally so unhealthy, and in autumn, quite pestilential; for the town is built in a complete swamp, and required to be protected by a dam, from being submerged by the river. It certainly was never intended by nature for the abode of man; at most, it is fitted for alligators, frogs and mosquitoes. It is the churchyard of the United States.

## HUNTING IN ARKANSAS.

Mr. Gerstaecker, in the course of his wanderings, made the acquaintance of another man, as fond of hunting as himself, to whom he gives the name of Slowtrap. We suspect that this, as well as all the other names he gives to real personages, is invented for the occasion.

The following is an account of his visit to Slowtrap's dwelling in Arkansas; and some of his hunting adventures in company with his hospitable friend:

At length the swamps were behind us. We crossed a small prairie, passed an old buffalo salt-lick, and arrived at Slowtrap's dwelling, planted on a spur of the hills which ran out into the plains. It was in no way different from the usual log-houses, sixteen feet square, from nine to ten high, with an enormous fireplace, no window, and weighted roof; close by was a field of about seven acres, planted with maize. His wife and children stood at the door as we arrived, and although I knew that they were much attached to each other, and lived happily together, and he had been about three weeks absent, not the least word was exchanged that could be construed into a greeting. "Take my saddle in," said S. to his eldest son, a boy of eight years old, who was leaning on the fence, looking at us as if we were perfect strangers, in whom he had no concern. At last, when the horse was cared for, and all things in their places, S. went into the house, took a seat, and lifted his youngest child into his lap; and then he said, "How do you do, all of you?" This distant reserve of the Americans, so prevalent even in their own families, often struck cold on my heart, and made me regret my native land. Man and wife are often as reserved towards each other as two strangers who meet for the first time, and care not about meeting again. I have seen Americans leave home, to be absent for months, without shaking hands with their wives, or saying "good-bye," and it is the same on their return. I must believe, for the honor of the Americans, that this reserve is mere custom, and does not proceed from any real want of affection, as I have seen proofs of deep feeling amongst them, but it always made a disagreeable impression on me. But still worse was it to see Germans aping this fashion, as often happened to be my lot.

When quietly seated, I took a survey of the dwelling. In two corners stood two large beds, covered with good stout quilts of many colors; between the beds, about four feet from the ground, was a shelf holding a few more quilts, and the linen of the family, which was not over-abundant, comprising three or four articles for each person. Under this shelf were two "gums," trunks of a hollow tree, about a foot in diameter, and two and a half or three feet high, with a piece of board nailed on the bottom. They are applied to all sorts of purposes: I have seen them used as beehives; these, I subsequently found, were one for flour, and the other for salt. Two wooden hooks over the door, supported my host's long rifle, with his powder-horn and shot-pouch. A shelf held some shoemaker's tools, leather, &c., Gun's Domestic Medicine, a family Bible, the Life of Washington, the Life of Marion, Franklin's Maxims, an almanac, and a well-worn map of the United States. Various files, awls, broken knives, and a bullet-mould, were stuck into the crevices of logs near the fireplace. On the left of it were two short shelves, with four plates, two cups, three saucers, some tin pots, and a large coffee-pot, all as bright and clean as possible. In the corner of the fireplace, was an iron pan with a cover, for baking bread, and two saucepans, one broken. Several joints of smoked meat hung from the roof, surrounded by strips of dried pumpkin, suspended on poles.

The above-named boy, a girl of ten, a blue-eyed, flaxen-haired, rosy-cheeked girl of four, diligently munching a bunch of wild grapes, and the little one on my friend's lap, formed the family; they all looked shyly at me, though they had seen me six months before, so that I was not quite a stranger to them.

We had agreed to set off for the mountains at once—but Slowtrap found some business to detain him at home, so it was put off till the next week, and I amused myself in the mean time as well as I could; and as I was acquainted with the country, I took my rifle, and paid a few visits to old acquaintances, returning to Slowtrap's on the 12th December, partly on account of the cold wet weather, and partly to mend my moccasins, which had suffered severely from the sharp stones of these mountains. Slowtrap happened to be mending a pair of shoes at the same time. It is a general practice with the backwoodsmen to make their own shoes, and a regular shoemaker is a scarce article in this part of the world. As they are thrown on their own resources from their youth, these Americans are very skillful in providing for their necessary wants, and are particularly expert with the axe, which they begin to wield as soon as their arms are strong enough to lift it. They use it for a variety of purposes—building houses, laying roofs and floors, forming the chimneys and doors, the only other tool used being an auger; and nothing amuses them more than to see the awkwardness of a new comer, when first he handles an axe. Besides making their own shoes, they under stand enough of tanning to prepare the leather; they make their own ploughs, dig wells, &c.; for all which operations Europeans require so many different workmen.

As we sat together before the fire, there was no difficulty in getting Slowtrap to relate some of his adventures with the Indians in his early days. In the evening we brought in some pumpkins, and as we cut them into thin rings to hang on the poles to dry he began to speak in the following words of the perils he had been exposed to in Kentucky, and his narrow escapes from the Indians: "Kentucky was at that time a wilderness, when my father, my uncle, and myself, arrived near the dwelling of Daniel Boone, to look about for a spot that would suit us; for North Carolina, where we then lived, began to be too populous, and a man who wanted to shoot a turkey or partridge was tired before he had walked half an hour, from the number of fences he was obliged to climb over. I was then just eighteen, as strong as a four-year-old bear, and was delighted at the thought of meeting the Indians. It was about this time of the year, and the game we saw made our hearts bound: numbers of bears, deer, and buffaloes; while the turkeys would hardly get out of our way. It would tire you to tell you of all the sport we had, for no country in the world could boast of more game than Kentucky thirty years ago; but now it is no better there than it was then in North Carolina, and five years hence, a man who wants to shoot a bear in Arkansas, will have many a weary mile to tramp. One evening we arrived at the edge of a cane-brake, and as there was good feeding for the horses, we resolved to pass the night there. We hobbled the forelegs of the horses with some bark of the papao tree, and hung a bell round the neck of my uncle's mare. Yet, not being sure of escaping the vigilance of the Indians, we kept watch by turns. Nothing suspicious occurred till about midnight, when the sound of the bell ceased, which I, having the watch at the time, thought rather extraordinary, as the horses were not in the habit of lying down till morning. The dogs also were restless, particularly a greyheaded bearhound, who gave a howl when the wind came from the quarter where the horses had been left. I did not awake the two seniors, but I passed an anxious night. Towards morning I heard the bell again, but further off, and more to the right. My father woke about daybreak, and I told him what had disquieted me. It seemed rather suspicious to him also, but he thought the horses might perhaps have strayed a little in search of fresh reeds. As soon as it was broad daylight, he took his bridle and rifle, and went with 'Watch,' the old dog, towards the sound of the bell, to bring back the horses. My uncle woke in the mean time. We had set a delicate morsel to broil. I was catching the dripping from some roasting bear's meat, in a piece of hollow bark, to baste the turkey, when my father came back without the horses, and said he had found infallible traces of Indians near our camp. My uncle wished to examine the marks; so we shouldered our rifles, and proceeded to the place where the horses had been feeding the evening before. In one rather moist place there was a very clear impression of a moccasin, and one of the savages had inconsiderately stepped on the trunk of a fallen tree, which being rotten, had yielded to his weight, leaving the mark of a foot. While examining it, we heard a noise in the canes. In an instant our rifles were all directed to the spot; but it was only my horse sticking his head out of the canes, and neighing at sight of us. My uncle now settled that, as he was best acquainted with the cunning and tricks of the Indians, he would seek the horses alone, and nothing we urged could dissuade him from his purpose. He took my father's bridle, and my horse, and was soon mounted, slowly and cautiously following up the trail. Losing sight of him, we went back to the camp to look after our breakfast, which we had forgotten in the first excitement. We remained constantly listening for the sound of the bell, when we heard a shot, and directly afterwards three more in quick succession. We were up in an instant, started towards the sound, and soon heard the gallop of a horse, and saw my uncle advancing at full speed. When he reached us he pulled up short, so that the horse reared. His eyes were glazed;—he was very pale, reeled in his saddle, and fell into my arms, which I extended to receive him. It was well for us that the Indians had not followed him, or we should have fallen an easy prey. My uncle recovered after a short time, and told us, with failing voice, that as he was following up the trail, he distinctly heard the bell again at a little distance, and riding cautiously forward, rather distrustful of the deep silence, he saw my father's horse standing by a fallen tree. He rode up to him, keeping a sharp look-out all round; and just as he leaned over to take hold of the bell-strap which was round his neck, an Indian appeared not fifteen paces off, took aim, and fired; feeling himself hit, he let go the horse, brought forward his rifle, and fired, when more dark figures appeared right and left. He turned his horse, and gave him the spurs. He sank fainting to the ground, and the dark blood flowed out as we opened his clothes. He was hit in three places, and two of the wounds were mortal. After a few minutes he raised himself again, gave us each a hand, which we pressed in silence, drew a deep breath, and fell back a corpse. We buried him on the spot, and vowed a deep revenge, which we faithfully consummated: a few nights afterwards, the wolves were tearing the flesh from three corpses over the fresh grave."

Having finished his tale, my host sat for some time with his head leaning on his hand, thinking of times long past. His wife had fallen asleep: she had, probably, heard the tale many times before, and as it was rather late, we were all glad to retire.

The dogs barked several times during the night, and about an hour and a half before daylight, they were quite furious; supposing their excitement to be caused by raccoons, or opossums, we started up, and took our guns, called the dogs, and went into the piercing cold morning air, though it was too dark to see one's hand; my thin deer-skin moccasins were soon frozen, which by no means added to my agreeable sensations. The bark of the dogs soon showed that they had chased something to a tree. As our feet were dreadfully cold, and it was still too dark to shoot, we lighted a fire, and though the dogs enjoyed its warmth, they never forgot the object of our being there, keeping their eyes fixed on the tree, and giving, from time to time, a short impatient howl. At length a gleam appeared in the east; gradually the forms of the nearest objects became visible; as the light increased, we could make out, on one of the upper branches of a tree, a dark spot, which afterwards was distinctly seen to be a raccoon. S— raised his rifle slowly, and took aim; the dogs jumped up, and looked to and fro from the muzzle of the gun to the dark spot on the tree, giving a slight whine—the piece became steady—a flash—a sharp report—and the creature fell dead from the top of the tree. The dogs seized it instantly, and it cost some trouble to rescue it from their fangs, before the skin was quite spoiled.

We returned to the house, and rested again till breakfast. After breakfast I went out to shoot turkeys, which were very numerous; but when I descended to the lower valley of the river, I found such an abundance of winter grapes, that I thought no more of my shooting, but gathering a good quantity, I lay down under a tree to enjoy them. After lying there about a couple of hours, I was roused by hearing the turkeys calling; so, hiding myself behind a fallen tree, I used my decoy pipe, and ten or a dozen stout fellows came strutting along. When they arrived within about twenty paces I gave a whistle, which brought them to a stand, and I shot the largest through the head. Satisfied with my prize, I returned to the house, and found that the grapes had quite spoiled my dinner.

As the weather turned out fine and warm in the afternoon, determined to hunt in the wood for a swarm of wild bees, which we had sought for in vain about six months before. We took some bait with us, and went to a spot about half a mile off.

To induce bees to take bait in the fall of the year, the hunter looks out for a small open space in their neighborhood, and if he cannot find one, he must make a clearance with his knife and tomahawk, stick a branch upright in the ground, and lay some leaves on it, spread with a little thinned honey. The bees soon discover it, and when they have got as much of the honey as they can carry, they rise in circles, which become larger and larger, till they attain a certain height, then they dash off direct for their own tree, to deposit their store in the general warehouse. The bee-hunter must take particular notice of the line of their flight, which requires a good eye, and then carry his bait some two-hundred yards further in that direction, when the bees will soon flock round it again. If, when loaded, they keep the same course, it is a sign that the tree is still in that direction, and the bait must be carried further, until they fly the other way. Then the bee-hunter will know that he has passed the tree, and that it must be between his present and his last station, and he is not long in finding it. When he comes near the tree, and the bees are at work, their unsteady zigzag flight will betray its proximity.

The first time we moved our bait, the bees flew backward, so we knew that we could not be more than a hundred yards from their tree; but the approaching night prevented our discovering it. Next morning, about ten o'clock, as it began to get warm, we returned to our hunt, and in less than half an hour, found the hole where the little laborers were passing in and out. It was in a nearly decayed, not very large post-oak, a tree that prefers moist soils, though it also grows on hills. It bears small and rather sweet acorns; its wood is very durable, and will remain long in the ground without rotting. I rode hastily back to the house, for we had taken a horse with us for the chase, and returned with a pail, an axe, a knife, and a spoon. The tree soon fell under our blows—smoke was made, the bees stupefied, an opening cut, and a most beautiful sight for a bee-hunter presented itself, in a number of well-filled cells. We filled the pail with the best, ate as much as our stomachs would bear, set the tree on fire, that the bees might not lead us astray in our next hunt, and returned to the house.

As there were several things to be done about the house, we remained at home, cut down firewood, and carried it to the house, ground flour in Slowtrap's excellent steel mill, and when the evening shadows began to lengthen fast, we sat by the fire, and the old fellow, rendered good-humored by the successful bee-hunt, began again with his stories. In the course of the day, we had seen a man pass by with a smooth-bored gun, and as such a thing was a rarity in the backwoods, the conversation turned on this circumstance. He said: "I once had a smooth-bored gun, called a musket, and not far from the house where we then lived, was a small lake, generally covered with wild fowl. One morning I took the old thumper, for it kicked tremendously, and lounged towards the lake to have a shot. I had not gone far along the bank, when I saw through a gap, a number of ducks swimming quietly on the other side of a thick bush; a fallen tree stretching out into the lake, seemed to offer a good bridge to approach them by. When I got to the end of it, and was about sixty yards from the birds, I raised the heavy old musket to take aim, but knowing how old kill-devil kicked, I leant as far forward as possible, with the firm conviction that the recoil would drive me back on the tree. Three ducks were swimming in a line, and thinking this a good chance, I pulled the trigger, leaning, if possible, still further forward in the act; but it only snapped, the expected recoil failed, and I fell head over heels into the lake. I had some trouble in getting back again to the shore, and never saw ducks or musket again."

The sky seemed to promise a continuance of fine weather, and as there was no prospect at present of Slowtrap's visit to the mountains, I resolved to take a little shooting excursion alone. The shooting on the north of the river was not so good as on the south, as there were fewer settlements; so I determined to cross over, and try my luck. A young man of the name of Curly, lived close to the south bank; he was certainly strongly suspected of horse-stealing, but in other respects was a good fellow, and a capital sportsman; his little weakness respecting horse-flesh was a matter of indifference to me, he could not steal any of mine, so I went to the river and hailed, when he soon brought his canoe and carried me across.

He was easily persuaded to accompany me for a few days, first requesting time to prepare some provisions. He lived in a small block-house, close to the river, surrounded by trees, and without an inch of cultivated land; he subsisted mostly by shooting. He had only lately arrived; his mother, wife, and sister lived in the house with him. As he had no flour in store, it was necessary to grind some, but his mill was more like a mortar than anything else. Such mills are frequent in Arkansas. A sound tree is cut off about three feet from the ground, and hollowed by fire, knife, and chisel, till it will hold about as much as a pail; it is made as smooth as possible, and a logger-head, or pestle of hard wood, is suspended to a balanced pole, such as is frequently fitted to wells. It may be imagined that pounding corn in this way is hard work, and as only a small quantity at a time can be prepared, it has to be done before every meal; but this is the only resource of all those who are too poor to buy a steel mill. At last Curly had as much as would serve for two days, in case we shot nothing. He rolled up in his blanket all the things he meant to take, hung his tin pot and tomahawk to his belt, and off we set into the glorious freedom of the forest.

We might have gone about three miles, when we came on the trail of several deer, though we had seen nothing of the precious creatures themselves; and as it began to grow dark, and we found ourselves near a bubbling spring, and a black hawberry bush looked very attractive, we resolved to camp there, and to begin our sport as early as possible in the morning. We cast off our blankets, laid down our rifles, and collected wood for a fire, the night promising to be rather cold. We soon had a fire, of which a volcano need not have been ashamed, and lay down to repose. Our supper consisted

## A PRIZE—CURLY'S MISHAP.

of dried venison, slices of bacon, maize bread, and coffee; a princely repast for the forest; but we hoped to have fresh meat on the morrow.

We breakfasted with the first gleam of light, fed the dogs, and related stories until it was light enough to see the sights on the muzzles of the rifles; then taking our preconcerted directions, we trod lightly and cautiously over the dried leaves. A little before sunrise I heard the crack of Curly's rifle; a few minutes later a second report, then a third. I stood still for about a quarter of an hour, in case a frightened deer should bound past. Nothing moved; I continued my march. I had not gone far when I saw a majestic buck at a walk. I crept lightly to a right angle with his course; when about eighty yards off, I gave a hail: he stopped, and my ball pierced his shoulder; after a few bounds, he lay struggling in the yellow leaves. Bearsgrease rushed after him, but finding him already dead, he only licked the wound, and lay quietly beside him, waiting for his share of the prize. I took the skin and the two legs, hanging the latter on a tree with the skin over them, cut a few bits of the rest for Bearsgrease, leaving the remainder for the wolves and vultures, and continued my march. Soon after I heard a shot, about a hundred yards off on the other side of a thick jungle, and proceeded towards the sound. It turned out to be Curly, who had killed a turkey; he was lying under a tree, and told me, with a mournful visage, that, having wounded a buck, he was following him over some loose stones, when he sprained his ankle, and could hardly move, being obliged to leave the wounded deer to its fate.

As we had traversed the country in a circle, we were not far from our last night's camp. I helped him to it as well as I could, and both being hungry, we roasted the turkey. But Curly had lost all heart for shooting, and, with the help of a big stick, limped slowly homewards, where he could lay up his leg to nurse. I could not tear myself away so soon, and continued my sport alone.

As the sky grew cloudy and threatening, I made a tent of my blanket, and collected wood enough to defy any quantity of rain that might fall. When all this was arranged, I went to the tree where I had left my venison and skin, and to give Bearsgrease another feed from the carcase. But I was too late; the vultures had left nothing but the bones, and had torn the skin on the tree, which, however, I was in time to rescue, and hanging it over my shoulders, with the legs safe in my arms, I returned to my camp. Having made a good fire, and roasted a slice of meat, the coffee being all gone, and the bread reduced to one small piece, I fed my dog, and lay down to repose. About midnight I was awakened by a formidable thunderstorm. Bearsgrease began to howl dreadfully, and close behind me an oak burst into flames. Flash followed flash, while the thunder was incessant; the whole forest seemed to swim in a lake of fiery brimstone, the rain poured in torrents, and the little stream swelled to a foaming river. When the storm ceased, silence and darkness took its place, only disturbed by the rustling of the rain falling perpendicularly on the leaves. My blanket protected me well; I was perfectly dry, and soon fast asleep again. Towards morning it cleared up, and the weather was the most glorious for shooting that could possibly be imagined. I was on foot by daybreak, and by ten o'clock I had three deer hanging to the trees. My last night's repose having been broken by the storm, and yesterday's and to-day's exertions having fatigued me very much, I threw myself under a tree, and enjoyed a delightful nap. The sun was near the horizon when I awoke, and there was hardly time for me to return to camp and collect wood before dark, for the night threatened to be very cold: but it was bright starlight, and my blanket was dry,—so I rolled myself comfortably in its folds.

I lay awake till past midnight, giving the reins to my imagination; and when I fell asleep I dreamed of stretched deerskins, and that Bearsgrease was chasing an immense buck, when his loud barking and howling awoke me. I patted him to keep him quiet, and found his hair all bristling up. I thought wolves must be near us; and listening attentively, I heard the cautious tread of some heavy beast over the dry frosty leaves.

I laid some dry fir branches, which were near me, on the fire, to make it burn up bright, and placed myself between it and the noise of the footsteps, in order to distinguish the eyes of my untimely visitor, and shoot him. Three times I caught sight of two glowing balls, and from their rapid disappearance I was convinced that I had to do with a panther. He went round and round the fire several times, but never close enough for me to distinguish his form;—and I passed half an hour with my rifle at my cheek, in the greatest anxiety, the dog pressing close to my side, with all his nerves on the stretch, following the tread of the panther, and giving a fearful howl every time he passed across the wind.

The brute, not possessing courage enough to attack, at length withdrew; but I remained a good quarter of an hour longer on the watch, till the dog, persuaded that all was safe, had lain down again, when I followed his example, wrapped myself in my blanket, and was soon fast asleep.

The morning was bitterly cold; and as I had nothing on my feet but a pair of thin deer-skin moccasins, not even stockings, I thought of a plan I had learned from an old sportsman, and bathed my feet in the icy cold water of the stream, dried them well, and put on my moccasins. My feet were soon in a glow, and remained warm all the morning.

I started at daylight, and followed the course of the stream downwards; but the bushes grew thicker and thicker, and I was about returning to cross the hill to another brook, when I caught sight of a noble stag in the thicket on my right. I crept quickly and silently round the bush to cut him off, when suddenly I heard a most heart-rending cry from a deer. My first impulse was to rush towards the sound, and on the first movement I made for this purpose, Bearsgrease bounded forwards; but I thought better of it, and a sharp whistle stopped the dog in his career. A second fainter whistle brought him to my side; then, hiding behind a tree, I reflected on what was best to be done.

The shriek certainly came from a deer, and nothing but a panther could have caused it; for if it had been a wolf, all would not have been silent again so soon, as a wolf could not have overpowered a deer so quickly.

Now, I had often heard from Americans how the panther darts on his prey, kills it in an instant, and, after eating his fill, buries or covers up the rest for a future meal. I resolved to try and make sure of the panther, and, if possible, to creep up to him unperceived. I did not then know how difficult it was to outwit a panther; but this time fortune favored me.

After waiting about half an hour, I thought I might make the attempt, and crept lightly and cautiously towards the thicket; the dog, well knowing my object, crept as silently after me. Just as I gained the edge of the thicket, and was looking out for the best place to enter it with the least noise, I heard a light rustling. My heart began to beat violently, the bush opened, and my eyes encountered the fierce orbs of the panther. Doubtless, in the first moment of surprise, he did not know exactly what to do; but his surprise did not last long: a panther has a bad conscience, and justly supposes a foe in every living being not belonging to his own race; and, crouching down about twenty paces from me in the yellow grass, he was preparing either to make a spring, or to hide himself, I could not tell which. But I was not idle; during the time he stooped, my arm had recovered its steadiness, the rifle cracked, the animal made one spring upwards, and fell dead to the earth. Bearsgrease seized him on the instant, and seemed to take exquisite pleasure in shaking the skin of his deadliest foe, and he cast many a longing look behind, when, at my command he followed up the panther's trail. We soon came to the place where he had killed the buck, and covered it with leaves; the skin had been so mauled that it was useless, but I stripped off the panther's, and set out on my return to my camp, deciding to go back to old Slowtrap's, and to commence my march on the Ozark mountains as soon as possible.

On arriving at the camp, I tied up the skin with strips of bark, and although I took very little of the venison with me, I had a heavy load. I reached Curly's in the evening. As it was nearly dark, I had no fancy for crossing the river at night, and creeping for half an hour through a cane-brake, with the chance of getting my eyes poked out; so I remained with Curly. The house was small, but it contained two large bedsteads, one table, three chairs, two plates, and one cup; a hole in the wall did duty for the absent window.

We passed a very pleasant evening. Curly sang well, and gave us a number of Irish comic songs, till, tired with laughing and the severe exertions of the day, I rolled myself in my blanket, and laid myself by the fire. I was up at daybreak, and the river being low, waded through, hastened to Slowtrap's, and spread out my skin. Slowtrap was out shooting wild fowl, which had collected in such numbers on a little river, running into the Fourche le Fave, that I never saw anything like it; they positively covered the water, and a good double-barrelled gun might have done immense havoc, particularly as the steep banks favored the approach to within thirty yards of the ducks.

Supposing the old fellow not to be far off, I took my rifle, and lounged down to the brink of the river; not

DUCK SHOOTING.

with any intention of shooting, as my rifle had too large a bore; but I came upon a string of ducks, not more than fifteen yards off. This was too enticing; I raised the gun, and off went the golden green head of the largest of them. I reloaded, fished out my bird, and was turning up the stream, when I heard Slowtrap's gun above a mile off, and as I had no intention of walking so far, I took my duck by the neck, and walked home. Where was my home? Wherever I happened to be—where I had erected a bark shed, or spread my blanket, or lighted a fire, or where the hospitable roof of a farmer or backwoodsman received me; though the next morning might find me with all my goods on my back—no heavy burden—seeking new shooting ground, and new home. What then?—I went home and commenced mending my old moccasins once more, though they were almost worn out; and as I had some tanned deer-skin, I cut out a new pair, for the others would have never survived a long march.

## HUNTING BEARS AND PANTHERS.

MEANTIME it grew dusk, continues Gerstaecker, and Slowtrap returned with seven ducks, three of which had had their heads shot off. Meat was now plentiful. After S. had made himself comfortable, that is to say, had taken off his hat, laid aside his rifle and pouch, pulled off his wet shoes and stockings, taken unto himself a slice of cold turkey, with its appropriate maize bread and boiled pumpkin, seated himself with his feet to the fire, cut off a piece of his chair to make a toothpick, and begun complacently to pick his teeth, a sure sign that he felt comfortable, all which operations took about three quarters of an hour, he asked, " Well, what's the news?" As the answer was not encouraging, another long pause ensued. When it was quite dark, and a good fire was burning, his wife brought us some bread and milk, of which he partook largely, and then began to thaw, and speak of his exploits; he had fired eleven times, and his piece had missed fire twenty-seven times, a habit the old flint gun had; but he had nevertheless brought home seven ducks, and he had seen a fresh panther trail, the panther had probably seen him from a tree, and jumped down and escaped.

He took particular notice of my panther skin, and thought that there must be a number of them about, but that formerly there were more than twice as many in Kentucky. "Ah, at that time," said he, a man might shoot five or six deer before breakfast, and once I had got up at daylight, and shot two noble bucks, and stalked a third for half a mile, when he got scent of me and escaped. I was tired with my exertions, and had scarcely any sleep all night, for a rascally panther had been howling near me, and several times came so close to the fire that I could make out his form, though he never gave me time to put a ball into him with certainty. So I threw myself under a tree, to rest a little, meaning then to continue my sport; but somehow my eyes closed unconsciously, and I can't say how long I may have lain there, when, still half asleep, I heard a strong rustling among the dry leaves which surrounded me, and felt that they were being thrown over me, so that I was quite covered in a few minutes. Surprise at first, and then an instinct of danger, which I did not quite understand, kept me motionless, awaiting the result: before I had formed any resolution, I heard something moving stealthily away, and cautiously raising my head, saw a panther disappear in the thicket. My first act was to jump up and look to my priming, and as I saw nothing more of the beast, though I was sure that it would return, I resolved to oppose cunning to cunning. A piece of a broken bough lay near; I dragged it to the spot, and covered it carefully with dried leaves, then slinging my rifle on my back, I mounted a neighboring oak, to await in patience, but with a beating heart, the conclusion of the adventure, as the panther might return at any moment. I may have sat for rather more than half an hour, my eyes steadfastly fixed on the place where the panther had vanished, when the bough began to move, and the female panther (for a female it turned out to be) reappeared with two cubs, intending, no doubt, that I should serve as supper for the family. This time she had reckoned without her host. I remained silent and motionless in the tree, watching every movement and keeping the rifle in readiness. She crept stealthily to within fifteen paces of the spot where she had left me covered up with leaves, and crouched down with her green eyes glaring upon the log; the next instant she made a spring, struck the claws of both her fore-feet into it, and buried her sharp fangs deep into the rotten wood. When she found herself deceived, she remained for a moment or two in the same attitude, quite confounded. I did not leave her much time for consideration; my ball crashed through her brain, and she fell dead on her supposed prey without a moan. I killed the two young ones easily enough."

He had hardly finished the anecdote, when the dogs began to bark, and, by-and-by, we jumped up to see what was the matter. It was a neighbor named Collmar, from the other side of the hill. I took the saddle off his horse, and laid it under one of the beds, tied up the horse to a young tree, shoved a roughly-hewn trough before him, which I filled with maize, and his eager munching proved how well he was satisfied with all the proceedings. Collmar had come over the hill to invite us to assist in erecting a new house. He had collected all the logs on the spot, and now, according to American custom, was calling on his neighbors to come and assist in raising them. S. was his nearest neighbor but one, and lived nine miles distant; the next dwelt eight miles further.

I promised to come at all events, but it was against Slowtrap's habit to promise anything two days in advance. Besides, his wife and his youngest child were both unwell. We shortened the evening with stories and anecdotes. Collmar was off with the dawn, to prepare for the following day. I took my rifle and lounged into the forest with Bearsgrease, to look for a turkey. He drove a gang into the trees, at less than half a mile from the house; but the wood was so thick and overgrown, that before I could come up to see which trees they had perched in, they had so hidden amongst the branches that there was not a trace of them to be seen. I therefore whistled for my dog, and hid behind a tree, to await the time when they would think themselves safe, and begin to call. I had not long to wait; ere long they began to cry, and about a hundred yards in front of me, a large cock raised himself on a branch, where he had nestled without my perceiving him. Without trying to get nearer, I took aim at once, and hit the turkey, which fell flapping from the tree; but the bushes were so thick that I should have lost him, had not Bearsgrease dashed in with the greatest intrepidity, in spite of thorns and creepers. The turkey, whose fall had been broken by the wild vines, had no sooner touched the ground, than he made a quick run for a cane-break, and disappeared, with Bearsgrease bounding and barking on his trail. On forcing my way through the canes, I witnessed an interesting struggle between the two. The dog was still young, and the turkey a fellow of twenty or twenty-two pounds, and Bearsgrease, knowing that he must not injure him, tried to hold him with his fore paws, whilst the turkey, which was only wounded in the left wing, constantly succeeded in escaping, and running a yard or two before the dog could pin him again. After watching them for some time, I put an end to the struggle by cutting off the turkey's head with my knife, and carried him home. I then saddled Slowtrap's old pony, and set off over the mountain, to gain Collmar's house before night, leaving Bearsgrease behind me.

The hills and rivers south of the Arkansas, almost all

run like that river, from west to east, and the hills have a peculiar formation. The middle row, or backbone ridge is the highest, and generally on either side are two or three lower ranges of hills, running parallel to the main range, and sloping more and more towards the plain. All the smaller rivers which run into the Arkansas from this side, have such hills between them. I rode slowly up and down these hills looking out for game. I had left my hunting-shirt behind, and a sharp north wind began to chill me a little; but I did not like covering myself with the blanket which lay across my saddle. Suddenly I saw a fox watching me, from the side of a hill beyond a little brook. I raised myself slowly in the saddle, and fired; but my hand shook so with the cold that I missed him. After the report, when the smoke cleared away, the fox had disappeared; I jumped off and ran to the place where he had been standing, to see if I could find traces of the ball, finding none, I reloaded, and returned to the horse, which was quietly grazing. With my left foot in the stirrup, and in the act of throwing my right leg over the saddle, what was my astonishment to see the fox in the same place as before, looking as unconcerned as if nothing had happened! I had to turn my horse before I could take aim, and the fox turned at the same time. A loud whistle made him stop for a moment to see what it was; he was off again before I could fire, but not quick enough to escape my ball. The jump he gave showed he was hit; so, throwing myself off the horse, I hastened after him. When he heard the bushes rustling, he stood still to listen. This allowed me to approach him: the shot had broken his left hind leg; and throwing away everything that hindered me in running, I darted after him. Dragging his wounded leg, he limped along the side of the hill; but, finding that I gained on him, he turned towards the summit. I had run for a good half mile, and too much out of breath to breast the hill, I soon lost sight of him. Heated and tired, I returned to the horse, picking up my rifle, powder-horn, pouch, and cap, by the way, enveloped myself in my blanket, and mounted my patient steed.

I soon crossed the highest summit of the range, and running down by the side of a small stream southwards from the hills, in about an hour and a half arrived at the place where Collmar's house was to be built, and where some of those who had arrived before me were occupied in cutting the logs.

The ground was already prepared and planks cut; other neighbors arrived from time to time with their dogs and guns, and the clearing was filled with laughing, talkative groups.

The horses were hobbled near some reeds, with plenty of maize shaken down in a dry place. In the evening, we all assembled at Collmar's hut, or rather shed, formed of boards fastened together, supported by poles, and containing three roughly-hewn bedsteads, a weaver's loom, and two spinning-wheels. It may have been about fifty feet long and twenty wide, with the floor as nature supplied it. Rifles and saddles lay about; three pairs of deer hams adorned one corner, and dried pumpkins hanging to poles, formed the sky to this paradise.

Immense blazing logs were heaped up in one blackened

corner, and from time to time it was necessary to throw a pail of water over the fire to prevent the planks from burning; and then clouds of ashes threatened us with the fate of Herculaneum and Pompeii.

All sorts of cooking utensils were crowded round the fire—a turkey was stuck upon a stick to roast by the side of an opossum, dangling on a string from the roof. Notwithstanding my long abode amongst people who were passionately fond of this article of food, I could never bring myself to eat a thing with a rat's head and tail, and hand-like claws. The prospect of a good supper was a delight to my hungry stomach. Meantime, I was much diverted by a bargain about cows going on between two old backwoodsmen: but, before discussing this subject, it will be as well to say something of the inmates of the shed. Collmar's wife, a stout, strong-built woman of about thirty-four, with two daughters of fourteen and ten, were all that belonged to the fair sex. They were busily employed about the fire with long-handled spoons, turning the meat in the frying-pans, and basting the turkey and opossum; five smaller figures, with a tin pot of milk in one hand and a lump of maize bread in the other, huddled near the fire, stared at the strangers with all their eyes. The hostess soon made room for the company by sending the children to bed. But to return to the bargainers about the cows. Instead of each praising his own cow, they found so much fault with them, that their own calves, if they had heard it, must have felt ashamed of them. After above an hour's discussion on the faults and failings of their horned property, they observed that they could not part with them without giving something into the bargain, as even their hides were worth nothing. These calumnies were put an end to by the announcement, "Supper is ready." Boxes, chairs, and logs, were placed round the table for seats. Turkey, venison, pork, opossum, maize bread, and the favorite beverage of the backwoodsman, coffee, disappeared so rapidly that soon nothing was left but the bones of the animals, the remembrance of the bread, and the grounds of the coffee. One after another rose when he had had enough, and then the women-folk, who had wisely kept something for themselves, took their places. This is one of the customs of the West which always displeased me. The hostess seldom sits down to table with the men, except now and then at tea or coffee. The other custom, that of rising when they had had enough, without regard to those who remained at table, was not so bad.

After supper the company formed various groups, and the conversation turned on shooting, pasture grounds, the survey of the land that had recently been accomplished, and then on religion. Words soon ran high; for among the company were Methodists, Baptists, Presbyterians, and unbelievers—but all disputes were put an end to by the arrival of two large jugs of whiskey, each containing about four bottles, which Collmar had sent his eldest son, a lad of fifteen, to fetch from a distant store. The boy had been obliged to ride slowly for fear of breaking the jugs.

The old bear-shooters were highly amused at the following account one of the party gave of a bear-hunt that had occurred in North Carolina, and which gave a sad picture of the low state to which field sports had fallen there. "In order to have a bear-hunt several farmers met, and let loose a tame two-year-old bear, giving him half an hour's law, and then following with horse and hound. The bear made straight for some hills, and in about an hour and a half's time was chased into a tree. Not wishing to kill him, no one had brought a rifle; so I went to a house about half a mile off, and borrowed an axe to cut down the tree. The bear looked with inquisitive eyes on the proceedings below, and did not appear to suspect danger, till the tree fell with a tremendous crash; men and dogs threw themselves on the half-stunned bear, to secure him and take him home; but the majority voted for another hunt, so the dogs were held in and the bear let loose. After a time, we all went after him again; this time the chase lasted longer, as the bear swam a river, and to avoid a wetting we turned off to a bridge, giving the bear a great advantage. At length, when we got close to him, he took to an enormous fir-tree, and we all assembled under it; none of us knew how to get him down again. We were several miles from any house, and had left the axe behind us, and he seemed to set us at defiance in his lofty position. Nevertheless he did not seem quite at his ease, and kept looking anxiously first on one side, and then on the other, at the dogs who were jumping and barking round the trunk of the tree. This inspired an old Virginian of the party with a new idea. There were several pine branches lying about; so, taking up one of the heaviest and longest, he commenced striking the tree with all his force. At the first blow, the bear gave a start as if electrified, and at the second or third he darted down like lightning among the dogs, when he was soon secured and taken home. He was once more allowed to run about for a couple of years, when he grew very fat, and in good condition for killing, and he was slaughtered accordingly." When the story was ended, we wrapped ourselves in our blankets, and slept soundly, though occasionally disturbed by some thirsty souls who rose to get a drink. It was lucky for those who were lying in the outer rows that most of the water seekers wore moccasins.

We were up at daybreak, and prepared to build the house by first making a large fire to warm our hands and feet. A man with an axe stood in each corner of the rising house, to cut the mortices and fit them into each other, while the rest of the party raised the logs; no trifling labor, as the house was to have two stories. By the evening, it was all up except the roof, when rain began to fall, and the logs became too slippery to admit of our standing on them; so the completion was left till dry weather.

We remained the night at Collmar's, and departed next day on our various ways, after a very frugal breakfast, for we had devoured all his store.

It was cold and foggy, and I was glad to get to Hogarth's, where I passed the night, returning next day to Slowtrap's. On relating the extraordinary behavior of the fox, he gave one of his smiles, and told many droll stories of the tricks of foxes, and one of a wild-cat, which attacked a man in the marshes of the Cash. The man had gone out early in the morning to shoot a turkey, and hearing a cock gobbling away with all his might, he placed himself behind a fallen tree, and began to use his call, when a wild-cat, probably deceived by the sound, sprang upon him like a fury, and attempted to bite through the veins of his neck. He found it impossible to pull the beast off, and was obliged to kill it behind his back with his scalping-knife; he was confined to his bed for several weeks, before he recovered from the ugly wounds caused by the cat's teeth and claws.

The weather cleared up next morning, and as old Slowtrap was still unprepared for his journey, I resolved to cross the river to shoot, and went to Curly's on the same day. As the deer kept themselves close hid in the daytime, we determined to have a shot in the night. An iron pan was soon prepared, and with my old German game-bag, which had accompanied me in all my wanderings, full of kindlers, our rolled-up blankets on our shoulders, we set off as soon as it was dark. A sharp wind had made the leaves so dry in the course of a few hours, that our footsteps might be heard at three hundred yards off; consequently we saw no deer, and after carrying the pan to and fro for about three hours, we got tired of such useless trouble. On arriving at a small stream, we made a good fire, and after a frugal supper had set our chins for a very short time in motion, we rolled ourselves in our blankets, and lay down each with his dog pressed close to his side.

We rose at daybreak, and following different routes, appointed a rendezvous at Curly's, as we did not mean to make a long affair of it. Bad luck seemed to stick to us, for though we found plenty of trails, we saw no game. At length Bearsgrease found a fresh trail, and followed it up, often looking round to see if I was near

him; so I kept as close as possible. Suddenly he stood still, and pointed, and an old buck got up about fifty yards from us, and made a half circle round us. When I gave a hail, he stood still as if to ask what I wanted. It happened that I was to windward of him; and snuffing the air he gave a bound, which caused my ball to strike too far backwards under his spine, bringing him on his haunches. Bearsgrease had been observing it all with remarkable patience, only turning his head from one to the other; but now giving vent to his eagerness, he darted on the deer, seized him by the jaw, and springing over his back, brought him to the ground. I had now a good opportunity of cutting the deer's throat, but I wished to give the dog a little practice, and I watched the struggle with the greatest interest. The buck was one of twelve branches, and had the full use of the forepart of his body. He strove to hit the dog with his sharp hoof, and to run his horns into him, but the dog cleverly eluded all his attempts, and at last seizing him by the throat, held him fast, while I ended his torments with my knife.

As Slowtrap had assured me that he would be ready to make the long expected journey, in a few days, I would not delay. I skinned the deer, packed the two haunches in the skin, fed the dog, and trudged away heavily laden, up and down hill to Curly's house.

## A KENTUCKIAN'S ACCOUNT OF A PANTHER FIGHT.

I NEVER was down-hearted but once in my life, and that was on seeing the death of a faithful friend, who lost his life in trying to save mine. The fact is, I was one day making tracks homeward, after a long tramp through one of our forests—my rifle carelessly resting on my shoulders—when my favorite dog, Sport, who was trotting quietly ahead of me, suddenly stopped stock still, gazed into a big oak tree, bristled up his back, and fetched a loud growl. I looked up and saw, upon a quivering limb, a half-grown panther, crouching down close, and in the very act of springing upon him. With a motion quicker than chain-lightning, I levelled my rifle, blazed away, and shot him clean through and through the heart. The varmint, with teeth all set and claws spread, pitched sprawling head foremost to the ground, as dead as *July*us Cæsar! That was all fair enough; but mark! afore I had hardly dropped my rifle, I found myself thrown down flat on my profile, by the old she panther, who, that minute, sprung from an opposite tree, and lit upon my shoulders, heavier than all creation! I feel the print of her devilish teeth and nails there now! My dog grew mighty loving; he jumped a-top and seized her by the neck; so we all rolled and clawed, and a pretty considerable tight scratch we had of it. I began to think my right arm was about chawed up; when the varmint, finding the dog's teeth rayther hurt her feelings, let me go altogether, and clenched him. Seeing at once that the dog was undermost, and there was no two ways about a chance of choking off, or let up about her, I just out jack-knife, and with one slash, prehaps I didn't cut the panther's throat deep enough for her to breathe the rest of her life without nostrils! I did feel mighty savagerous, and big as she was, I laid hold of her hide by the back, with an alligator grip, and slung her against the nearest tree hard enough to make every bone in her flash fire. "There," says I, "you infernal varmint, root and branch, you are what I call used up."

But I turned around to look for my dog, and—and—tears gushed smack into my eyes, as I see the poor affectionate cretur, all of a gore of blood, half raised on his fore-legs, trying to drag his mangled body towards me; down he dropped. I ran up to him, whistled loud, and gave him a friendly shake of the paws—(for I loved my dog!) But he was too far gone; he had just strength enough to wag his tail feebly, fixed his closing eyes upon me wishfully, then gave a gasp or two, and—all was over.—*James H. Hackett.*

## ANGLING FOR BASS.*

THE best, and one of the most universal fish of the Mississippi, is the black bass. They vary from one to seven pounds in weight, are taken with a fly, the min-

* From Lanman's "Adventures in the Wilds of the United States."

now and the frog, and in my opinion, as a game fish, are only second to the trout. They are found in great abundance at all the rapids in the river, but afforded me the finest sport at the Falls of Saint Anthony. When I was there the water was uncommonly low, so that pool fishing was in its prime, and I enjoyed it to perfection. I captured no less than thirty-five superb bass in the space of two hours, and that too, without once moving the anchor of my boat. I took them with a hand-line, baiting with a minnow, and the majority of them weighed over two pounds apiece.

The only respectable trout of the region of the Mississippi extends from Prairie du Chien to Lake St. Croix. An expert angler may here capture an occasional pounder, out of the river itself; but the rarest of sport is afforded by all the neighboring brooks, which run through a hilly country, and are rapid, rocky, and clear. The trout of these streams average about eight ounces in weight. As I sailed up the Alpine portion of the river in a steamboat, my opportunities for wetting the line were not frequent or particularly successful, as the following illustration will testify.

I had just arisen from the breakfast table, when the pilot of the boat informed me that he was about to be delayed for two hours, and that there was a fine trout stream a little farther on, which I might investigate. I immediately hailed a couple of my traveling companions, and with our rods in prime order, we all started for the unknown stream. Owing to a huge rock that lay on the margin of the river, we were compelled to make an extensive circuit over a number of briar-covered hills, and

ANGLING FOR BASS.

we found the bed of our pilot's trout brook without a particle of water. What aggravated our condition was the intense heat of the sun. In about an hour, however, we succeeded in reaching the Mississippi once more, and there, comfortably seated in the shadow of a bluff, we threw out our lines and awaited the arrival of the boat. We happened to be in the vicinity of a deep hole, out of which we brought five black bass, weighing three or four pounds apiece. We did not capture a single trout, but the sight of one immense fellow that I *lost*, agitated my nerves. Something very heavy had seized my hook, and after playing it for some minutes I was about to land it, when I saw that it was a trout, (it must have weighed some three pounds,) but making a sudden leap, it snapped my line, and was, like a great many objects in this world, entirely out of my reach; and then I was the victim of a loud and long laugh. The only thing that kept me from falling into a settled melancholy was the incident which immediately followed. When the boat came along, a Frenchman who was a passenger, and happened to have a canoe floating at the stern, volunteered his services to take us on board the steamer. Knowing that my friends had never been in a canoe before, I would not embark with them, and in about two minutes I had the *pleasure* of seeing them capsized, and after they had become completely soaked, of seeing them rescued from all danger minus the three fine bass which they had taken. This feat was performed in the presence of quite a number of ladies, and to the tune of a hearty peal of laughter.

## HUNTING ON THE OZARK MOUNTAINS.

It was Christmas eve, and growing dark, says Mr. Gerstæcker.* My heart sunk as I remembered former joys of this season, and thought of my present loneliness. Strange! that recollections should be so sweet and yet so bitter.

In good time we arrived at old Conwell's, Slowtrap's father-in-law. He lived in a block-house, surrounded by mountains covered with trees, close to the bank of the White river, which was narrow enough to be bridged by a tree. The family were assembled round the fire; Conwell himself was absent. A matron of pleasing appearance rose from her seat on the entrance of her son-in-law, and cordially shook his hand, while two fine boys of eleven and eight jumped up to welcome him; another person in the room, a young graceful girl, who at first kept modestly in the background, then came forward to greet her brother-in-law, who addressed her as Sophy; neither was the stranger overlooked, but received a hearty welcome from all. I, who, a few minutes before, had felt so deserted and miserable, now experienced a silent joy, as I looked upon the amiable, honorable countenance of the mother, the mild expression of the daughter, and the open, happy faces of the two boys. It was as if I had found new relations, and was once again at home. Never in my life had I felt, from the first moment, so completely domesticated as with these people.

* Wild Sports in the Far West.

In about half an hour old Conwell came in: if ever uprightness was stamped upon any countenance, it was upon his; his hair was white as snow, but his step was as springy as he moved about in his hunting-shirt, leggins, moccasins, and bare neck, as if he had seen but twenty years. After we had been seated about an hour, it seemed as if I had known him from childhood, and the evening flew past with incredible swiftness.

The cold was very sharp on Christmas-day, and we were delighting in a glorious fire, when John, the youngest boy, ran in, and said there was a large gang of turkeys in the corn. I seized my rifle, called Bearsgrease, and was soon in the field. No sooner had the dog found the scent, than he was amongst them, and they flew to the neighboring trees. I knocked over one, loaded, and tried for another, leaving Bearsgrease to watch the prize, as several pigs were near us. Not being able to get another shot, I returned to the dog, and found him with his paws full of business. Another larger dog had come to have a smell at the turkey; Bearsgrease, mistaking his intentions and my instructions, attacked the stranger, threw him over, and held him fast, with the fiercest countenance in the world; but when he saw me coming he began to wag his tail, being thus, like Janus, severe in front and amicable behind. I released the stranger from his disagreeable position, and patted and soothed Bearsgrease to express my approbation and satisfaction at his good behavior; but he continued to give an occasional growl and scowl at the other dog.

I amused myself for a couple of days with turkey shooting, leaving Slowtrap time to arrange his affairs, when he informed me that he had concluded his business quicker than he had expected, and now meant to return home. This was disagreeable to me for two reasons—first, because he was a very pleasant companion; and, secondly, because he was so well acquainted with the mountains. However, there was no persuading him to remain, and he fixed on the following morning for his departure.

In the afternoon, as the sun was bright and warm, we formed a merry party in front of the house; but S., who never could bear lying or sitting on the cold ground, sat himself on the fence, which was about five feet high, and told us some of his humorous stories with his usual gravity. Meantime, several cows had assembled on the other side of the fence. It has already been said that S. wore a shabby old coat, whereof the tails hung low outside the fence. In the morning he had been walking about the hills, and had been very hot; and his pocket-handkerchief, moist with perspiration, was in one of his pockets. It is well known that cows are fond of salt and saline substances, and they had probably divined that something of the sort was in one of those pockets. One, rather bolder than the rest, had quietly approached, taken the flap in her mouth, and was contentedly chewing it. I had observed the whole proceeding with great amusement; but fearing that his coat was in danger of being reduced to a state of pulp, I called out to him to look behind. He looked round, beheld the cow chewing his coat-tails with the greatest placidity, and raised one of his long arms to drive her away. The cow, frightened at the long arm, made a retreat; but unluckily one of the buttons caught between her teeth, and she gave a sudden wrench to poor Slowtrap, who was nicely balanced at the top of the fence; in a moment his legs rose in the air, like the two chimneys of a steamer, and then his body tumbled to the ground. What happened afterwards, no one could tell, as we all followed his example, in a convulsion of laughter.

On the 28th December my old companion mounted his steed, and shaking hands with his relations and me, was soon out of sight in the forest. I prepared for the mountains, and Conwell said he would willingly go with me, but that he had business for some days; I answered, that I would go first, not to be a burden to him, at which he was much vexed, and requested me not to go without him, concluding his kind invitation to remain in his house, by saying that I was "as welcome as the flowers in May." I could not withstand this, and remained with much pleasure. He rode away the same day, and returned on the following evening. In the afternoon it came on to snow, and continued till late at night, so that we expected glorious weather for shooting; but our joy did not last long, for it soon became warm again. Nevertheless we got every thing in readiness, mended moccasins, cast balls, sharpened knives, and, on the 30th, we proceeded to the Pilot rock, at the source of the Hurricane. After crossing the Boston divide, we stopped on the slope, where we found a spring of delicious water, and "struck camp." The night was clear and cold, but the heat of the day had spoiled all the beautiful snow. Stretched before the fire, we rested our weary limbs after the exertions of the day, and were soon sound asleep, with our dogs beside us.

As we were not yet on our intended ground, we rose early, descended the mountain, crossed the Hurricane, and fixed upon a spot for a night's camp, where we left Conwell's horse, with our blankets and provisions. Here we separated to mount the hill on different routes. The Hurricane is a mountain stream, taking its name from a hurricane which raged near its mouth some time ago, leaving traces that are still visible. It runs into the Mulberry, and flows with it into the Arkansas.

Conwell went to the left, I to the right; the hill was in places so steep, that I was obliged to lift the dog up before me. At length I gained a flat terrace. The terrace formation is characteristic of these mountains; seen from below they do not appear very high, because only the top of the next division is visible; but when one is surmounted, another and another arises, and people maintain that when you come to the highest there is always one more.

The terrace on which I found myself was about one hundred and eighty paces wide. Advancing cautiously towards the middle, keeping a sharp look-out, I perceived a doe quietly grazing, and coming towards me. I whistled, she stopped, bounded upwards with the shot, ran about fifty paces towards me, and fell dead. She was in excellent condition—I hung her up, and went on. At the end of the terrace, where a spring dashed down the rock, I observed signs of a bear; he had turned over several stones to find worms, and had bitten off some of the bushes to make a bed; seeing nothing more, I returned to the camp, to have the help of my companion to follow up the trail next day, taking half the doe on my shoulders as I went along. I found Conwell occupied with a very fat turkey.

Tired with all the climbing, we wrapped ourselves in our blankets, and threw ourselves down for a nap; but the sun setting, and wind getting colder and sharper, did not allow us much repose, but warned us to make a fire, and a good fire too, for the night. Wood was abundant, and we had only to move a few steps for as much as we wanted. The sun had hardly disappeared behind the trees on the western mountains, when it became dark in our ravine; the twilight did not last more than ten minutes. It was the last day of the year. In my native land, many a happy pair were forgetting past pains and sorrows in the tumult of the dance in lighted halls; while I was stretched under the starry skies beside a crackling fire in the forest, my trusty rifle and faithful dog by my side. I had no mind for dancing or music; for seven months I had not heard from home, and seemed to have got wedged in among the mountains, with the world closed behind me, all retreat cut off, and nothing left but to advance: and yet the future offered no inviting picture; alone. in the endless wilderness, I stood, with hair turning gray—a solitary hunter, leaning on my rifle, separated from all I loved.

Old Hawkeye must have had many a sorrowful hour.

Meantime, my companion, leaning on his elbow, was gazing on the fire, and lost in recollections of the past; but his past must have been a happy one, for he often smiled to himself. He had lived an active life, and looked forward to a happy old age, in the circle of an amiable family in the vicinity of his married children, in the enjoyment of health and strength. Wherefore should he be unhappy?

I stood up to change the current of my thoughts, poked at the fire, laid the logs together, which were burnt through the middle, and reposed again on my blanket. Conwell told me he was sixty-two years old to-day, 31st of December, 1841; and yet he was so strong and active that I had to exert myself to keep up with him. He spoke of his past life; how he had continually preceded civilization, first in Carolina, then in Kentucky, Tennessee, Missouri, and now in the Ozark mountains, and he complained that people were gathering too thick about him, and said he felt a strong inclination to make another move. He mentioned how fortunate and happy he was in his family. He spoke of his children, and as I listened to him my troubled thoughts were soothed; it was as if one of my own family was speaking. Thus passed our evening till sleep weighed down our eyelids, and wrapped in our blankets past and future were forgotten.

Next morning, as the tips of the western mountains were lighted up with the first rays of the rising sun, we woke from our lairs, shook off the wreaths of frost, and joyfully inhaled the fresh morning air; it was bitter cold, the water in our tin cups was all frozen, as was the meat; but a breakfast fit for a prince was soon smoking before us—juicy venison, fat turkey, good strong coffee, and maize bread. Where was the hotel that could afford fare as good? but man is fated never to be satisfied—my companion sighed for bear.

Before breakfast was quite ready, I went to the creek which flowed at a few paces from our camp, to have a good wash, and finding a hole with deep water as clear as crystal, I threw off my clothes, and plunged under the cool element. It was a delicious treat, and I did not feel the cold till I got out; but I was soon by the fire, and by the time I had my clothes on, I felt such an animating glow, and such strength, that I could almost have torn an oak up by the roots. Old C. looked on smiling, but thought it too cold to plunge in, and contented himself with washing face, breast, hands, and feet. Thus refreshed we sat down to breakfast; turkey, venison, coffee, and bread disappeared with terrific rapidity; even Bearsgrease appeared surprised, sitting with his mouth wide open, though Conwell maintained that he held it open more conveniently to catch the morsels I threw to him, from time to time; perhaps he was right.

After these trifles, half a turkey, and the greater part of a haunch of venison had been safely disposed of to the general satisfaction, we set off to look for the bear, tokens of whose whereabout I had seen the day before. On arriving at the place, the dogs showed signs of excitement, and running down the steep they soon began to give tongue. We followed as fast as we could, and came to a large detached rock, behind which a cave ran into the mountain. Several marks showed that the bear was at home; the dogs barked furiously, and I laid aside my rifle and pouch, and was about to enter the cave with my drawn knife, when bruin began to suspect mischief. He was right opposite the entrance, but a slight bend in the cave, which was only eight feet deep, prevented our seeing him. He would not have cared much for the dogs, but as I approached, the wind was behind me; the moment he discovered me, he began snorting and growling, and made a rush which nearly upset me, although I sprang on one side. Conwell, who had seen many such affairs, cooly stood at the entrance with his rifle cocked, watching my proceedings. The report of the rifle was heard before I and the dogs had recovered our composure after the rush; the bear seemed to be determined that nothing should stop him, and disappeared in a gorge; but the dogs roused by the shot, were soon on his traces. The old man laughed heartily as he saw me standing, knife in hand, quite disconcerted at the mouth of the cave, and regretted that he had not been able to give all his attention to my admirable jump, as he was obliged to look after the beast.

We followed the dogs, and on examining a rock which the bear had crossed, we found drops of dark blood, and were tolerably sure of him. Weakened with loss of blood, he had not run far before the dogs came up with him. As they were both young and untrained to bears, he had not much trouble in keeping them off, but they answered our purpose in stopping him. I came up just as he had shaken off the dogs, and was climbing a steep bluff. I fired and struck his right paw, and as he fell, the dogs seized him again; my companion now arrived, and coolly taking aim, sent a ball through his heart. He was a fat two-year-old, and promised a delicate repast; we decided on taking him home. So, while C. skinned and cut him up, I returned to the camp, to fetch the horse with our blankets and game, and as I rode past, I brought away the other half of the doe, which was too good to leave behind. As the day was now far advanced, and the horse had about 200 lbs. to carry, we resolved to camp for the night near the first spring we came to.

As we crossed a flat on the top of a mountain, we heard a horrible noise from a large gang of turkeys, a sure sign of bad weather. Conwell sprang from his horse, and we ran towards the sound. When near enough, I cheered on the dog, and in an instant the whole forest was alive with turkeys. A great big fellow flapped into a tree about sixty yards in front of me, and fell to the ground with a ball from my rifle. While loading, I observed Conwell going about with his rifle at his cheek, carefully watching all the long necks; then he stopped, took aim, and fired. But the turkey only reeled on the bough, and recovered himself. As soon as I was loaded I knocked over a second, and by this time the greater part of the gang had made off; but the one Conwell had hit, sat still, badly wounded, with the blood dropping fast. Conwell had now loaded again, and shot him through the head. On my asking why he had not selected another, as he was sure of this one, he answered that this was the fattest and heaviest of the whole gang, and he was right. Mine were both large birds, but his weighed more by three pounds. He laughed, and said he had not looked out for the best in vain, and told me "when the turkeys are all sitting on the trees, frightened at the dogs, there is no occasion to be in a hurry to shoot the first that comes—a good sportsman should 'choose the best, which is easily done; a short thick neck is the infallible sign. The leaner the turkey, the longer and thinner his neck. The bird seems larger, but take care to shoot the thick-necks, and I'll wager that they ain't so bad to eat." Long experience has since taught me that he was right, but it required some time before I was cool enough to look at the turkeys on their perch, and make a choice amongst them. We opened them on the spot, for it is extraordinary how soon they spoil, even in cold weather, if this is not done. We threw two of them over the horse, while I shouldered the third, and, in a very short time we came to a spring of good water, and made a camp for the night.

One of the results of our camping out, with supper and breakfast, was the disappearance of one of the turkeys, and half the bear's ribs. With strength well recruited, we set off for the dwelling of my old friend, and reached it about two in the afternoon. It was dark by the time when the skins were stretched and the meat salted, when we sat round the fire and talked over old times.

We were tired and went betimes to bed, intending to sally forth early next morning; but the rain poured down the whole night, and we had forgotten to take our blankets in from the fence, so that, it may be supposed, they were rather damp; however, we were not vexed. We had plenty of provisions; a little repose would not hurt us, especially as we were looking forward to fresh adventures.

We made ourselves comfortable, provided wood, and had placed ourselves in a half circle round the fire, when

little John ran in and told us that he was just come from a neighbor's, who had sent out his negro to count the little pigs, which a sow was bringing with her out of the forest. After a little while he came in, and said gravely, that he counted nineteen, but that one had run about so, that he could not count him. Conwell now commenced a story of his early days, in the following words :—
"About forty years ago my parents moved into the Cumberland mountains; and as the land was good and fertile, and game plentiful, a little settlement was soon made. We were very comfortable, grew as much Indian corn as we wanted, had plenty of venison, bear, and wild-honey, and we could always procure powder, coffee, and whatever else we wanted in exchange for our bear's fat, skins, &c.: so that every one would have allowed that we could not be better off, but for one circumstance that embittered our existence and exposed us to numberless dangers. There was a tribe of Tuskarora Indians in our vicinity, who had been driven out of the north, probably by the French, and who plundered and murdered whenever they found an opportunity. Amongst other things, they had stolen a number of horses, and that so cunningly, that for a long time they eluded all our efforts to trace them. The mountains ended in a bluff several miles long, and from twenty to thirty feet high, so steep that no bear, let alone a horse, could have descended it. As soon as a horse was missed, those who went to seek him examined each end of the cliff, without ever finding any traces of the animal. I was then about twenty-two years old, and one day I was out with my dog,—and such a dog I have never seen since. Old Beef here is a

good fellow, but that one had a cross of a bull in him; well, we came on the trail of a fat bear—for fat he was—of that I had infallible signs; in the first place, because he had crossed a sandy bed of a small stream where his footsteps were deeply impressed, showing the balls round and full; secondly, I found that he had not eaten the acorns with their cups, but had taken the trouble to separate them. I fancied he could not be far off, and followed up the trail, which led towards the bluff; at about two hundred yards from it, he had entered the stony bed of a brook. I kept close up with the dog, making as little noise as possible, and only taking my eye off the trail when a turn or higher ground gave me a chance of seeing the beast. As I proceeded I was astonished to find traces of horses leading towards the bluff. Two capital horses had been stolen from us a few nights before, and we had looked everywhere for traces of them, without success; of course, no one thought of looking on the edge of the cliff.

"My previous astonishment was nothing to what I experienced, when I came to the place, where, after heavy rain, the brook falls over the cliff, but which in dry weather does not contain a drop of water, and found, where the depth might be about twenty feet, two fir-trees, rounded, and placed standing against the rock, just so far apart that a horse might slide down them, but could not fall through; that this was the use they had been put to was evident from the marks of the struggles of the horses, before they were launched, and from patches of horsehair sticking to the poles. That the bear had decended by these means was clear from the marks of his claws in the wood.

"It would not have done for the dog;—besides the discovery was too important for delay, and I hastened home to give information. We had not long to wait to turn it to account. The Indians, who had stolen a couple of horses a few nights before, returned for some more the same evening. Luckily, our watchmen gave the alarm in time, and they had hardly made off with their booty, when we started by a nearer road, as they were obliged to choose the most stony paths, in order to leave as few traces as possible, and thus made a long circuit.

"About nine in the morning we arrived opposite the fir-trees, and hid ourselves in the trees and behind rocks to await the redskins. About noon we began to think that they must have discovered our trail, and would not appear; but we resolved to wait till dark. We were fifteen in all, and decided not to fire till every man was sure of his mark; and, with beating hearts, we listened for the slightest sounds. We had almost given up the hopes of seeing them, when a single warrior appeared, in blanket dress, and descended the cliff. He was sent to reconnoitre, and had not the slightest suspicion of danger; for he passed close before my uncle Ben, who, not able to resist the temptation, or fancying that he was discovered, I know not which, contrary to his usual caution, fired. The savage leaped high in the air, and fell on his face without a groan.

"Now, whether the Indians thought that their spy had shot something, or whether they thought themselves strong enough to disregard a single man, whom chance might have brought to the spot, in less than five minutes the whole troop were on the edge of the bluff, about eighty paces from our hiding-place. They had with them only the four horses which they had lately stolen, and as we well knew that it would be vain to seek them if once their suspicions were roused, we took aim in silence. The party consisted of nine men, four of them on horseback; we might easily have killed them all, but were too eager to recover the horses; so it happened that all aimed at the riders. I had not been in quite such a hurry, and when the others turned to fly I aimed at one just as he was entering the thicket; he gave a spring and threw off his blanket; I saw the blood spurt out, but he was soon out of sight, and as I could not find his body, I think he must have escaped.

"We took the arms and dresses of the slain, bound them on the horses, left the corpses to the wolves and vultures, and entered the settlement in triumph the same evening. It was long before we saw anything more of the Tuskaroras, who withdrew in alarm towards Lake Ontario."

By this time dinner was ready, and after dinner we took a siesta; then, what, with reading and conversation, it was evening before we were aware. I was now asked to give information about the old world, and to tell them whether kings would take off people's heads when they chose—and how houses were built when there was so little wood—and what people did in the winter. They were much astonished when I mentioned that we did not grow Indian corn, nor let the cattle run wild; but when

I said that we sometimes planted trees, the children shook their heads, and even the old ones thought that I was practicing on their credulity; they also wanted to know if kings and queens always wore their crowns, and if they walked about with their sceptres, and what the nobility looked like.

Next morning, starting with the rising sun, we took a direction towards the Richland and War-eagle, two streams which flow into the White river. We took no provisions with us, but rode out with only the blankets on the horses, as Conwell supposed we should find plenty of game. On arriving on our ground, we turned the horses loose, who bent their steps homewards, grazing as they went. We took different courses, agreeing to return in the evening to the place where our blankets were hanging up. I walked cautiously and slowly, but saw nothing of either deer or turkey; once I heard the report of C.'s rifle. When I returned to the camp I made a good fire, spread my blanket, placed my rifle in readiness, and laid me down to rest. About sunset I heard a light step; at first I thought it was a deer—it was Conwell, without game or dog. He sat down by my side on the blanket, and observing that he supposed I must be very hungry, he gave a faint smile, and said that he could fast until to-morrow evening. He might well laugh. He said his dog was after a deer which he had shot, and, judging from the marks, he must have been hit in the fleshy part of the haunch; the dog, being young, could not be called off after once catching the scent, and dog and deer were soon out of sight.

While he was talking, Bearsgrease rose up and snuffed

the air; Conwell thought it must be his dog who had found his trail. As I supposed so too, I took no notice, until I thought I heard a short bark, and Bearsgrease, growling lightly, gave me a significant look. I jumped up with my rifle, and in a minute a noble buck, with horns laid back, rushed by at full speed, at about twenty paces from the camp. I sent a ball into him, and my dog was instantly close on his heels. He did not run far; my ball had broken the left leg, and passed through the right. After running about 200 paces, he sprang into the Richland, on whose banks we were encamped, and seemed resolved to sell his life as dearly as possible. The dogs were upon him, but, as they were forced to swim, while he touched the bottom, he had not much difficulty in shaking them off again. Conwell remained lying as if it were no concern of his, so I seized his rifle, ran to the bank, ended the poor animal's torments with a ball through his brain, and plunged into the water to pull him out. Now we had meat in plenty; the skin and haunches were hung up, the ribs roasted, and the dogs fed before dark.

We slept well all night, and were up early, but the leaves were so dry that we found nothing but one turkey, which Conwell knocked over. However, the sky began to get cloudy, and as we had meat for the present, our hopes rose. It came on to blow from the north, but we were protected by a bank of about ten feet high, and though we could not sit close to it on account of sharp stones, yet it kept off some of the cold wind, and a glorious fire soon made us forget it.

Supper was over, and Conwell had taken off one of

his moccasins to take a stone out, when he said that it reminded him of something that had happened to him a long time ago when he was a child. I was already covered up in my blanket, but finding that he had a mind to talk, I roused up, gave the fire a poke that made the sparks fly, and leaning back, with Bearsgrease for a pillow, who seemed well pleased with the arrangement, I waited the commencement of his narrative.

When I got up, Conwell stopped; but now passing his hand over his face, he began:—

"I was between five and six years old when my father made my first pair of moccasins, for he was a very good shoemaker, and had always made strong shoes for children, though he himself always wore moccasins; but, at my earnest, repeated request, he made a pair for me, and warned me particularly not to lose them. On this same day a peddler had been in the house, and had persuaded my father to buy a pair of large boots, as very serviceable for bad weather;—and as it had rained a great deal lately, he put them on, took his rifle, and sallied forth to the forest. He was hardly gone when I wished to wear my new moccasins; and, to my horror, found that one was missing. In vain I searched the house from top to bottom; it was gone, and the other seemed to be there only to remind me of my loss, and the punishment awaiting me. With a beating heart I saw my father return earlier than I had expected, out of humor with the bad weather and bad sport; and he asked roughly why I was running about barefoot. With tears in my eyes I told him that I could not find one of the moccasins, and that I thought the cat must have run off with it. He said he would *eat* me, and that if I did not find the other before night I should suffer for it. With a sorrowful heart I recommenced my search, and all my brothers helped me. Meantime my father had sat himself by the fire, and complained that something in his boot had plagued him the whole day; so, pulling it off, and feeling inside, what should he find but my much-bemoaned moccasin? It is easier to imagine my delight than to express it."

Conwell rolled himself in his blanket and fell asleep, still smiling at the recollection. I could not sleep; his story had recalled events of my own childhood, and I kept gazing at the strange and changing figures in the fire. Bearsgrease was lying close to me, with his head on my shoulder; he had raised it several times, and snuffed the air, and again lain down. At length he roused up and gave a slight growl. I thought I heard something, and looking up to the bank behind me, I was astonished to find two glowing eyeballs steadily fixed upon me. My head being between the fire and the animal, I could see them plainly just above the bank. It must be a panther, and judging from the position, ready to spring. My rifle, as usual, lay ready; so, half raising myself, that I might have the fire in a line with the two sights, I aimed between the two fiery balls, and the rocks reëchoed the report.

Old Conwell was up like lightning with his rifle ready, and the dogs hunted about while I reloaded, but all was as silent as the grave. The old fellow shook his head, and asked what on earth I had been firing at. I finished loading without a word, then taking a brand from the fire and going about twenty paces to a slope in the bank,

I mounted, and found an immense panther, quite dead. I threw him over, and Conwell dragged him to the fire; the ball had pierced his brain through the right eye. He was a very powerful beast, had enormous fangs, and when we cut him open, his stomach was found quite empty. He must have been attracted to the fire by hunger, and Conwell thought he might have smelt the venison; he would probably have ventured a spring as soon as the fire burnt low; the dogs could not scent him, as he was so much above us. After skinning him we threw the carcass into the river below the camp, as the dogs would not touch it. We slept the rest of the night undisturbed.

A light rain fell next morning, which, in about an hour, moistened the dead leaves sufficiently for us to walk without making a noise; so I made haste to stretch the panther's skin, and we set off, each as before taking a separate path. Before I had gone half a mile I saw two deer grazing; just at this moment Conwell's gun was heard at some distance, and they both raised their heads and listened attentively, but perceiving nothing suspicious, they began to feed again. They were a doe and a year-old fawn, and when they were in a line I fired; the doe, which was nearest, fell at once, and the fawn after running about fifty yards. They were very fat, and I hung them up.

In hanging up deer it is necessary to take precautions against the vultures, which are a great annoyance to sportsmen. The best way of securing the deer, whose skin they would ruin with their beaks, is to hang them up by their heads, so that their vultures may have no point of support, and must content themselves with pecking at the skull. There is also a large crow, which tries to steal the fat; but they may be kept off by placing two peeled sticks crosswise on the deer—for the crows will not venture their heads between two such suspicious-looking objects.

Continuing my march, I came to the bank of a stream running into the Richland, when I saw a wolf spring out of a thicket on the opposite side, about eighty paces off; he ran about fifty yards and then stopped, but not long enough for me to take aim; finally he disappeared among some rocks. I crossed over to the thicket to see how Bearsgrease would take the scent of a wolf; all his hairs bristled up the moment he came to the yet warm lair.

Late in the afternoon, on my way to the camp, I struck a fresh bear's trail, and followed it up, though it led me out of my way. Meantime it began to rain harder, and coming to a broad stream, which the bear had crossed, my dog lost the trail. As it was too late to return to the camp, I considered myself lucky in finding a cave, two feet deep in leaves driven in by the wind. Without making a fire, which would have been dangerous, I crept in, taking Bearsgrease for a pillow, who was much pleased thereby, and, spite of wet clothes, I slept well till morning, covered up with the leaves.

The morning was cold and wet, my clothes were still damp from yesterday's rain, and I was as hungry as a lion; so altogether I did not feel quite so comfortable as I could wish. But walking quick to warm myself, in about an hour's time I reached the place where I had left the two deer, hung the fawn over my shoulders, and not long after gained the camp.

The fire was burning bright which Conwell had only lately left, and it was no small quantity of venison that I put down to roast. Having appeased my appetite, and fed Bearsgrease, I laid down again to rest. After an hour's time, as Conwell did not return, I set off again; it was still very cold. As I was passing a small ravine I saw a young buck feeding, without the slightest suspicion of danger. As I was within distance, I aimed and fired; he fell as if shot through the brain, but my ball had struck too high, so that at the moment when I came up to seize him he recovered himself, and rose on his forelegs. I saw on the instant that there was no time to lose, and threw myself upon him. The dog had also seized him, and I was in the act of drawing my knife to plunge in his throat, when he made a sudden effort, and we all three tumbled down a declivity of nine or ten feet. In falling I had dropped my knife, which fell among the stones, and I felt much pain in my head and left side; but neither I nor Bearsgrease had let go our hold. The poor animal made most desperate efforts to escape, and with our greatest exertions it was hardly possible for us to hold him. Without a knife there was but one method of securing him; a cruel one, indeed, but if I had to bite his neck through with my teeth I would not let him go. I threw him over on his side, and smashed his forelegs with a sharp stone. Thus crippled, Bearsgrease could hold him; I jumped up, found my knife, and ended the poor creature's torments.

I succeeded in slinging it with a great deal of trouble, my left side paining me exceedingly; however I managed to climb up the steep, recovered and loaded my rifle, and hobbled towards the camp, intending to remain quiet the rest of the day.

I found my old friend awaiting me. He had killed four bucks, and brought away their haunches, the rest not being good eating at this season. We settled to shoot towards the house next day, and then to take horses to carry home the game we had shot.

On our way homewards we only killed three turkeys. We caught the horses the same evening, and once more reposed our weary limbs among my old friend's family circle.

At midnight it began to rain, and towards morning it poured in torrents. The game was not to be thought of, and we sat round the fire amusing ourselves with old stories and anecdotes. As we were talking of the prairies, Conwell told us one of his adventures after buffaloes.

"Not many years ago, when I lived in the Kickapoo prairie, in Missouri, four of us set out one morning to shoot buffaloes. It was bitter cold, and we rode rapidly over the frozen ground. On gaining an elevation, we descried a herd in the distance, and made towards them. When about half a mile from them they discovered us, and ran off, we after them helter-skelter. The hindmost was a cow, too fat to keep up with the others, so we all singled her out for our mark. After galloping for about a mile, she received all our balls, and fell, when we secured her. The wind was now blowing from the northwest, almost cold enough to freeze the marrow in our bones, and the dry buffalo dung, the only fuel in the prairies, made but a poor fire. The nearest wood was about a mile from the place where the cow fell, and a debate arose whether we should fetch the wood to the buffalo, or carry the buffalo to the wood. We thought the latter easier. One of the party, named Turner, began to strip off the skin; we offered to help him, but he would not permit it; so, willingly leaving the cold work to him, we made as good a fire as we could for him to warm his hands by. When the skin was off, we cut off the prime pieces, took the marrow-bones, packed them in the skin, threw them over a horse, and brought them to the nearest wood, where we luckily found water. Our four tomahawks soon cut wood enough, and we made a roaring fire; when it was burnt to charcoal we stuck in the marrow-bones, first one end, then the other; and certainly there is no more delicate eating for the backwoodsman than buffalo marrow, except bear's ribs, and wild honey. The meat was rather tough, and nothing particular.

"It was now getting dark, and we began to prepare our camp. One of the party proposed, instead of each rolling himself separately in his blanket, that we should spread the skin, which was large enough to hold us all, and then lay all the blankets over us. But Turner objected, and maintained that as he had skinned the cow alone, he alone would sleep in it. It was all the same to us; we all had good blankets, and could make ourselves comfortable by the fire, which we closely surrounded, while Turner wrapped himself in his heavy skin, with the hairy side inwards;—and we were all soon asleep.

"The weather was extremely cold, and we were obliged to get up several times in the course of the night, to lay on fresh wood though Turner never moved out of his warm skin. Towards morning the wind changed to the north-east, and the sky threatening a snow storm, we decided on returning home as soon as possible, to avoid the approaching storm, or at any rate to get better shelter than the open prairie afforded. So we swallowed our breakfast quickly, and saddled the horses, which had been feeding on the dry grass, and now approached as close as they could to the fire. We called Turner several times to make him get up, but a slight motion of the hide was the only answer. At length, a half smothered cry for help issued from the skin. We rushed to Turner in alarm, fearing something serious, but burst into a roar of laughter, on finding that he was frozen in, and could not move a limb. We rolled him to the fire, to thaw the skin, and set him free; the rolling and the heat made him feel rather giddy, but a hot marrow-bone restored him;—and then loading the horses with the softened skin, and the remainder of the meat, we reached home before the storm, which came on that evening with a tremendous force."

The weather continued gloomy enough, the clouds hanging about the trees, as if they were seeking shelter from the wind, which was driving them from the rocky mountains. All the cattle collected near the house, with their tails to the wind, and pendant ears, looking very wretched. Luckily I found a few books,—such as "A Dialogue of Devils," "The Life of Marion," "The Life of Washington," "The Pilgrim's Progress," "The United States' Reader," &c., and killed some of the time by turning over their leaves.

The rain lasted till the 12th January. The various streams had become cataracts and rivers, so we were obliged to remain at home two days longer. Meantime our store of meat had fallen very low, and there appeared little hope of being able to use that which we had left hanging in the forest. However we hastened away to save the skins, if there was yet time. The streams were still so swelled that we could only pass them on horseback. We reached our last camp about noon, and found, as we had expected, that the meat was tainted, and the greater part of it devoured by vultures. We stretched the skins, in the hope that the wind, with the help of a faint sun, which was peering bashfully through the clouds, might dry them.

As it grew late, and we had no other provisions than bread and salt, we set off with the dogs to look for turkeys, and came upon a gang just as they were making themselves comfortable for the night. We killed two, and might have shot more, but did not wish to increase the quantity of decaying meat in the neighborhood. On this account we removed our camp about half a mile off, stretched our blankets to keep off a light drizzling rain, hobbled the horses, and fed them with maize. The wolves made a dreadful noise all night at our old quarters. In the morning the rain held up, and the clouds separated a little; so I set off to try and steal a march on them, and spoil their howling. The leaves were wet, and going round to gain the wind, I crept for about two hundred yards on my knees up to a large tree, and counted eight of them. Although they were to windward of me, one of them raised his head and began snuffing the air, then turned sharp round, and they all made off with their peculiar long gallop for the bush. Now was my time or never; I aimed at one of the largest, which covered another with its body. When the smoke cleared away not a wolf was to be seen; they had vanished like magic—but following up the trail, I found one dead, and signs of another being wounded; but I found nothing more of the latter,—he was probably torn to pieces by his comrades. I scalped my prize, and returned to the camp; the scalp is valued, as before stated, at three dollars.

Meantime Conwell had employed himself in roasting turkeys, and we made an excellent breakfast. We then started off again. When I came to the place where I had hung up the buck, whose capture nearly cost me my neck, I found that the wolves had succeeded in dragging it down, and eaten nearly all but the bones. I knocked over another, and also killed a wild-cat; returning to camp in the afternoon, where Conwell had arrived before me. He had killed a couple of deer, and we decided on bringing them to the camp, as there were so many wolves about.

Finding no traces of bears, we determined to leave the Richland and try the Mulberry again ; so next morning we loaded our horses, and set off on our return. As we were descending a hill, Conwell stopped suddenly at the foot of a large oak, and after examining the bark attentively, he said that a bear was either in the tree, or had very lately left it. The weather had improved, and it was again rather cold. We had nothing better than our tomahawks for cutting down the tree, and they were not very sharp; a few strokes proved the fact. Luckily for us it was hollow, and we set-to with a will.

After hacking at it for three hours, the tree began to crack. We seized our rifles, called the dogs, and hastened towards the direction in which the tree must fall, to be ready to receive him. A couple of small splinters broke first; then a large one; then the top began to bend slowly down the hill; then with a loud crash, and smashing its branches in the fall, the tree measured its length on the ground. No bear appeared; the nest was empty, though there could be no doubt it had lately been tenanted, for the sides were beautifully smooth and clean. There was a bough about five feet below the hole, where the bear went in and out, on which an Indian must formerly have stood, and tried to make an opening with his tomahawk, but without success; probably the bear, disturbed by the blows, had made his way out in time. Judging by the bark, this must have occurred about four or five years ago.

While we were looking at it, Conwell asked what the dogs were about; they appeared to be very eagerly licking up something from the ground, and we found that, accidentally, we had cut down a tree with honey in it. The bees were all torpid with the cold, and the dogs were enjoying the honey, which the breaking boughs had brought to light. Our plans were soon arranged; Conwell went to look for a deer; I took my tomahawk to cut a trough, and was soon busy about the upper part of the trunk, which was sound enough. As it was freezing, and the honey would not run, there was no occasion to make the trough very deep; so it was soon finished, and

I loaded it with great lumps of the frozen delicacy. This done, I collected wood and made a fire, expecting we should pass the night here; but just then I heard the report of Conwell's gun quite near, followed by his hail: I answered, and was soon by his side. He had killed a large fat doe, which we hung up by the hind legs, made a cut above the haunch, and drew off the skin without another touch of the knife, except at the knees, hocks, and head; stopping the holes, we turned it with the hair outwards, and so made a bag to carry the honey. When it was all in, I mounted, Conwell handed it to me, and away we went homewards, leaving the greater part of the last deer behind.

## BEAR AND PANTHER HUNTING.

WE had no trifle to carry, and were very glad to reach home; but our feet were hardly out of the stirrups when we heard that some Indians had looked in. They had discovered a cave which certainly contained a bear, but the Cherokees, who had first found it, had not ventured to penetrate far, as it was deep and narrow. This was grist to our mill. The skins and meat were stowed away, the rifles discharged and cleaned, horses fed, and all prepared for a regular hunt. We passed the evening in telling stories about bears; among others Conwell related the following anecdote respecting their winter sleep: "In this southern climate, the bear generally lays up

about Christmas, or the beginning of the year, and remains till the end of February; if the weather is then mild he comes out occasionally, and sometimes he does not return to his winter-quarters, but prepares a new lair by biting down branches, and making a bed for himself in the most secluded and thickest jungle, as far removed as possible from the haunts of man. If they go into a cave, they do not take any provisions with them, but keep sucking their paws, whining all the time; when they become torpid, they lie with their head doubled under them, and their fore-paws above it. I myself have crawled into a cave, and poked bears with the end of my rifle, to make them raise their heads, so that I might conveniently fire into their brains; and the bears were always cowardly in the cave, except they had young, when they fight furiously—but even then, only when they have no other choice. When the weather is warm and they come out to drink, it is extraordinary how exactly they always step in the same place; but as the marks are thereby made so much deeper, these 'stepping paths,' as they are called, are easily discovered."

The night was bitter cold; the day broke as fine as a sportsman could wish. One of Conwell's married sons, who lived in the neighborhood, joined our party, and another young man named Smith, and as we rode by the school, the master dismissed all the boys and girls, as the temptation to accompany us was too strong to be resisted. We took plenty of fir splinters for torches, and our guide was young Smith, who was one of the party who had tracked the bear, but not ventured very far into the cave.

We reached the entrance about two o'clock in the afternoon, and prepared a good dinner to strengthen us for the exertions in prospect. While the meat was roasting, I took a survey of the outside, which presented a wall of limestone rock, about thirty feet high, and about three hundred feet long, with four openings. After having well fortified the inner man, we prepared to enter the cave. We took only one rifle with us, but each had his large hunting-knife, and I buckled my powder-horn close to my side; then with my rifle in my right hand, and a torch of at least twenty inches in my left, we entered a dark passage about four feet high and two feet wide; young Conwell came next to me with another torch, followed by his father with a bundle of splinters to replace the torches as they burnt out. For about eighty yards it was all hard rock, and we advanced easily enough. But now came a sudden turn to the right, and the cave was so low that we were obliged to crawl on our hands and knees; the bottom was stiff clay, with numerous marks of bears, some quite fresh. As we advanced the passage became still smaller, and we were obliged to crawl on our stomachs. Thus far the Indians had penetrated, as we found by splinters of fir, and marks of their elbows and knees in the clay. The passage was now so small that I was obliged to lie quite flat, and push myself along by my feet assisted by my left elbow, holding the torch in my left hand, and the rifle in front with the right. The aperture was quite round, and rubbed smooth by the passing in and out of wild animals, who may perhaps have made this their winter-quarters for hundreds of years. Here and there we found stalactites, which were a great hindrance, and we often had considerable difficulty in pushing ourselves through.

Apparently, we were the first whites, indeed the first men, who had ever ventured into the place, for the ground retained every impression that had been made in it. In some places the marks of the bears were petrified, having perhaps been left centuries ago. Once the thought occurred to me: should we ever get out again, or perish here from hunger? I went on however, all my senses on the stretch, to discover the sleeping bear.

We disturbed immense numbers of bats with our torches, and found also several crickets and a few bluebottle flies. When my torch was nearly burnt out, I stopped for a supply from young Conwell; the moment I remained quite still, I thought I heard a low whining not far off; and listening attentively, I distinctly heard the sound bear cubs make in sucking, and a low deep growling; so there was no longer any doubt but that we were near a she-bear with cubs.

The place where I had stopped was rather more roomy, so that I could sit up, and I turned to the two Conwells and asked if they heard the sound, which they answered with a whispered "Yes;"—and we held a short council as to further proceedings. In the first place, the cave was smaller further on—secondly we had only expected a sleeping bear, instead of a she-bear awake and with cubs, for which it was rather early in the season; though C. told me afterwards, that in Arkansas he had occasionally met with bear cubs as early as January. Whoever has seen a she-bear defend her young, with ears laid back and open jaws, may form some idea of our feelings. We were all bear-killers, and knew well enough the danger we were encountering in a space almost too narrow to admit of any movement. But at all events there we were, and there was the bear—and no one even hinted at a retreat.

I examined my rifle closely to see that all was right, and as we slowly worked our way forwards, the elder Conwell warned me to make sure of my shot, adding drily, by way of comfort, that it would be all the better for me; for if I missed I should be the first to suffer from the animal's fury.

We came nearer and nearer to the growling bear, who certainly must long since have heard us, and was now listening with all her might. At length the mingled whining and growling appeared to be quite close, and holding the torch behind my head, I plainly saw fiery eyeballs. I now halted, cleared the sight of the rifle, which had got clogged with the clay, refreshed my torch, and crept as silently as possible towards the dark mass.

The decisive moment was come; and as I could now distinguish the animal's head through the surrounding darkness, I put myself in an attitude to take aim. The bear had risen on her hind legs, and sat with their usual swinging motion; as I was trying to fix one of her eyes with the rifle, she suddenly disappeared through the almost palpable darkness.

Following her up, we came upon three cubs, nice little things, which roared lustily when for the first time they saw a light. These sounds were by no means agreeable to us, for we had reason to fear that the cries of the cubs might still more enrage the dam. We wished to save them alive, and asked old Conwell to stay with them and quiet them and to make a fire, while we went after the old one. Conwell sat down, and soon quieted them by giving them a finger to suck.

About ten feet from the lair the cave divided into two passages of equal size. The fresh marks showed that the bear had taken the one to the right. Presently the cubs began to cry again with renewed force, which rather alarmed us, for we should have been in an awkward predicament if the bear had endeavored to hasten to their help, and found the way blocked up by our bodies; for, with the best will in the world, she could neither pass over us, nor by our sides, and there was no other way left than to kill us, and eat her way through. While we were consulting together about this matter, in a low voice, the cry suddenly ceased, and we pushed on silently in better spirits; for, from all that we had seen, this bear was rather more cowardly than usual.

We went on and on, to the great annoyance of our ribs and elbows, and there seemed to be no end to the cave. There was a peculiarity about it, which I never found in any other, namely, several flat stones about one and two inches thick, which rang like steel when slightly struck with the finger. One place was very remarkable. It was about fifty or sixty feet long, with similar flat stones on each side, approaching to within six inches of each other in the middle, so that one could have passed through in a sitting posture, with the neck in the narrow part, and the head in the upper compartment; but to say the least, this would have been a rather inconvenient position for receiving the attack of an enraged bear.

After clearing this double passage, we arrived at a spring, which had worn itself a channel of about eighteen inches deep, and eight or nine wide. After working our way through another difficult pass, as I was in the act of drawing a long breath, I heard a deep growl very near me. Although I had been listening for this sound every foot of the way for several hours, yet, on hearing it so suddenly and so close, I was rather startled, and nearly let fall the torch; but quickly recovering, and raising the torch as high as possible, to the discomfort and horror of several innocent bats, I could make out Mrs. Bruin, about ten yards off, sitting upright, gnashing her teeth, digging into the ground with her sharp claws, and apparently in the worst possible humor.

Young Conwell, who was close behind me, laid his hand lightly on my foot, and whispered that he heard the bear. As I had obtained this intelligence for myself, I whispered to him to be quiet, and creeping forward a couple of paces, I came to a place from whence I thought I could fire with effect. I placed my right foot in the channel of the stream, raised myself as well as I could on my left knee, and brought up the rifle. Young Conwell, who was anxiously watching all my motions, whispered me for God's sake to aim carefully, for if I made a bad shot we were both done for. Although I was nearer the danger than he was, I would not have changed places with him, as he could not see what was going on, and must naturally fear the worst; and in such cases, it is preferable to be in the post of danger, than to remain in a state of suspense.

The bear, by no means pleased with our intrusion, laid back her ears, snapped her teeth, and kept constantly swinging to and fro; as she did not sit quite upright I had no other choice than to aim at the head, in the hope that if I missed my aim, the ball might pierce the breast. As I was taking aim, the thought crossed my brain for a moment (why should I deny it?) how helpless I was if the shot failed; but it lasted only a moment, and, in the excitement of the present, I forgot both past and future.

I took a long aim, and yet, as the bear was not still for one second, I pulled the trigger too soon. The cave was filled with thick smoke; a fearful groan announced that the beast was wounded; we did not wait to examine the state of affairs, but crept back as fast as the narrow space would allow, to a spot where there was more room to move, in order to reload and return to the attack.

We had retreated, backwards, for about a hundred yards, and had halted in a more convenient part of the cave, when we heard the bear coming towards us snorting and snapping her teeth, till the cave echoed with the sound. My first thought was "Good-bye to the light of the sun." But I had not much time for consideration, and called to young Conwell to make haste if he valued our lives, for the old one was coming. He did not require much pressing, and I never saw crabs crawl backwards quicker than we tried to do; yet, however great our hurry, and imminent our danger, it was very slow work, and the snorting came nearer and nearer.

I had dropped my rifle, as it very much hindered my retreat, and keeping a sharp look-out in front, where I constantly expected to see the bear, I suddenly discovered the glowing eyes, only a few paces off. Just at this moment, my left elbow struck against a projecting bit of rock; the torch fell out of my hand, and all was dark as pitch; for although young Conwell had a second torch, my body filled up the space so completely that not a ray of light could pass. I took up the glimmering splinter, and threw it at the bear, which checked her, but only for a moment. Suddenly young Conwell stopped, and said he could not find the passage, and making a slip with his right hand, which held the torch, he dropped it in the water. I could not answer for the bear, who had followed us slowly, as if she knew that we were doing our best to get out of her way; she must have been so near, that I felt sure that if I stretched out my arm to its full extent, I should touch her, for I could feel her hot breath on my face. With my left arm a little in advance, the right with the hunting-knife drawn back, I awaited, with every stroke of the pulse, the beast's attack, thinking of nothing else than selling my life as dearly as possible; for I had no hopes of getting out alive.

Meantime, young Conwell had not been idle. Aware that we could do nothing without a light, he had felt for his tinder-box, and the noise of his flint and steel was the only sound that broke a silence like that of the grave, for at the first blow, the bear had ceased growling to listen to the strange sounds.

After a painful and anxious pause, he called out, "I have got a light, give me the powder-horn and a rag." I cut away the first from its sling, then tore off a piece of my hunting-shirt, and passed them behind me. In a few minutes he recovered his splinter; this gave us, or rather me, new hopes, for he had no fear—firstly, because he could not know how near the bear was; and, secondly, because, as he assured me afterwards, he was so intent on striking a light, that he could think of nothing else. He had also succeeded in turning himself round, and his voice sounded to me like an angel's song when he called out that he had found the passage. He had now the advantage of creeping forwards, while I was still obliged to show front to the bear; but he gave me a few more splinters of fir, and a light, and we again began our slow retreat towards the entrance.

As I held the torch forwards, the bear gave a deep growl, gnashed her teeth, and retreated a pace or two, but followed again as soon as she saw that I was retiring. Necessity sharpens invention, I laid a couple of burning sticks crosswise on the ground, and saw, to my inexpressible delight, that she did not venture to pass them. Shuffling back as fast as I could, I heard Jim (young C.) call out to his father to go back, as the bear was coming. No other words were spoken, and indeed the growling came nearer; the fire had probably gone out on the moist ground, and then she followed us again.

I now crawled over the place where we had first discovered her, and found out the reason why the cubs had so suddenly ceased their cry. When we stopped, uncertain what to do, old C. had dashed their heads against the rock, and thus, most likely, saved our lives; for a cry from the cubs when our torches had gone out, would have enraged the wounded animal so much, that she would certainly have attacked us, and we should have been either killed, or so dreadfully crippled, that we must have perished miserably in the cave.

At about a hundred paces from the lair, I stopped to listen again, but could hear nothing. I now called to the others to wait for me, and when we came to a more roomy place, which had also been the retreat of a bear, we held a consultation. Old C. thought that the bear had lain down by her dead cubs, and that one of us had better return to the mouth of the cave, and fetch another rifle, as it was out of the question trying to pass the furious animal to get at mine. However, before attempting the long and difficult way back to the entrance, I resolved to creep again to the lair, and see if she was not dead, for I could not but think that my ball must have had some effect. When I got there I could see nothing of her. My shout brought the others to the spot; so, advancing a little, and examining closely, we saw thick dark blood, and found, that instead of returning to her lair, she had taken the left-hand passage. I instantly proceeded to regain my rifle, which I found covered with blood and slime, about three hundred yards off. I returned as fast as I possibly could, cleaned it, and reloaded, when we all started again for a fresh attack.

The left-hand passage was as bad as the right, but luckily the bear had not gone far. We soon reached the place where, grinding her teeth, she awaited our approach. I halted about eight or nine feet from her, raised myself as high as the space would allow, laid the rifle over my left arm, in which I held the torch, and seizing the time when her head was quiet for an instant, I fired. Again the cave echoed the crack of the rifle, and all was enveloped in thick smoke. I heard the bear groan and move, but stood my ground, as this time I knew that my ball had struck the right place: as the smoke cleared away, she lay dead before me.

Young Conwell and I were half dead from our exertions, and it would have been impossible for us to get the bear out;—for the time we had been crawling in the close air of the cave and smoke of the torches, and the long-continued excitement of constant danger, were almost too much for the constitution of any man; so we decided on returning to the fresh air as fast as we could. It took us about half an hour to do so, and I shall never forget the effect of the delightfully cool night air, as I drew it in long inspirations, and gazed on the bright-blue starry skies.

Young Smith and the schoolmaster were fast asleep, but as the dogs barked they both jumped up, and almost fell down again from fright, for they swore that they had never seen such horrible figures as we looked in the red light of the torches, covered with blood and slime, and blackened with smoke. Judging by the stars, it must have been about two o'clock in the morning. Although as hungry as lions, we were too exhausted to touch any thing; so we lay down and slept till daybreak. We made a good breakfast, and then, leaving old Conwell behind, who had done rather too much for his time of life, we four again entered the cave to bring out our prizes. We fastened a cord round the old bear's neck; I squeezed past, and shoved from behind, while Smith and the schoolmaster pulled, and young Jim Conwell held the light. We gained ground inch by inch, and about noon, amid a general hurrah, we cast down the carcase by the camp fire, where it was instantly taken possession of by Bearsgrease, who laid himself growling by its side.

As we had some way to go home, we only opened and cleaned her, and broke the spine, so that the carcase might lay better across a horse. We reached home by the evening; I took a plunge in the river, and then settled down to sleep.

We rose refreshed the next morning ready for further efforts, and concluded to try some caves that old Conwell knew of. We provided ourselves with cords and food, and made two large wax candles, which are less disagreeable in a close cave than pine torches, give a better light, and are not so liable to go out. We arrived at the place in the afternoon, and found eight or nine caves, from forty to eighty feet deep, but all empty. We now separated to try different paths, and agreed that as soon as any one found a trail, he was to make a signal so that all might join in the chase.

I found a small cave with fresh marks, but no bear. On returning to the mouth, I heard the dogs, and listening attentively for a minute or two, I felt sure they were coming towards me. Presently the noise of rushing

SHOOTING THE BEAR.

through breaking branches was very distinct, and at last a bear broke cover. Throwing himself without hesitation down a precipice of about ten feet, he came towards me as fast as his legs would carry him. I stood still to see how near he would come. At about fifty paces distance he winded me, stopped short in his career, snuffed the air for an instant, and then made off in a different direction. I seized the opportunity offered, and sent him a ball; but I was not quite cool enough, and only wounded him in the hip. Meantime, the dogs having been stopped by the bluff which Bruin had so unceremoniously disposed of, he gained a good space in advance; but the wound checked his speed, and I could soon distinguish by the dogs' bark that they had come up with him again, but they were keeping out of reach of his paws. A young man named Erskine, who was shooting near us, attracted by the report of my gun and the barking of the dogs, came up and gave the mortal wound. The two Conwells joined soon after, and we broke him up together.

Erskine told us that he had found a cave, which he was sure contained a bear; and asked one of us to go with him and try it, as he had neither torches or wax candles. I was ready at once, took one of the candles, and explaining to the others where they might find us, we set off, and reached the place about sunset. We first made a large fire before the entrance of the cave, and then crept into it, Erskine preceding. Further on, the passage grew larger, so that we could walk upright, side by side. After going some distance, we heard the regular low whine of the bear, who was sucking his paws, and Erskine, also a regular bear-hunter, asserted that he was fast asleep. Passing a sharp turn in the cave, we discovered him at our feet, and, as my comrade had stated, fast asleep, his head between his paws, uttering a low monotonous whine. Erskine set the muzzle of the rifle to the back of his head, and fired; he gave a convulsive start, and lay dead. I probed the wound with my fore finger to see how far the ball had penetrated; the rifle threw a ball of twenty-two to the pound; the skull was completely shattered.

We now decided on getting out of the cave for a little repose and refreshment, and to await the Conwells. We found them sitting by the fire, and young Conwell offered at once to take the cord and fasten it round the bear's neck, and try and pull him out alone. Lighting one of the candles, he soon disappeared in the cave. They had examined several other caves, but had not found any more signs. Extraordinary to relate, we had not seen a single deer during the course of our hunt; the forest seemed deserted, excepting by a bear or two in the caves, and a very few turkeys.

We had rested and talked for about half an hour, when young Conwell reappeared without the bear, having found it too heavy, and requiring help. We went, one and all, taking fresh torches with us, to the scene of action, and dragged him out, though with considerable difficulty, as many parts of the route were ill-adapted for the transport of such a mass of flesh. Lying down by the fire, we slept comfortably till late next morning. It was near noon ere we could tear ourselves away from our couches of soft leaves, but as we all agreed that we must move sooner or later, we got up, loaded the horses with our prizes, and moved off towards Conwell's dwelling in as direct a line as the nature of the country would allow. We kept no look-out for game on our way home, having meat enough, and being almost tired to death.

We received a hearty welcome from Conwell's family, and we resolved to enjoy a little repose after all our hard work. In spite of the bears and bats that I encountered in my dreams, I awoke quite refreshed, and did full justice to the beautiful breakfast of bear-collops, milk, and maize bread. Perhaps the wild out door life which we had been leading may have lent more charms to the quiet life of this happy home, than under other circumstances I should have been sensible of; but, be that as it may, I shall never forget this amiable family. Old Conwell and I sat the whole day by the fireside, mending our leggings and moccasins. He was certainly the last man in the world to neglect spinning a yarn when he had a good opportunity, and he told me so many anecdotes, and related so many adventures, that the day passed away only too soon.

About an hour before sunset, a neighbor came in to inquire whether we would go with him to the debates. "Debates!" I asked, quite astonished, "what does that mean?" He seemed still more astonished at my ignorance, and explained that, on every Friday, it was the custom to hold a meeting at the school-house, about two miles off, to debate on any subject which might be proposed, and in which the scholars took part. The account excited my curiosity still more, and I decided on no account to miss such an opportunity. Old Conwell had frequented these meetings too often to be induced to leave his comfortable fireside; but I saddled a horse at once, and was soon at the school.

Imagine a large smoky building in the midst of a forest, with dark, dusty windows; a broad, well-worn doorstone; a heavy iron-bound door; and rules and regulations pasted here and there in the room. A number of horses, fastened to the surrounding trees, showed that several of the debaters were already assembled. A bright fire burned in the chimney, and the room was nearly full, and almost everybody was talking. At length order was established, and the company proceeded to the business of the evening. Two judges and two leaders were selected. The judges took their places in the centre, while the leaders stationed themselves on opposite sides, each taking it in turns to choose a follower from the persons present. The question to be decided was this: "In a thickly inhabited district, where much cattle was reared, there was only one parish bull. The district was on the bank of a broad river, and the inhabitants were obliged to cross it very often, as all the mills and tanneries were on the other side—but there was only one ferry-boat, passed to and fro by a single rope. The bull got down to the ferry, and on board the boat, and gnawed the rope in two; the boat floated down the river with the bull, and boat and bull were never seen again." These were the facts, now comes the question, "Who is to pay the damage for the loss? The owner of the boat for carrying off the bull, or the owner of the bull, because, from some malicious though undiscovered intention, he stole the boat?"

It was highly amusing to see one after another stand

up, and seriously defend the cause of the bull, or the boat; others again talked all sorts of nonsense for a quarter of an hour, and then sat down with the remark that it was unnecessary to say more, as the case was so clear that the judges could not do otherwise than give a decision in their favor. After all had been heard, myself included, the judges consulted together, and the owner of the bull was condemned to pay the expenses. The next question was: "Which is better, a single or a married life?" The judges were not quite impartially chosen. The wife of one had run off with a young man to Texas, three years ago; the wife of the other had three times borne twins. I was chosen on the married side with the schoolmaster, three or four other young men, and six or seven of the scholars. We defended our cause with glowing animation—but one judge thought of Texas, and the other of the twins, and our scale kicked the beam. Several other questions were discussed; among them, "Which is worse, a smoky chimney or a scolding wife?" Left undecided. At last I was invited to propose a subject, but I would not consent until I received assurance that it should be discussed: "Which enjoys life most, has fewer cares, and lighter sorrows—a short or a long-tailed dog?" But by this time it was late, and time to adjourn; so the house was soon left to its solitude in the forest, and the party dispersed in all directions to their dwellings.

On the morning of the 22nd January, old Conwell and I shouldered our rifles, and each provided with meat and bread, we wandered towards the waters of the Richland. Lucky was it that we took provisions, for not a shot did we fire. Next day was almost as bad, and if Conwell had not knocked over a turkey, we should have been reduced to chew sassafras. At length on the third day, he shot a deer, and I a turkey, which put a little life into the dogs. Disgusted with our bad luck, we decided on returning home next day, besides, the weather was bad, and threatened to be worse. To our inexpressible joy, snow fell during the night, and all thoughts of return vanished. We took different directions, with the agreement to return to camp in the evening. I had not gone far when I saw footsteps of a young buck in the four-inch deep snow, followed him up and shot him. I heard the report of Conwell's rifle about the same time. Hanging up the deer, I walked on. After lounging along slowly for above an hour, without seeing anything, I came across the track of Conwell, who, with his dog, had been following up the bloody trail of a panther; I gathered from the signs that he had broken his left hind leg. I followed it up on the instant, as fast as my legs could carry me; in rather more than an hour, I arrived at the mouth of a cave, where Conwell was awaiting me, knowing that I should cross his trail, and follow it up as soon as I saw the marks of the panther.

The wounded brute had taken refuge in the cave, leaving us to act as we pleased, probably thinking himself quite safe. We held a short consultation—Conwell said that he had hidden a bundle of kindlers in a hole, and that if I would keep watch here, he would go and fetch them. I consented, of course, and laid myself down before the cave, with bare knife and cocked rifle.

Lying in the snow, however, was anything but agreeable; at first, when I was warm with running, I thought nothing of it, but by degrees I became colder and colder, till my teeth chattered. I could not venture to lay aside the rifle to make a fire, for fear the panther should escape. I managed to keep up a little warmth, by running and jumping, but was very glad when my old friend returned and made a good fire.

As soon as we were well warmed, we made torches, and entered the cave as cautiously as possible, each with a burning torch in his left hand, and a rifle in the right. I went first, but the cave was soon roomy enough to admit of our walking upright, beside each other. Some distance in, it took a turn to the left, and about two hundred paces in advance, we saw the fiery eyeballs of the beast, who kept shutting them from time to time. Conwell, taking my torch, stepped behind me, while I took aim and fired. We heard a noise after the shot, but could not make out the result; I reloaded as fast as possible, while Conwell went in advance, but we could see nothing more of the animal's eyes. We went on with cocked rifles on our left arm. Moving silently and cautiously forward, we suddenly discovered the panther in a little hollow close to our feet, a beautiful but alarming sight, his ears laid back, his teeth gnashing in wild rage, and his glowing eyes so wide open, that they seemed half out of their sockets. Inspired by one impulse, we both fired so exactly together, that neither knew that the other had done so. Our enemy was hit, but whether mortally or not was more than we could tell. Dropping our rifles like lightning, we drew our knives; a sore need we had of them, for before the sound of the rifles expired, we felt the weight of the panther upon us. I drove my knife into him, and sprang back; our torches were extinguished; it all passed so quickly, that I did not recover full possession of my senses, till I stood beside my old friend, in the fresh air, at the mouth of the cave. I can only remember that, in the impenetrable darkness and thick smoke, I did not know which way to turn, and that Conwell dragged me out. When we came into the light of day, we found ourselves covered with sweat and blood, and our clothes all torn.

Conwell complained of pain in the breast. Tearing open his shirt, we found two deep gashes from the left shoulder to the pit of the stomach; I had escaped with only a few scratches. We had neither of us felt when we were wounded; but before we troubled ourselves about it, we made a fire in the mouth of the cave to prevent the panther from coming out; then washed and bound up our wounds, and sat by the fire to consider what was next to be done. There was the panther in the cave, whether alive or dead we knew not. At any rate he was badly wounded, for both our knives, with blades nine inches long, were bloody to the hilt. But indeed we had no choice; our rifles, and Conwell's ball-pouch, which the brute had torn away, were still in the cave.

It might, perhaps, have been possible to suffocate the panther with smoke, but there might have been another opening, and then we should have had our trouble for nothing. We soon made up our minds, and entered the cave again with fresh torches and bare knives, but not without beating hearts. We moved silently and cautiously on, holding the torches well before us, so as not to be so agreeably surprised a second time. We recovered our rifles without seeing the enemy. I held both the torches while Conwell loaded his rifle, and then gave them to him while I loaded mine, and having our faithful weapons once more in our hands, we stepped forward again still slowly and silently, but with lighter hearts. "There!" suddenly called out C., holding his torch aloft, and staring before him. It was the first word spoken since we re-entered the cave. The panther lay stretched on the ground, no longer dangerous, for the last convulsions were over. We skinned him and cut him up; all the balls had taken effect, and both our knives had pierced his body, so that it was only in his death-struggle that he sprang upon us. We took the skin, although it almost looked like a sieve, and returned to our fire.

It was night by the time we came out of the cave, and, with hungry stomachs, lay all four by the fire; for neither we nor the dogs had any fancy to eat the panther. Conwell suffered very much from his wound, but towards morning he fell into a tolerably quiet sleep. We moved off with the first gleam of day to the place where I had hung up the buck, breakfasted there, and started for fresh game.

Meantime it had become warmer. The snow had disappeared, but all the game seemed to have gone on their travels; for although we saw signs enough, not a shot could we get. In the night we were awakened by a thin cold rain, and having no mind to get wet through, we jumped up, cut poles with our heavy knives, and spreading my blanket, which was the largest, over them, and laying ourselves on the other, underneath it, after making up the fire afresh, that the rain might not put it out, we were soon fast asleep.

Next morning brought fresh troubles, but no reward. Dispirited, we wandered the whole day through the wet forest, without seeing a turkey. The meat we had brought with us was getting low, as we had not been very saving of it, and had given the larger share to the dogs; after breakfast there was one small piece left for each to share with his dog at night; still hoping, we walked on cautiously and attentively till late at night, without seeing even so much as a vulture.

On the morning of the 29th of January, we sat by the fire with empty stomachs, and stared sorrowfully at the crackling flames. At length Conwell burst out with a loud laugh, and asked whether we were forced to remain in this deserted spot, and why we should not go home. But I would not give it up yet; to go home with nothing but a panther's skin full of holes was too bad, and I begged for one more day; at any rate, if we found nothing before twelve o'clock, we could then meet at the camp and return home. In silence, and on the watch for the merest trifles, I wandered with Bearsgrease through all the places where hitherto I had almost always found game, without meeting a sign; and my hunger was quite painful. How I thought of shooting parties at home, where one was sure of finding some sort of a house every half hour; here, was only thick forest, where one wet dripping tree looked exactly like another. And yet it was not without its charms. For instance, every now and then you were entangled by the thorns of the black locust, or if your slippery moccasins caused you to fall, you might be sure of finding some of them conveniently placed to receive you.

I returned to the camp about noon, exhausted and dispirited, and found my old comrade stretched quietly by the fire. He said he had been waiting for me about a couple of hours; that it was very clear there was no game to shoot; and I was now of the same opinion. Heartily sick of the useless fatigue, we shouldered the skin and our blankets, and left the place with heavy hearts and weary limbs.

It was long after dark when we arrived at Conwell's home, and received the usual kind welcome, and we were heartily laughed at, when, instead of bringing provisions, we fell, like famished wolves, upon every thing eatable that came in our way. A long draught of fresh milk did me, above every thing else, an immensity of good.

I would willingly have enjoyed a day's rest; but Conwell—who, in spite of his deep gashes, which were not yet healed, was as fresh and strong as ever after his first meal, and could not remain quiet under the circumstances—impressed on me the necessity of trying again, otherwise people would believe that we had lost the power of shooting a deer. So we were off again before noon, gained the source of the Hurricane, rode across the "Devil's Stepping Path," a narrow rock with a precipice on each side, left the Pilot-rock on our left, and came towards evening into the pine forests, where we were sure of finding kindlers. Descending the steep side of a mountain, we observed a column of thin blue smoke by the side of a stream, showing that some hunters were encamped there. We went straight towards it, and found it to be an Indian camp, and our former acquaintance, young Erskine, among them. They were Cherokees with three young Choctaws, those two tribes being on good terms. Like ourselves, they were out bear-hunting, but had had better luck. A quantity of bear meat was hanging about the camp, and even the dogs could eat no more. Casting ourselves down by the fire, one of the squaws—for there were several women in the camp—immediately cooked some bear for us, with which we duly regaled ourselves.

Night came on, and soon all were sunk in deep repose. I was not inclined to sleep, and Bearsgrease, who had tired himself with chasing a gang of turkeys, which escaped at last by flying across a ravine, lay close to me, with his head on my left arm. Soon he began to dream, scrambling with his feet as if running, and barking in a low voice. Watching him brought to my mind a story which was told me by an old bear-killer, to the effect, that if a man lays his pocket-handkerchief over the head of a dreaming dog, letting it stay till the dream is out, then lays it under his own head, and falls asleep, he will have the same dream that the dog had. A pocket-handkerchief was a luxury I had dispensed with, but I laid my Scotch cap on my dog's head, under which he went on dreaming, and when he awoke I laid it under my own head, and was soon asleep. It was perhaps owing to the idea under which I fell asleep, although in general I can never dream what I wish, but, be that as it may, I soon found myself running desperately after turkeys, and never stopped, till I had chased them into a tree, when I stood looking up at them without thinking of shooting. Just then my dog gave a loud bark, and I jumped up. One of the Indians had risen to look to the fire, and Bearsgrease thought it rather suspicious. My beautiful dream was gone, and I could no longer recollect whether I barked or not. I fell asleep again, but the dream never returned.

Early in the morning we began to move, dividing into two parties, for the better chance of finding game. Conwell went with some of the Indians, amongst whom he had found an old acquaintance, to make a circuit round the Pilot-rock, while Erskine and I, with three Cherokees proceeded to the sources of the Frog bayou.

About ten o'clock we came to a cave, which seemed worth examining. We made torches, there being plenty of strips of pine lying about; it was settled that I should try my luck, with one of the Indians. Erskine remained with the two others by the fire, saying he had searched so many caves within the last four days without finding anything, that he was tired of it. The entrance was rather small, but it became gradually larger, and we went a long way in. There were evidences of its having been tried before, as we found moccasin marks, and pieces of burnt wood. An unexpected sight suddenly arrested our progress—the skeletons of a man and of a bear, lying peaceably within three feet of each other. A rifle thickly covered with rust, and a corroded knife, lay by the side of the first, and some glass beads convinced us that it was the skeleton of an

Indian, who had bravely attacked the bear single handed, and had fallen in the struggle, the skeleton of the bear proving that he had sold his life dearly.

The skeleton was perfect, except some of the small bones which rats or snakes might have carried off. The Indian pointed in silence to the upper bone of the right arm, which was broken, and the knife was lying on the left side.

The sight of these remains of a human being, which may have lain there for years, while his footsteps were still so fresh in the moist earth, was deeply affecting. As I was about to pass on, the Indian laid his hand on my arm, and shook his head, saying, in broken English, "The spirit of the red man is in the cave, and Wachiga goes no further." Nothing could induce him to go on, all my persuasions were fruitless; pointing to the bones, he said, "The bones of the red man belonged to a great chief; the bear seeks no bed where the hunter sleeps." As this last remark seems well founded, and as the sight had shaken me too much for me to go alone, we turned back without touching the remains.

We found Erskine alone, and told him what we had seen, but he did not seem at all inclined to visit the remains. We found three other caves, but no bear: Erskine and the Indians tried the two first, Erskine and I the last. The cave separated into two passages; Erskine took the right, I the left, and as I proceeded I found plenty of marks. The cave was so small that I was obliged to leave everything but a torch and my knife; I could not even turn myself from one side to the other, to change my attitude. I had taken off my hunting-shirt, and had on nothing but a cotton shirt and leggings, and was working on inch by inch, with tolerable certainty of finding a bear. The passage was quite round, and in many places as smooth as glass, from being rubbed by wild beasts. In one place I found the skin of a rattlesnake.

At length I got so completely jammed in, that I could neither move backwards nor forwards. The perspiration burst from every pore, and for a minute or two I lay motionless. Then I again exerted all my efforts to force myself backwards, and to my indescribable satisfaction, at length succeeded, leaving, however, the greater part of my shirt behind me, and my delight may be imagined when I again inhaled the fresh air. My hair stood on end at the fearful thought of sticking fast in such a hole, buried alive, and dying of hunger.

Night found us far from our camp, so we made one for ourselves where we were. Wachiga, who had become very pensive, sat smoking his tomahawk and staring at the fire. Notwithstanding that he had been converted to Christianity, he had still some remains of the old superstition. Erskine was in high good humor, and told one droll story after another.

On the next morning, February 1st, we had hardly started ere we heard the dogs. Wachiga declared instantly that they were his brother's, and disappeared behind the rocks without another word. As we stood listening, the sound seemed to take a different direction; we ascended the mountain as fast as we could, to cut off the chase, but found that we must have been mistaken, for in a few minutes all was silent as the grave;

once we thought we heard a shot, but could not be certain. We ascended to the highest terrace and walked slowly on, looking out for fresh signs, and listening to catch the sound of the dogs; below, amongst the broken masses of rock, they might be near without being heard, while on the mountain tops, they are audible at a great distance.

It may have been about two in the afternoon, and we had hitherto seen nothing, when Bearsgrease raised his nose in the air, remained for an instant or two in a fixed position, then giving a short smothered howl, dashed down the mountain side. Listening attentively, we heard the chase coming down the Hurricane river. Erskine called out triumphantly, "We shall have plenty of bear this evening," and dashed after the dog. I was soon by his side. I must observe by the way, that we were both very hungry. Presently a bear broke through the bushes; a projecting rock stopped him for an instant, when Erskine saluted him with a ball: he received mine as he rushed past, and disappeared. The dogs, encouraged to greater efforts by our shots and the stronger scent, followed him out; Bearsgrease, who was quite fresh, leading the van. They soon came up with him and stopped him. We rushed to the spot without waiting to reload, and arrived in time to see the beast, excited to the greatest fury, kill four of our best dogs with as many blows of his paws; but the others only threw themselves on him with the greater animosity, and if our rifles had been loaded, we could not have used them. Just as a large powerful brown dog, which had furiously attacked the bear, was knocked over bleeding and howling, Erskine

THE FATAL BEAR HUNT.

called out, "Oh, save the dogs," threw down his rifle, and rushed on with his knife among the furious group; I followed on the instant. When the bear saw us coming, he exerted still more force to beat off the dogs, and meet us. Seizing his opportunity, my comrade ran his steel into his side. The bear turned on him like lightning, and seized him; he uttered a shrill piercing shriek. Driven to desperation by the sight, I plunged my knife three times into the monster's body with all my force, without thinking of jumping back; at the third thrust, the bear turned upon me. Seeing his paw coming, I attempted to evade the blow, felt a sharp pang, and sunk senseless to the ground.

When I recovered my senses, Bearsgrease was licking the blood from my face. On attempting to rise, I felt a severe pain in my left side, and was unable to move my left arm. On making a fresh effort to rise, I succeeded in sitting up. The bear was close to me, and—less than three feet from him lay Erskine, stiff and cold. I sprang up with a cry of horror, and rushed towards him. It was too true; he was bathed in blood, his face torn to pieces, his right shoulder almost wrenched away from his body, and five of the best dogs ripped up and with broken limbs lying beside him. The bear was so covered with blood that his color was hardly discernible. My left arm appeared to be out of the socket, but I could feel that no bones were broken.

The sun had gone down, and I had hoped that the other hunters might have heard our shots and the barking and howling of the dogs. It grew dark. No one came. I roared and shouted like mad; no one heard me. I tried to light a fire, but my left arm was so swelled that I gave up the attempt. But as it would have been certain death to pass the night under these circumstances without a fire, I tore away part of the back of my hunting shirt, the fore part being saturated with blood, sprinkled some powder on it, rubbed it well in, all with my right hand, shook a little powder into my rifle, and placing the muzzle on the rag, I fired, when it began to burn immediately. Blowing it up to a flame, I piled on dry leaves, twigs, &c., and succeeded in making a good fire, though with great pain and trouble. It was now dark. I went to my dead comrade, who was lying about five yards from the fire. He was already stiff, and it was with great difficulty that I could pull down his arms and lay him straight; nor could I keep his eyes closed, though I laid small stones on him.

The dogs were very hungry, but as it was impossible for me to break up the bear, I only ripped him up, and fed them with his entrails. Bearsgrease laid himself down by the corpse, looking steadfastly in its face, and went no more near the bear. In the hope of obtaining help, I loaded and fired twice, but nothing moved: the forest appeared one enormous grave.

I felt very ill, vomited several times, and my shoulder was excessively painful. Winding my blanket round me as well as I could, I laid myself down beside the fire, and lost all consciousness of my wretched situation; whether I slept or fainted is more than I can tell, but I know that I dreamed I was at home, in bed, and my mother brought me some tea and laid her hand on my breast; I heard the children in the street making a noise, and saw the snow on the roofs of the houses, and thought it must be very cold out of doors.

Such an awakening as I had was worse than I could wish to my bitterest enemy. Bearsgrease had pressed close to my side, laying his head on my breast; the fire was almost out, I was shivering with cold, and the wolves were howling fearfully around the dead, keeping at a distance for fear of the living, but by no means disposed to lose their prey. I rose with difficulty, and laid more wood on the fire. As it burnt up, the face of the corpse seemed to brighten. I started, but found it was only an optical delusion. Louder and fiercer howled the wolves, and the dogs, of whom five were alive besides Bearsgrease, answered them; but the answer was by no means one of defiance—rather a lament for the dead. Partly to scare away the wolves, partly in the hope of finding help, I loaded and fired three times; my delight was inexpressible as I heard three shots in return. I loaded and fired till all my powder was expended. As morning broke, I shot two shots not far off, and soon after, a third. A shipwrecked mariner, hanging on to a single plank, could not raise his voice more lustily to hail a passing ship, than I did then—and, joy upon joy, I heard a human voice in answer. The bark of the dogs announced a stranger, and Wachiga advanced out of the bush. "Wah!" he exclaimed, starting at the shocking spectacle. He felt poor Erskine, and shook his head mournfully. He then turned to me. I showed him my swollen arm, which he examined attentively, without speaking. Forming a hollow with his two hands, and placing them to his lips, he gave a loud piercing shout.

The answer came from no great distance, and in a few minutes my dear old Conwell, and most of the Indians, were at my side. I grasped Conwell's hand sorrowfully, and told him in few words how it had all happened. The old man scolded, and said it served us right; there was no great danger in sticking a knife into a bear's paunch, when he is falling, with the dogs upon him, but if he has been thrown, and then catches sight of his greatest enemy, man, he exerts all his force to attack him, and woe to him who comes within reach of his paws. It was all very well talking; he had not been present, and seen one dog after another knocked over never to rise again; five minutes more, and not one would have been saved, and who knows whether the enraged beast would not have attacked us, then.

Meantime, the Indians had been digging a grave with their tomahawks. Wrapping the body in a blanket, they laid him in it, and covered him with earth and heavy stones. Conwell cut down some young stems, and made a fence round the solitary grave. I could not avoid a shudder at the quiet coolness of the whole proceeding, as the thought struck me, that the same persons, under the same circumstances, would have treated me in the same cool way, had I fallen instead of Erskine. Like me, he was a lonely stranger in a foreign land, having left England some years before, and his friends and relations will probably never know what has become of him. Thousands perish in this way in America, of whom nothing more is heard, and perhaps in a few months the remembrance of them has entirely passed away.

After the dead was quietly laid in the grave, Wachiga

came with an elderly Indian to look at my arm. Wachiga moved it, while the other looked steadfastly in my face: the pain was enough to drive me mad, but I would not utter a sound. Next the old Indian took hold of my arm, laying his left hand on my shoulder, and while Wachiga suddenly seized me round the body from behind, the other pulled with all his force. The pain at first was so great that I almost fainted; but it gradually diminished; in spite of my resolve to show no signs of it, I could not suppress a shriek. Conwell soon after asked if I could ride. On my answering "Yes," he helped me on a horse; then throwing the bear's skin and some of the meat on his own, we moved slowly homewards. My sufferings on the way were very great, but I uttered no murmur. I only longed for repose. At nightfall we had still four miles to go. He asked me if I could support the pain and fatigue, or if we should camp where we were, as there was plenty of wood and water. I would rather have ridden forty miles, let alone four, with the hope of rest at the end of them. We arrived in about an hour. I was so stiff that I could hardly get off the horse. On entering the room I threw myself on a bed, and had a violent fever during the night, and talked wildly—fortunately in German. Towards morning I began to feel better, had a quiet sleep, and woke up about noon much refreshed. Meantime, old Conwell had related all that had occurred, and they attended me like a son. It took two more days before I could move out of bed and was able to stand.

I was hardly so far recovered as to be able to crawl about, when Conwell proposed another hunt, and although

I had suffered so much, I could not say "No." On the 6th of February we rode out again, but there was no longer any life in the thing; we found the same Indians, hunted with them a few days, shot a few deer, some turkeys, and a young bear, returning on the 12th, Conwell with two deer-skins and some haunches, I with a turkey.

By this time my arm was quite healed. Nevertheless, I had made up my mind to leave the mountains and go southwards, partly from a returning fit of my old love of change, partly because I longed for news from home, not having received any letters for several months, and partly also because game had become so scarce through the number of hunters, that there was hardly enough to subsist on. We heard that a party of twelve men had been along the Richland and killed or driven away everything, and that during the last three days not a turkey was to be seen. The news of game from other quarters was no better; in short there was nothing for it but off! off! When I was once more surrounded by my old friend's amiable family, and passed another evening amongst them, my resolution was indeed shaken; however, during the night I gave it mature consideration, and in the morning I told them that I should that day take my departure. Attempts were immediately made to dissuade me from it, and old Conwell asked in downright earnest if I could not stay with them always, and take the school. The present schoolmaster was ignorant and a drunkard, and they would have been glad to be rid of him. For a moment, indeed, but only for a moment, my fancy depicted the delights of a home amongst the mountains, then the image of my old village schoolmaster flashed across my mind, with his threadbare black coat, false collars, and shirt-front, and his frame as thin as a skeleton. I shook my head mournfully. He changed his plan, and proposed that I should take a farm. But that I had also reflected on: I was too poor, and although the kind people would have done every thing in their power to help me, I should have been too dependent; for although much is not required to set up farming in America, still there must be something, and it does not look well for the beginner to be always borrowing horse or plow, axe, spade, saw—in short, every farming and household utensil, until at last the most patient man would be worn out, and everybody would be alarmed the moment they saw the borrower coming. I was once witness of such a beginning: a family that came to the forest without any means, were at first most liberally assisted by their neighbors; they helped them with their fences, in building their house, in clearing and ploughing the land, and lent them every thing, even to flour and pork; but how could people who began thus ever become independent? It took years before they could procure the most necessary articles for themselves.

My old friend acknowledged the truth of the picture, and my journey was settled for the morrow.

## DRIVES.

The following graphic and very interesting account of the drives, common in newly settled countries, is extracted from "A Sketch of the Settlement of the Township of Tallmage, in Summit county, Ohio," by Charles Whittlesey.

This region was originally very well stocked with bear, wolves, deer, and turkeys. The flesh of the two last was not only a luxury, but a necessary article of food. Deer skin breeches, and deer skin facings to woolen pantaloons, (after one season's service,) were the height of fashion. Red foxes were not common. The wolf made great havoc with the few sheep introduced here; committing depredations at the same time upon the wild deer. He has been known to attack cows. The bear confined himself to hogs, and many instances are given of his boldness in capturing and carrying away provisions of this kind. He springs suddenly upon his victim, grasps him in his arms or forelegs, with a force which is irresistible, erects himself upon his hind legs like a man, and makes off in an instant with his load. The piercing squeal of the hog is the first warning of his presence to the owner. A large bear, who meets with no obstruction, will make his way through a thick wood in this manner, with a hog of good size, faster than a man on foot can follow. The groans and struggles of the animal in his embrace, become weaker and weaker, and soon cease entirely. One of these creatures took a shoat from a drove belonging to captain J. Hart, of Middlebury, in his presence. The captain followed him closely, but the bear evidently gained in the race, till he came to a brush fence, and not being able to climb it with sufficient expedition, dropped the dying pig in order to secure himself. Mr. Edmund Strong was chopping on his land, when one of his hogs was taken near by. After a severe contest with clubs, Mr. Strong recovered the body of his hog; and, using it as a bait, afterwards caught the offender in a trap. Another seized a full grown hog belonging to A. Whittlesey, near the centre, and, notwithstanding men were near by, and made close pursuit, he carried it off without difficulty.

When Mr. Ephraim Clark lived in a log-house, a few rods north of the parsonage, on the same side, his hogs were fed across the road at a trough in the field. One morning, as he returned from feeding them, a large bear fell upon the hogs before he had reached the house. By the time he had seized his rifle, and re-crossed the road, the bear had secured one, and as he rose preparatory to a retreat, received a bullet in the chest. He then let the hog fall, and made fiercely toward Mr. Clark, but in making an effort to scale the bars, fell backward and died.

Mr. John Caruthers and his dogs fell in with one of a moderate size, while traversing the woods near the east line of the township, in search of horses. An engagement followed, in which the bear had apparently the advantage. To an early settler, the loss of a dog, his companion and faithful sentinel, was a misfortune that affected, not only his interest, but the best feelings of his heart. Mr. Caruthers had nothing in his hand but a bridle, and could therefore bring no weapon to the assistance of his friends, but such dry clubs as lay about him. The animal paid very little attention to these; but at length finding a young sappling, he broke it into a good stick, and managed to give several hard knocks, repeatedly on the same spot, just behind the ear. By this means he was killed, and the dog released.

By the assistance of a large and valuable wolf dog, Mr. D. Preston and Mr. Drake Fellows killed one with clubs and stones, at the south end of "Stony Hill."

If the body of a hog was recovered partly eaten, the same bear could generally be taken in a trap, within the next twenty-four hours. He invariably returned for the remainder, and showed little or no sagacity in avoiding his fate. For this purpose, a heavy steel trap was used, with smooth jaws and a long drag chain, with iron claws at the extremity. It was not fastened to the spot, because the great strength of the animal would enable him to free himself, but as he ran, after being caught, the claws would catch upon the brush, retarding his flight, and leaving a distinct trail. He was generally overtaken within two miles, exhausted of strength. Here the dogs were first allowed an opportunity to exhibit their courage and natural animosity, before the rifle put an end to his degradation and sufferings. In these conflicts if the shackles were upon his hind legs, leaving the fore paws free, there were but few dogs desirous of a close combat the second time.

In the winter of 1824-5, the inhabitants of this and the adjoining townships, determined to make an effort to clear the country of the bear, and of the wolf at the same time. There were four *drives*, or large hunts, organized during the winter; *two* in Brimfield, one in Springfield, and one in Portage. They were frequently got up in the new country by those who were not professed hunters, for the purpose of taking a few deer and turkeys, then so common. A large tract of wild land, the half or fourth of a township, was surrounded by lines of men, with such intervals that each person could see or hear those next to him, right and left. The whole acted under the command of a captain and at least four subordinates, who were generally mounted. At a signal of tin horns, or trumpets, every man advanced in line towards the centre, preserving an equal distance from those on either hand, and making as much noise as practicable. From the middle of each side of the exterior line, a blazed line of trees was previously marked to the centre as a guide, and one of the sub-officers proceeded along each as the march progressed. About a half or three-fourths of a mile from the central point, a ring of blazed trees was made, and a similar one at the ground of meeting, with a diameter at least equal to the greatest rifle range. On arriving at the first ring, the advancing lines halted till the commandant made a circuit, and saw the men equally distributed and all gaps closed. By this time a herd of deer might be occasionally seen driving in affright from one line to another. At the signal, the ranks move forward to the second ring, which is drawn around the foot of a eminence, or the margin of an open swamp or lake. Here, if the drive has been a successful one, great numbers of turkeys may be seen flying among the trees away from the spot; deer in flocks, sweeping round the ring, under an incessant fire, panting and exhausted. When thus pressed, it is difficult to detain them long within the ring. They become desperate, and make for the line at full speed. If the men are too numerous and resolute to give way, they leap over their heads, and all the sticks, pitchforks, and guns, raised to oppose them. By a concert of the regular hunters, gaps are sometimes made purposely to allow them to escape. The wolf is now seen skulking through the bushes, hoping to escape observation by concealment. If bear are driven in, they dash through the brush in a rage, from one part to another, regardless of the shower of bullets playing upon them. After the game appears to be mostly killed, a few good marksmen and dogs scour the ground within the circle, to stir up what may be concealed or wounded. This over, they advance again to the centre, with a shout, dragging along the carcasses which have fallen, for the purpose of making a count.

It was at the hunt in Portage, that the bear were either exterminated or driven away from this vicinity. It embraced the "Perkins' Swamp," and several smaller ones, rendered passable by ice. At the close of this "*drive,*" *twenty-six* were brought to the centre ground and others reported.

Wolves were taken with difficulty in steel traps, but more readily in log pens, prepared like the roof of a house, shelving inwards on all sides, and containing the half devoured carcass of a sheep, upon which they had made a previous meal. The wolf easily clambered up the exterior side of the cabin, and entered at the top, which was left open; but once fairly within it, he could neither escape or throw it down.

Turkeys were taken in square pens, made of lighter timber, and covered at the top. They entered at an open door in the side, which was suspended by a string that led to a catch within. This string and catch were covered with chaff, which induced them to enter, and while engaged in scratching about the chaff to get at the grain mingled with it, some unlucky companion would strike the catch, and let the door down behind them all.

This town was much infested with rattlesnakes, during the first ten years of its settlement, though but one instance is known of a bite among the inhabitants. There were two kinds, the large yellow, (*crotalus durissus* of naturalists,) and the small venomous black rattlesnake, (*crotalus miliarius*,) or massassauga. The massassauga frequented the low grounds, to the terror of all cranberry hunters. The yellow rattlesnake, which was very large and more numerous, kept the open dry ground, particularly fields of standing grown wheat. It is said that eleven were killed in one day in a wheat field, one mile north of the centre. They resorted in the winter to a den in the rocks, at the southwest part of Stony hill. On the approach of spring, attracted by the warmth of the atmosphere, they would come out in a half torpid state, and were killed by the inhabitants by scores. At this day, a rattlesnake, a bear, or a wolf, would be equally an object of curiosity.

## HUNTING ADVENTURES OF ICHABOD MERRITT.

ICHABOD MERRITT was born in Massachusetts, in June, 1796. In 1804 his parents removed to the district of Three-Rivers, in Lower Canada. At that time there was an abundance of game in that part of Canada, and also in the adjoining parts of Vermont. For many months during the fall and winter, hunting and trapping was a regular, and also a profitable business. It was here, and in his youthful days, that Mr. Merritt inured himself to hardship, and self-possession in case of difficulty. He usually spent his winters in the woods, either trapping the martin and sable for their fur, or hunting the bear, moose, or deer, with which those woods abounded. In the fall of 1815, he, with a brother, killed ten bears, the skins of which they sold for one hundred dollars. I give his account of his killing one of them, as something of a specimen of the rest. "The dogs," (for a hunter in those days could not hunt without *two*, and sometimes with more dogs) he remarked, " had started a bear, and it appeared to be coming partly towards me. I moved in a direction to head it. Soon it came in sight, and when about twelve rods from me it jumped upon a log, and turned to look and listen for the dogs. At this time I fired at it. The ball struck the jawbone, and glancing, lodged in the skin in its neck. The bear was hurt but little, and continued in her course, coming near where I was loading. The dogs overtook and seized it. In my haste to load, I had not watched them; but the moment I had finished loading I looked up, and the bear had got clear of the dogs and was pitching at me. She was not eight feet off. I sprang and ran a short distance, every step of which I could not help cringing, for I almost felt the embrace of the bear, and expected every instant to see her huge paws coming around me. As soon as I dared to look behind me, I found my faithful dogs had seized the bear, and she had turned to fight them. This gave me the very chance I wanted, and I let drive at her head, and shot her square through. She died instantly."

In that climate (Canada) the bears usually den up in the winter, and lie in something of a torpid state. During a thaw, they sometimes venture out, but that is seldom. In warmer climates, they ramble more while the snow is upon the ground.

During those winter hunts, to find and kill the moose, was quite an object with the hunters. The moose is an animal similar to the deer or elk, except vastly larger. Their color is dark gray. The horns of the male are pronged, and very large in proportion to the size of their bodies. The body is thick-set, tail short, and they have a very large upper lip. Their usual gait is a trot, swinging their legs out so as to form a half circle in the snow when it was three or four feet deep. "I have often," says Merritt, "measured their steps in the snow, and found them seven feet apart." A man, five and a half feet high, could walk under the belly of a full grown one. They usually bring two young at a time. In winter, they herd together, and as the snow increases, they form yards, living upon browse, the twigs and bark of trees. Sometimes they will take a strip, following some ridge or swamp, feeding upon the brush until they fill themselves, and then lie down, the next day progressing on further.

"The last moose which I killed," said Merritt, "was out back of Brompton lake, in Canada. I was hunting with J. Bonney. It was near night, when we came upon a moose-yard. We had taken provisions but for one day. We were not expecting then to chase them, but merely to find their place of yarding, and then wait until the snow became deeper before we disturbed them. When the snow was deep, and particularly when there was an icy crust, we could soon run them down and shoot them. Bonney was for giving immediate chase. I persuaded him to camp that night, and in the morning to ascertain where we could get some provisions before we started them, as the chase might last, as it frequently did when there was but little snow, five or six days. The next day, it took us until about noon before we could find anything to eat. We then obtained three quarts of Indian-meal, and about four pounds of bull-beef. We had with us a small kettle, with the aid of which we made our meal into porridge. Our dogs shared our provisions with us. We did but little this day, the second of our trip, except to get back upon the trail. The third day we gave chase; but, before night, Bonney was for giving up the pursuit. I persuaded him to continue, told him that he had been fierce to begin the pursuit when we had nothing to eat, and now when we had beef and porridge, I was for going ahead. Near night the dogs came up with them, but too late for us to get a shot at them. We again encamped. The next day, after following five miles further, we overtook them back of a hill, which by the sound, they appeared to be going around. I immediately ran to the opposite side of the hill to meet them. They came around as I expected, and I partly met them. As they turned, a large one ran upon the ice of a creek and broke in. As he rose upon the ice, I was ready, and cut loose upon him, and shot him square through. This stopped his running. After securing our prize, and getting a hearty meal of fresh meat, we returned."

When Merritt came to the State of Ohio, in 1815, there were numerous elk in the forests of this State. The elk is of the deer species, although much larger, the male, like that of the deer, only having horns. They usually go in droves. "In 1823," says Merritt, "I started three in the northwest corner of this township; after following them around awhile, one separated from the others. I followed that one, and at night came within two miles of home. I went home and slept, and the next morning I took my brother with me, and a rope, determining to catch and bring it in alive. We took its track, there being a little snow, and often came in sight of it. Many times we might have shot it, but we were determined to halter it. The next night found us about fifteen miles from home. The third day the elk became worried and hungry, as we had not allowed it to eat. During the day it ran into a cleared field, and the dogs there stopped and held it. It was a cow elk. I came up and caught my right arm over its neck, and with my left hand I took it by the nose. She soon cleared herself from the dogs, and I found that I had a wild colt to handle. She carried me with ease—frequently striking at me with her fore-feet. I managed so that her feet usually went one upon each side of me, when she reared and struck, so that I was but little hurt. I would then have been glad to be out of that scrape; but the difficulty was in letting go. We soon arrived at the opposite side of the field, where was a high and strong fence. With my weight, the elk could not jump the fence, and I here, with my left hand, caught around a rail, and I found I was able to hold the creature down, until my brother came up with the rope. When this was fastened to her, both of us could hold her. With the aid of a crotched stick, to keep her off, we led her to a log stable, and there confined her. After getting help so as to have one with a halter upon each side, and one behind to whip up, we succeeded to lead her home, a distance of twenty-eight miles." Merritt says, that he has killed or caught with ropes, over thirty elk, in and near this place. They have now, for more than eighteen years, all disappeared from these parts, and it will soon only be known by tradition, or from history, that such animals ever roamed our forests.

# PERILOUS ADVENTURES OF MR. ROSS COX.

Mr. Cox's book is entitled "Adventures on the Columbia river, including the narrative of a residence of six years on the west side of the Rocky Mountains among various tribes of Indians; together with a journey across the Rocky Mountains." It is exceedingly entertaining; and as it abounds with curious hunting adventures, we shall make some extracts from it. Mr. Cox left Astoria with a trading party, (June 29th, 1812,) and went up the Columbia river to visit and trade with the Indians. The following extract gives an account of his most perilous adventure.

On the 17th of August we left our encampment a little after four A. M. During the forenoon the sun was intensely hot. Occasional bright green patches, intermixed with wild flowers, and gently rising eminences, partially covered with clumps of small trees, gave an agreeable variety to the face of the country; which we enjoyed the more, from the scorched and sterile uniformity of the plains through which we had passed on the two preceding days. We got no water, however, until twelve o'clock, when we arrived in a small valley of the most delightful verdure, through which ran a clear stream from the northward, over a pebbly bottom. The horses were immediately turned loose to regale themselves in the rich pasture; and as it was full of red and white clover, orders were given not to catch them until two o'clock, by which time we thought they would be sufficently refreshed for the evening's journey.

After walking and riding eight hours, I need not say we made a hearty breakfast; after which I wandered some distance along the banks of the rivulet in search of cherries, and came to a sweet little arbor formed by sumach and cherry trees. I pulled a quantity of the fruit, and sat down in the retreat to enjoy its refreshing coolness. It was a charming spot, and on the opposite bank was a delightful wilderness of crimson haw, honeysuckles, wild roses, and currants; its resemblance to a friend's summer-house, in which I had spent many happy days, brought back home, with all its endearing recollections; and my scattered thoughts were successively occupied with the past, the present, and the future. In this state I fell into a kind of pleasing, soothing revery, which, joined to the morning's fatigue, gradually sealed my eyelids; and unconscious of my situation, I resigned myself to the influence of the drowsy god. Imagine my feelings when I awoke in the evening, I think it was about five o'clock from the declining appearance of the sun! All was calm and silent as the grave. I hastened to the spot where we had breakfasted : I ran to the place where the men had made their fire: all, all were gone, and not a vestige of man or horse appeared in the valley. My senses almost failed me. I called out, in vain, in every direction, until I became hoarse; and I could no longer conceal from myself the dreadful truth that I was alone in a wild, uninhabited country, without horse or arms, and destitute of covering.

Having now no resource but to ascertain the direction which the party had taken, I set about examining the ground, and at the northeast point of the valley discovered the tracks of horses' feet, which I followed for some time, and which led to a chain of small hills, with a rocky gravelly bottom, on which the hoofs made no impression. Having thus lost the tracks, I ascended the highest of the hills, from which I had an extended view of many miles around; but saw no sign of the party, or the least indication of human habitations. The evening was now closing fast, and with the approach of night a heavy dew commenced falling. The whole of my clothes consisted merely of a gingham shirt, nankeen trousers, and a pair of light leather moccasins, much worn. About an hour before breakfast, in consequence of the heat, I had taken off my coat, and placed it on one of the loaded horses, intending to put it on towards the cool of the evening; and one of the men had charge of my fowling-piece. I was even without my hat; for in the agitated state of my mind on awaking, I had left it behind, and had advanced too far to think of returning for it. At some distance on my left, I observed a field of high, strong grass, to which I proceeded, and after pulling enough to place under and over me, I recommended myself to the Almighty, and fell asleep. During the night confused dreams of warm houses, feather-beds, poisoned arrows, prickly-pears, and rattlesnakes, haunted my disturbed imagination.

On the 18th I arose with the sun, quite wet and chilly, the heavy dew having completely saturated my flimsy covering, and proceeded in an easterly direction, nearly parallel with the chain of hills. In the course of the day I passed several small lakes full of wild-fowl. The general appearance of the country was flat, the soil light and gravelly, and covered with the same loose grass already mentioned; great quantities of it had been recently burned by the Indians in hunting the deer, the stubble of which annoyed my feet very much. I had turned into a northerly course, where, late in the evening, I observed, about a mile distant, two horsemen galloping in an easterly direction. From their dresses I knew they belonged to our party. I instantly ran to a hillock, and called out in a voice, to which hunger had imparted a supernatural shrillness; but they galloped on. I then took off my shirt, which I waved in a conspicuous manner over my head, accompanied by the most frantic cries; still they continued on. I ran towards the direction they were galloping, despair adding wings to my flight. Rocks, stubble, and brushwood were passed with the speed of a hunted antelope; but to no purpose; for arriving at the place where I imagined a pathway would have brought me into their track, I was completely at fault. It was now nearly dark. I had eaten nothing since the noon of the preceding day: and, faint with hunger and fatigue, threw myself on the grass, when I heard a small rustling noise behind me. I turned round, and, with horror, beheld a large rattlesnake cooling himself in the evening shade. I instantly retreated, on observing which he coiled himself. Having obtained a large stone, I advanced slowly on him, and taking a proper aim, dashed it with all my force on the reptile's head, which I buried in the ground beneath the stone.

The late race had completely worn out the thin soles of my moccasins, and my feet in consequence became much swollen. As night advanced, I was obliged to look out for a place to sleep, and after some time, selected nearly as good a bed as the one I had the first night. My exertions in pulling the long coarse grass nearly rendered my hands useless, by severely cutting all the joints of the fingers.

I rose before the sun on the morning of the 19th, and pursued an easterly course all the day. I at first felt very hungry, but after walking a few miles, and taking a drink of water, I got a little refreshed. The general appearance of the country was still flat, with burned grass, and sandy soil, which blistered my feet. The scorching influence of the sun obliged me to stop for some hours in the day; during which I made several ineffectual attempts to construct a covering for my head. At times I thought my brain was on fire from the dreadful effects of the heat. I got no fruit those two days, and towards evening felt very weak for the want of nourishment, having been forty-eight hours without food; and to make my situation more annoying, I slept that evening on the banks of a pretty lake, the inhabitants of which would have done honor to a royal table. With what an evil eye, and a murderous heart, did I regard the stately goose, and the plump waddling duck, as they sported on the water, unconscious of my presence! Even with a pocket-pistol I could have done execution among them. The state of my fingers prevented me from obtaining the covering of grass which I had the two preceding nights; and on this evening I had no shelter whatever to protect me from the heavy dew.

On the following day, the 20th, my course was nearly northeast, and lay through a country more diversified by wood and water. I saw plenty of wild geese, ducks, cranes, curlews, and sparrows, also some hawks and cormorants, and at a distance about fifteen or twenty small deer. The wood consisted of pine, birch, cedar, wild-cherries, hawthorn, sweet-willow, honey-suckle, and sumach. The rattlesnakes were very numerous this day, with horned lizards, and grasshoppers: the latter kept me in a constant state of feverish alarm, from the similarity of the noise made by their wings to the sound of the rattles of the snake, when preparing to dart on its prey. I suffered severely during the day from hunger, and was obliged to chew grass occasionally, which allayed it a little. Late in the evening I arrived at a lake upwards of two miles long, and a mile broad, the shores of which were high, and well-wooded with large pine, spruce, and birch. It was fed by two rivulets, from the north and northeast, in which I observed a quantity of small fish; but had no means of catching any, or I should have made a Sandwich Island meal. There was, however, an abundant supply of wild cherries, on which I made a hearty supper. I slept on the bank of the nearest stream, just where it entered the lake, but during the night the howling of the wolves, and growling of bears, broke in terribly on my slumbers, and "balmy sleep" was almost banished from my eyelids. On rising the next morning, the 21st, I observed on the opposite bank, at the mouth of the river, the entrance of a large and apparently deep cavern, from which I judged some of the preceding night's music had issued. I now determined to make short journeys, for two or three days, in different directions, in the hope of falling on some fresh horse tracks; and in the event of being unsuccessful, to return each night to the lake, where I was at least certain of procuring cherries and water sufficient to sustain nature. In pursuance of this resolution I set out early, in a southerly direction, from the head of the lake, through a wild barren country, without any water or vegetation, save loose tufts of grass, like those already described. I had armed myself with a long stick, with which, during the day, I killed several rattlesnakes. Having discovered no fresh tracks, I returned late in the evening hungry and thirsty, and took possession of my berth of the preceding night. I collected a heap of stones from the water-side; and just as I was lying down observed a wolf emerge from the opposite cavern, and thinking it safer to act on the offensive, lest he should imagine I was afraid, I threw some stones at him, one of which struck him on the leg: he retired yelling into his den; and after waiting some time in fearful suspense, to see if he would reappear, I threw myself on the ground, and fell asleep; but, like the night before, it was broken by the same unmusical noise, and for upwards of two hours I sat up waiting in anxious expectation the return of daylight. The vapors from the lake, joined to the heavy dew, had penetrated my frail covering of gingham; but as the sun rose, I took it off, and stretched it on a rock, where it quickly dried. My excursion to the southward having proved abortive, I now resolved to try the east, and after eating my simple breakfast, proceeded in that direction: and on crossing the two small streams, had to penetrate a country full of "dark woods and rankling wilds," through which, owing to the immense quantities of underwood, my progress was slow. My feet too were uncovered, and, from the thorns of the various prickly plants, were much lacerated; in consequence of which, on returning to my late bivouack, I was obliged to shorten the legs of my trousers to procure bandages for them. The wolf did not make his appearance; but during the night I got occasional starts from several of his brethren of the forest.

I anticipated the rising of the sun on the morning of the 23d, and having been unsuccessful the two preceding days, determined to shape my course due north, and if possible not return again to the lake. During the day I skirted the wood, and fell on some old tracks, which revived my hopes a little. The country to the westward was chiefly plains, covered with parched grass, and occasionally enlivened by savannas of refreshing green, full of wild flowers and aromatic herbs, among which the bee and humming-bird banqueted. I slept this evening by a small brook, where I collected cherries and haws enough to make a hearty supper. I was obliged to make farther encroachments on the legs of my trowsers for fresh bandages for my feet. During the night I was serenaded by music which did not resemble " a concord of most sweet sounds;" in which the grumbling-bass of the bears was at times drowned by the less pleasing sharps of the wolves. I partially covered my body this night with some pieces of pine bark which I stripped off a sapless tree.

The country through which I dragged my tired limbs on the 24th was thinly wooded. My course was north and northeast. I suffered much from want of water, having got, during the day, only two tepid and nauseous draughts from stagnant pools which the long drought had nearly dried up. About sunset I arrived at a small stream, by the side of which I took up my quarters for the night. The dew fell heavily; but I was too much fatigued to go in quest of bark to cover me; and even had I been so inclined, the howling of the wolves would have deterred me from making the dangerous attempt. There must have been an extraordinary nursery of these animals close to the spot; for between the weak, shrill cries of the young, and the more loud and dreadful howling of the old, I never expected to leave the place alive. I could not sleep. My only weapons of defence were a heap of stones and a stick. Ever and anon, some more daring than others approached me. I presented the stick at them, as if in the act of levelling a gun, upon which they retired, vented a few yells, advanced a little further, and after surveying me for some time with their sharp, fiery eyes, to which the partial glimpses of the moon had imparted additional ferocity, retreated into the wood. In this state of fearful agitation I passed the night; but as daylight began to break, Nature asserted her supremacy, and I fell into a deep sleep, from which, to judge by the sun, I did not awake until between eight and nine o'clock on the morning of the 25th. My second bandages having been worn out, I was now obliged to bare my knees for fresh ones; and after tying them round my feet, and taking a copious draught from the adjoining brook for breakfast, I recommenced my joyless journey. My course was nearly north-northeast. I got no water during the day, nor any of the wild cherries. Some slight traces of men's feet, and a few old horse tracks occasionally crossed my path: they proved that human beings sometimes, at least, visited that part of the country, and for a moment served to cheer my drooping spirits.

About dusk, an immense sized wolf rushed out of a thick copse, a short distance from the pathway, planted himself directly before me, in a threatening position, and appeared determined to dispute my passage. He was not more than twenty feet from me. My situation was desperate, and as I knew that the least symptom of fear would be the signal for attack, I presented my stick, and shouted as loud as my weak voice would permit. He appeared somewhat startled, and retreated a few steps, still keeping his piercing eyes firmly fixed on me. I advanced a little, when he commenced howling in a most appalling manner; and supposing his intention was to collect a few of his comrades to assist in making an afternoon repast on my half-famished carcass, I redoubled my cries, until I had almost lost the power of utterance, at the same time calling out various names, thinking I might make it appear I was not alone. An old and a young lynx ran close past me, but did not stop. The wolf remained about fifteen minutes in the same position; but whether my wild and fearful exclamations deterred any others from joining him, I cannot say. Finding at length my determination not to flinch, and that no assistance was likely to come he retreated into the wood, and disappeared in the surrounding gloom.

The shades of night were now descending fast, when I came to a verdant spot, surrounded by small trees, and full of rushes, which induced me to hope for water; but after searching for some time, I was still doomed to bitter disappointment. A shallow lake or pond had been there, which the long drought and heat had dried up. I then pulled a quantity of the rushes and spread them at the foot of a large stone, which I intended for my pillow, but as I was about throwing myself down, a rattlesnake coiled, with the head erect, and the forked tongue extended in a state of frightful oscillation, caught my eye immediately under the stone. I instantly retreated a short distance; but assuming fresh courage, soon despatched it with my stick. On examining the spot more minutely, a large cluster of them appeared under the stone, the whole of which I rooted out and destroyed. This was hardly accomplished, when upwards of a dozen snakes of different descriptions, chiefly dark brown, blue, and green, made their appearance; they were much quicker in their movements than their rattletailed brethren, and I could only kill a few of them.

This was a peculiarly soul-trying moment. I had tasted no fruit since the morning before, and after a painful day's march, under a burning sun, could not procure a drop of water to allay my feverish thirst. I was surrounded by a murderous brood of serpents, and ferocious beasts of prey, and without even the consolation of knowing when such misery might have a probable termination. I might truly say, with the royal psalmist, that "the snares of death compassed me round about."

Having collected a fresh supply of rushes, which I spread some distance from the spot where I massacred the reptiles, I threw myself on them, and was permitted, through Divine goodness, to enjoy a night of undisturbed repose.

I arose on the morning of the 26th considerably refreshed, and took a northerly course, occasionally diverging a little to the east. Several times during the day, I was induced to leave the path, by the appearance of rushes, which I imagined grew in the vicinity of lakes, but on reaching them, my faint hopes vanished: there was no water, and I in vain essayed to extract a little moisture from them. Prickly thorns and small sharp stones added greatly to the pain of my tortured feet, and obliged me to make farther encroachments on my nether garments for fresh bandages. The want of water now rendered me extremely weak and feverish, and I had nearly abandoned all hopes of relief, when, about half-past four or five o'clock, the old pathway turned from the prairie grounds into a thickly wooded country, in an easterly direction; through which I had not advanced half a mile, when I heard a noise resembling a waterfall, to which I hastened my tottering steps, and in a few minutes was delighted at arriving on the banks of a deep and narrow rivulet, which forced its way with great rapidity over some large stones that obstructed the channel.

After offering up a short prayer of thanksgiving for this providential supply, I threw myself into the water, forgetful of the extreme state of exhaustion to which I was reduced: it had nearly proved fatal, for my weak frame could not withstand the strength of the current, which forced me down a short distance, until I caught the bough of an overhanging tree, by means of which I regained the shore. Here were plenty of hips and cherries; on which, with the water, I made a most delicious repast. On looking about for a place to sleep, I observed lying on the ground the hollow trunk of a large pine, which had been destroyed by lightning. I retreated into the cavity; and having covered myself completely with large pieces of loose bark, quickly fell asleep. My repose was not of long duration; for at the end of about two hours I was awakened by the growling of a bear, which had removed part of the bark covering, and was leaning over me with his snout, hesitating as to the means he should adopt to dislodge me; the narrow limits of the trunk which confined my body preventing him from making the attack with advantage. I instantly sprung up, seized my stick, and uttered a loud cry, which startled him, and caused him to recede a few steps, when he stopped and turned about, apparently doubtful whether he would commence an attack. He determined on an assault; but feeling I had not sufficient strength to meet such an unequal enemy, I thought it prudent to retreat, and accordingly scrambled up an adjoining tree. My flight gave fresh impulse to his courage, and he commenced ascending after me. I succeeded, however, in gaining a branch, which gave me a decided advantage over him; and from which I was enabled to annoy his muzzle and claws in such a manner with my stick, as effectually to check his progress. After scraping the bark some time with rage and disappointment, he gave up the task and retired to my late dormitory, of which he took possession. The fear of falling off, in case I was overcome by sleep, induced me to make several attempts to descend: but each attempt aroused my ursine sentinel; and after many ineffectual efforts, I was obliged to remain there during the rest of the night. I fixed myself in that part of the trunk from which the principal grand branches forked, and which prevented me from falling during my fitful slumbers.

On the morning of the 27th, a little after sunrise, the bear quitted the trunk, shook himself, "cast a longing, lingering look" towards me, and slowly disappeared in search of his morning repast. After waiting some time, apprehensive of his return, I descended and resumed my journey through the woods, in a north-northeast direction. In a few hours, all my anxiety of the preceding night was more than compensated, by falling in with a well-beaten horse-path, with fresh traces on it, both of hoofs and human feet; it lay through a clear open wood, in a northeast course, in which I observed numbers of small deer. About six in the evening, I arrived at a spot where a party must have slept the preceding night. Round the remains of a large fire which was still burning, were scattered several half-picked bones of grouse, partridges, and ducks, all of which I collected with economical industry. After devouring the flesh, I broiled the bones. The whole scarcely sufficed to give me a moderate meal, but yet afforded a most seasonable relief to my famished body. I enjoyed a comfortable sleep this night, close to the fire, uninterrupted by any nocturnal visiter. On the morning of the 28th, I set off with cheerful spirits, fully impressed with the hope of a speedy termination to my sufferings. My course was northerly, and lay through a thick wood. Late in the evening, I arrived at a stagnant pool, from which I merely moistened my lips; and having covered myself with some birch bark, slept by its side. The bears and wolves occasionally serenaded me during the night, but I did not see any of them. I rose early on the morning of the 29th, and followed the fresh traces all day, through the wood, nearly northeast by north. I observed several deer, some of which came quite close to me; and in the evening I threw a stone at a small animal resembling a hare, the leg of which I broke. It ran away limping, but my feet were too sore to permit me to follow it. I passed the night by the side of a small stream, where I got a sufficient supply of hips and cherries. A few distant growls awoke me at intervals, but no animal appeared. On the 30th, the path took a more easterly turn, and the woods became thicker and more gloomy. I had now nearly consumed the remnant of my trousers, in bandages for my wretched feet; and, with the exception of my shirt, was almost naked. The horse-tracks every moment appeared more fresh, and fed my hopes. Late in the evening, I arrived at a spot where the path branched off in different directions; one led up rather a steep hill, the other descended into a valley, and the tracks on both were equally recent. I took the higher; but after proceeding a few hundred paces through a deep wood, which appeared more dark from the thick foliage which shut out the rays of the sun, I returned, apprehensive of not procuring water for my supper, and descended the lower path. I had not advanced far, when I imagined I heard the neighing of a horse. I listened with breathless attention, and became convinced it was no illusion. A few paces farther brought me in sight of several of those noble animals, sporting in a handsome meadow, from which I was separated by a rapid stream. With some difficulty I crossed over, and ascended the opposite bank. One of the horses approached me: I thought him the "prince of palfreys; his neigh was like the bidding of a monarch, and his countenance enforced homage."

On advancing a short distance into the meadow, the cheering sight of a small column of gracefully curling smoke, announced my vicinity to human beings, and in a moment after, two Indian women perceived me: they instantly fled to a hut which appeared at the farther end of the meadow. This movement made me doubt whether I had arrived among friends or enemies; but my apprehensions were quickly dissipated by the approach of two men, who came running to me in the most friendly manner. On seeing the lacerated state of my feet, they carried me in their arms to a comfortable dwelling, covered with deer skins. To wash and dress my torn limbs, roast some roots, and boil a small salmon, seemed but the business of a moment. After returning thanks to that great and good Being in whose hands are the issues of life and death, and who had watched over my wandering steps, and rescued me from the many perilous dangers I encountered, I sat down to my salmon, of which it is needless to say I made a hearty supper.

The family consisted of an elderly man, and his son, with their wives and children. I collected from their signs that they were aware of my being lost, and that they, with other Indians and white men, had been out several days scouring the woods and plains in search of me. I also understood from them that our party had arrived at their destination, which was only a few hours' march from their habitation. They behaved to me with affectionate solicitude; and while the old woman was carefully dressing my feet, the men were endeavoring to make me comprehend their meaning. I had been fourteen days in a wilderness without holding "communion kind" with any human being; and I need not say I listened with a thousand times more real delight to the harsh and guttural voices of those poor Indians, than was ever experienced by the most enthusiastic admirer of melody from the thrilling tones of a Catalani, or the melting sweetness of a Stephens. As it was too late, after finishing my supper, to proceed farther that night, I retired to rest on a comfortable couch of buffalo and deer skins. I slept soundly: and the morning of the 31st was far advanced before I awoke. After breakfasting on the remainder of the salmon, I prepared to join my white friends. A considerable stream, about ninety yards broad, called *Cœur d' Alene* river, flowed close to the hut. The old man and his son accompanied me. We crossed the river in a canoe; after which they brought over three horses, and having enveloped my body in an Indian mantle of deer skin, we mounted, and set off at a smart trot in an easterly direction. We had not proceeded more than seven miles, when I felt the bad effects of having eaten so much salmon after so long a fast. I had a severe attack of indigestion, and for two hours suffered extreme agony; and, but for the great attention of the kind Indians, I think it would have proved fatal. About an hour after recommencing our journey we arrived in a clear wood, in which, with joy unutterable, I observed our Canadians at work hewing timber. I rode between the two natives. One of our men, named François Gardepie, who had been on a trading excursion, joined us on horseback. My deer skin robe and sunburnt features completely set his powers of recognition at defiance, and he addressed me as an Indian. I replied in French, by asking him how all our people were. Poor François appeared electrified, exclaimed "*Sainte Vierge!*" and galloped into the wood, vociferating, "*O mes amis! mes amis! il est trouvé!— Oui, oui, il est trouvé!*"—"*Qui? qui?*" asked his comrades. "*Monsieur Cox! Monsieur Cox!*" replied François. "*Le voilà! le voilà!*" pointing towards me. Away went saws, hatchets, and axes, and each man rushed forward to the tents, where we had by this time arrived. It is needless to say that our astonishment and delight at my miraculous escape were mutual. The friendly Indians were liberally rewarded; the men were allowed a holiday, and every countenance bore the smile of joy and happiness.

## HUNTING ON THE COLUMBIA RIVER.

IN the great plains on the east side of the Columbia, says Mr. Ross Cox, between Oakinagan and the Spokan lands, there are, during the autumnal months, plenty of deer, grouse, wild ducks, and geese.

I spent a great portion of this period with a few of my men and some Indians, on shooting excursions, and had excellent sport.

We stopped one very sultry day about noon to rest our horses, and enjoy the cooling shade afforded by a clump of sycamore-trees with a refreshing draught from an adjoining spring. Several large hawks were flying about the spot, two of which we brought down. From their great size, immense claws, and large hooked beaks, they could have easily carried off a common-sized duck or goose. Close to our resting-place was a small hill, round the top of which I observed the hawks assemble, and judging that a nest was there, without communicating my intention to any of the party, I determined to find it out.

I therefore cautiously ascended the eminence, on the summit of which I perceived a nest larger than a common-sized market-basket, formed of branches of trees, one laid regularly over the other, and the least of which an inch in circumference. Around it were scattered bones, skeletons, and half-mangled bodies of pigeons, sparrows, humming-birds, &c. Next to a rattlesnake and shark, my greatest aversion is a hawk; and on this occasion it was not diminished by observing the remains of the feathered tribe, which had, from to time, fallen a prey to their voracious appetite. I therefore determined to destroy the nest, and disperse its inhabitants; but I had scarcely commenced the work of demolition with my dagger, when old and young flew out and attacked me in every direction, but particularly about my face and eyes; the latter of which, as a punishment for my temerity, they seemed determined to separate from their sockets.

In the mean time I roared out lustily for assistance, and laid about me with the dagger. Three men promptly ran up the hill, and called out to me to shut my eyes, and throw myself on the ground, otherwise I should be shortly blinded, promising in the mean time to assist me. I obeyed their directions; and just as I began to kiss the earth, a bullet from one of their rifles brought down a large hawk, apparently the father of the gang. He fell close to my neck, and in his expiring agonies made a desperate bite at my left ear, which I escaped, and in return gave him the *coup de grace*, by thrusting about four inches of my dagger down his throat. The death of their chieftain was followed by that of two others, which completely dispersed them; and we retired after breaking up their den.

Red foxes and wolves are also in great numbers about the plains; but their skins are not now purchased by the Company, as the price given for them would not defray the expense of their carriage.

The prairie wolves are much smaller than those which inhabit the woods. They generally travel together in numbers, and a solitary one is seldom met with. Two or three of us have often pursued from fifty to one hundred, driving them before us as quickly as our horses could charge.

Their skins are of no value, and we do not therefore waste much powder and ball in shooting them. The Indians, who are obliged to pay dear for their ammunition, are equally careful not to throw it away on objects that bring no remunerating value. The natural consequence is, that the wolves are allowed to multiply; and some parts of the country are completely overrun by them. The Indians catch numbers of them in traps, which they set in the vicinity of those places where their tame horses are sent to graze. The traps are merely excavations covered over with slight switches and hay, and baited with meat, &c., into which the wolves fall, and being unable to extricate themselves, they perish by famine, or the knife of the Indian. These destructive animals annually destroy numbers of horses; particularly during the winter season, when the latter get entangled in the snow; in which situation they become an easy prey to their light-footed pursuers, ten or fifteen of which will often fasten on one animal, and with their long fangs in a few minutes separate the head from the body. If, however, the horses are not prevented from using their legs, they sometimes punish the enemy severely; as an instance of this, I saw one morning the bodies of two of our horses which had been killed the night before, and around were lying eight dead and maimed wolves; some with their brains scattered about, and others with their limbs and ribs broken by the hoofs of the furious animals in their vain attempts to escape from their sanguinary assailants.

While I was at Spokan I went occasionally to the horse prairie, which is nearly surrounded by partially-wooded hills, for the purpose of watching the manœuvres of the wolves in their combined attacks. The first announcement of their approach was a few shrill currish barks at intervals, like the outpost firing of skirmishing parties. These were answered by similar barking from an opposite direction, until the sounds gradually approximated, and at length ceased on the junction of the different parties. We prepared our guns, and concealed ourselves behind a thick cover. In the mean time, the horses, sensible of the approaching danger, began to paw the ground, snort, toss up their heads, look wildly about them, and exhibit all the symptoms of fear. One or two stallions took the lead, and appeared to wait with a degree of comparative composure for the appearance of the enemy.

The allies at length entered the field in a semicircular form, with their flanks extended for the evident purpose of surrounding their prey. They were between two and three hundred strong. The horses, on observing their movement, knew from experience its object, and dreading to encounter so numerous a force, instantly turned round, and galloped off in a contrary direction. Their flight was the signal for the wolves to advance; and immediately uttered a simultaneous yell, they charged after the fugitives, still preserving their crescent form. Two or three of the horses, which were not in the best condition, were quickly overtaken by the advanced guard of the enemy. The former, finding themselves unable to keep up with the band, commenced kicking at their pursuers, several of which received some severe blows; but these being reinforced by others, they would have shortly despatched the horses had not we, just in time, emerged from our place of concealment, and discharged a volley at the enemy's centre, by which a few were brought down. The whole battalion instantly wheeled about, and fled towards the hills in the utmost disorder; while the horses, on hearing the fire, changed their course and galloped up to us. Our appearance saved several of them from the fangs of their foes; and by their neighing they seemed to express their joy and gratitude at our timely interference.

Although the wolves of North America are the most daring of all the beasts of prey on that continent, they are by no means so courageous or ferocious as those of Europe, particularly in Spain or the south of France, in which countries they commit dreadful ravages, both on man and beast:* whereas, an American wolf, except forced by desperation, will seldom or never attack a hu-

* During the late Peninsular war, the Duke of Wellington had occasion to send despatches by a mounted dragoon, to a general of division not quite a day's march distant from headquarters. The answer not having arrived at the period it was expected, his Grace despatched three others to ascertain the cause. They found the mangled remains of their unfortunate comrade lying beside those of his horse, and the greater portion of the flesh eaten off their bodies. His sword was firmly grasped in his mutilated hand, and the dead carcasses of seven or eight wolves which lay about him, exhibited strong marks of the sabre, and of the desperation with which he fought before he was overpowered by numbers.

man being; a remarkable instance of which is mentioned in the detail of my wanderings in the previous article. The lynxes are by no means so numerous as the wolves, but they are equally destructive, and individually more daring. They generally travel alone, or in couples, and seldom fly as the wolves do on the first approach of man. The largest American lynx, does not exceed in size, an English mastiff.

Bears are scarce about the plains, but they are found in considerable numbers in the vicinity of the woods and lakes. Their flesh is excellent, particularly in the summer and autumnal months, when roots and wild fruit are had in abundance. They are most dangerous animals to encounter, especially if they are slightly wounded, or that any of their cubs are in danger, in which case, they will rush on a man, though he were armed at all points; and wo to him if Bruin should once enfold him in his dreadful grasp.

I have seen several of our hunters, as well as many Indians, who had been dreadfully lacerated in their encounters with bears; some have been deprived of their ears, others had their noses nearly torn off, and a few have been completely blinded.

From the scarcity of food in the spring months, they are then more savage than at any other season, and during that period it is a highly dangerous experiment to approach them.

The following anecdote will prove this, and, were not the fact confirmed by the concurrent testimony of ten more, I would not have given it a place among my *memorabilia*.

In the spring of this year, (1816) Mr. M'Millan had despatched ten Canadians in a canoe, down the Flathead river, on a trading excursion. The third evening after quitting the fort, while they were quietly sitting round a blazing fire, eating a hearty dinner of deer, a large half-famished bear cautiously approached the group, from behind an adjacent tree; and before they were aware of his presence, he sprang across the fire, seized one of the men (who had a well-furnished bone in his hand) round his waist, with the two fore paws, and ran about fifty yards with him on his hind legs, before he stopped. His comrades were so thunderstruck, at the unexpected appearance of such a visitor, and his sudden retreat with *pauvre Louisson*, that they for some time lost all presence of mind; and, in a state of fear and confusion, were running to and fro, each expecting in his turn to be kidnapped in a similar manner; when at length, Baptiste Le Blanc, a half-breed hunter, seized his gun, and was in the act of firing at the bear, but was stopped by some of the others, who told him he would inevitably kill their friend, in the position in which he was then placed. During this parley bruin relaxed his grip of the captive, whom he kept securely under him, and very leisurely began picking the bone which the latter had dropped. Once or twice Louisson attempted to escape, which only caused the bear to watch him more closely; but on his making another attempt, he again seized Louisson round the waist, and commenced giving him one of those infernal embraces which generally end in death. The poor fellow was now in great agony, and vented the most frightful screams; and observing Baptiste with his gun ready, anxiously watching a safe opportunity to fire, he cried out, *Tire! tire! mon cher frère, si tu m'aimes. Tire, pour l'amour du bon Dieu! A la tête! à la tête!* This was enough for Le Blanc, who instantly let fly, and hit the bear over the right temple. He fell, and at the same moment dropped Louisson; but he gave him an ugly scratch with his claws across the face, which for some time afterwards spoiled his beauty. After the shot, Le Blanc darted to his comrade's assistance, and with his *couteau de chasse*, quickly finished the sufferings of the man-stealer, and rescued his friend from impending death; for, with the exception of the above-mentioned scratch, he escaped uninjured. They commenced the work of dissection with right good will; but on skinning the bear, they found scarcely any meat on his bones; in fact the animal had been famishing, and in a fit of hungry desperation, made one of the boldest attempts at kidnapping ever heard of in the legends of ursine courage.

## SHOOTING WILD TURKEYS.

WHILST speaking of the shooting of turkeys, says Mr. Audubon, I feel no hesitation in relating the following occurrence, which happened to myself. While in search of game, one afternoon late in autumn, when the males go together, and the females are by themselves also, I heard the clucking of one of the latter, and immediately finding her perched on a fence, made towards her. Advancing slowly and cautiously, I heard the yelping notes of some gobblers, when I stopped and listened in order to ascertain the direction in which they came. I then ran to meet the birds, hid myself by the side of a large fallen tree, cocked my gun, and waited with impatience for a good opportunity.* The gobblers continued yelping in answer to the female, which all this while remained on the fence. I looked over the log, and saw about thirty fine cocks advancing rather cautiously towards the very spot where I lay concealed. They came so near, that the light in their eyes could easily be perceived, when I fired one barrel, and killed three. The rest, instead of flying off, fell a strutting around their dead companions; and had I not looked on shooting again as murder without necessity, I might have secured at least another. So I showed myself, and marching to the place where the dead birds were, drove away the survivors. I may also mention, that a friend of mine shot a fine hen, from his horse, with a pistol, as the poor thing was probably returning to her nest to lay.

Should you, good natured reader, be a sportsman, and now and then have been fortunate in the exercise of your craft, the following incident, which I shall relate to you as I had it from the mouth of an honest farmer, may prove interesting. Turkeys were very abundant in his neighborhood, and, resorting to his cornfields, at the period when the maize had just shot up from the ground, destroyed great quantities of it. This induced him to swear vengeance against the species. He cut a long

* See vignette on the title page.

trench in a favorable situation, put a great quantity of corn in it, and having heavily loaded a famous duck gun of his, placed it so as that he could pull the trigger by means of a string, when quite concealed from the birds.

The turkeys soon discovered the corn in the trench, and quickly disposed of it, at the same time continuing their ravages in the fields. He filled the trench again, and one day seeing it quite black with the turkeys, whistled loudly, on which all the birds raised their heads, when he pulled the trigger by the long string fastened to it. The explosion followed of course, and the turkeys were seen scampering off in all directions, in utter discomfiture and dismay. On running to the trench, he found nine of them extended in it. The rest did not consider it expedient to visit his corn again for that season.

During spring, turkeys are *called*, as it is termed, by drawing the air in a peculiar way, through one of the second joint bones of a wing of that bird, which produces a sound resembling the voice of the female, on hearing which, the male comes up, and is shot. In managing this, however, no fault must be committed, for turkeys are quick in distinguishing counterfeit sounds, and when *half civilized*, are very wary and cunning. I have known many to answer to this kind of call, without moving a step, and thus entirely defeat the scheme of the hunter, who dared not move from his hiding-place, lest a single glance of the gobbler's eye should frustrate all further attempts to decoy them. Many are shot when at roost, in this season, by answering with a roll ing gobble to a sound in imitation of the cry of the Barred Owl.

But the most common method of procuring wild turkeys is by means of *pens*. These are placed in parts of the woods where turkeys have been frequently observed to roost, and are constructed in the following manner. Young trees of four or five inches diameter are cut down, and divided into pieces of the length of twelve or fourteen feet. Two of these are laid on the ground parallel to each other, at a distance of ten or twelve feet. Two other pieces are laid across the ends of these, at right angles to them, and in this manner, successive layers are added, until the fabric is raised to the height of about four feet. It is then covered with similar pieces of wood, placed three or four inches apart, and loaded with one or two heavy logs to render the whole firm. This done, a trench about eighteen inches in depth and width, is cut under one side of the cage, into which it opens slantingly and rather abruptly. It is continued on its outside to some distance, so as gradually to attain the level of the surrounding ground. Over the part of this trench within the pen, and close to the wall, some sticks are placed so as to form a kind of bridge about a foot in breadth. The trap being now finished, the owner places a quantity of Indian corn in its centre, as well as in the trench, and as he walks off, drops here and there a few grains in the woods, sometimes to the distance of a mile. This is repeated at every visit to the trap, after the turkeys have found it. Sometimes two trenches are cut, in which case the trenches enter on opposite sides of the trap, and are both strewn with corn. No sooner has a turkey discovered the train of corn, than it communicates the circumstance to the flock by a cluck, when all of them come up, and searching for the grains scattered about, at length come upon the trench, which they follow, squeezing themselves one after another through the passage under the bridge. In this manner the whole flock sometimes enters, but more commonly six or seven only, as they are alarmed by the least noise, even the cracking of a tree in frosty weather. Those within, having gorged themselves, raise their heads and try to force their way through the top or sides of the pen, passing and repassing on the bridge, but never for a moment looking down, or attempting to escape through the passage by which they entered. Thus they remain until the owner of the trap arriving, closes the trench, and secures his captives. I have heard of eighteen turkeys having been caught, in this manner, at a single visit to the trap. I have had many of these pens myself, but never found more than seven in them at a time. One winter I kept an account of the produce of a pen which I visited daily, and found that seventy-six had been caught in it, in about two months. When these birds are abundant, the owners of the pens sometimes become satiated with their flesh, and neglect to visit the pens for several days, in some cases for weeks. The poor captives thus perish for want of food; for, strange as it may seem, they scarcely ever regain their liberty, by descending into the trench and retracing their steps. I have more than once found four or five, and even ten dead in a pen, through inattention. Where wolves or lynxes are numerous, they are apt to secure the prize before the owner of the trap arrives. One morning, I had the pleasure of securing in one of my pens, a fine black wolf, which, on seeing me, squatted, supposing me to be passing in another direction.

## HUNTING THE COUGAR.*

THERE is an extensive Swamp in the section of the State of Mississippi which lies partly in the Choctaw territory. It commences at the borders of the Mississippi, at no great distance from a Chickasaw village, situated near the mouth of a creek known by the name of Vanconnah, and partly inundated by the swellings of several large bayous, the principal of which, crossing the swamp in its whole extent, discharges its waters not far from the mouth of the Yazoo river. This famous bayou is called False river. The swamp of which I am speaking, follows the windings of the Yazoo, until the latter branches off to the northeast, and at this point forms the stream named Cold Water river, below which the Yazoo receives the draining of another bayou inclining towards the northwest, and intersecting that known by the name of False river, at a short distance from the place where the latter receives the waters of the Mississippi. This tedious account of the situation of the Swamp, is given with the view of pointing it out to all students of nature who may chance to go that way,

* Audubon's Ornithological Biography.

and whom I would earnestly urge to visit its interior, as it abounds in rare and interesting productions: birds, quadrupeds, and reptiles, as well as molluscous animals, many of which, I am persuaded, have never been described.

In the course of one of my rambles, I chanced to meet with a squatter's cabin on the banks of the Cold Water river. In the owner of this hut, like most of those adventurous settlers in the uncultivated tracts of our frontier districts, I found a person well versed in the chase, and acquainted with the habits of some of the larger species of quadrupeds and birds. As he who is desirous of instruction ought not to disdain listening to any one who has knowledge to communicate, however humble may be his lot, or however limited his talents, I entered the squatter's cabin, and immediately opened a conversation with him respecting the situation of the swamp, and its natural productions. He told me he thought it the very place I ought to visit, spoke of the game which it contained, and pointed to some bear and deer skins, adding that the individuals to which they had belonged formed but a small portion of the number of those animals which he had shot within it. My heart swelled with delight, and on asking if he would accompany me through the great morass, and allow me to become an inmate of his humble but hospitable mansion, I was gratified to find that he cordially assented to all my proposals. So I immediately unstrapped my drawing materials, laid up my gun, and sat down to partake of the homely but wholesome fare intended for the supper of the squatter, his wife, and his two sons.

The quietness of the evening seemed in perfect accordance with the gentle demeanor of the family. The wife and children, I more than once thought, seemed to look upon me as a strange sort of person, going about, as I told them I was, in search of birds and plants; and were I here to relate the many questions which they put to me in return for those which I addressed to them, the catalogue would occupy several pages. The husband, a native of Connecticut, had heard of the existence of such men as myself, both in our own country and abroad, and seemed greatly pleased to have me under his roof. Supper over, I asked my kind host what had induced him to remove to this wild and solitary spot. "The people are growing too numerous now to thrive in New England," was his answer. I thought of the state of some parts of Europe, and calculating the denseness of their population compared with that of New England, exclaimed to myself, "How much more difficult must it be for men to thrive in those populous countries!" The conversation then changed, and the squatter, his sons and myself, spoke of hunting and fishing, until at length tired, we laid ourselves down on pallets of bear skins, and reposed in peace on the floor of the only apartment of which the hut consisted.

Day dawned, and the squatter's call to his hogs, which, being almost in a wild state, were suffered to seek the greater portion of their food in the woods, awakened me. Being ready dressed, I was not long in joining him. The hogs and their young came grunting at the well known call of their owner, who threw them a few ears of corn, and counted them, but told me that for some weeks their number had been greatly diminished by the ravages committed upon them by a large Panther, by which name the Cougar is designated in America, and that the ravenous animal did not content himself with the flesh of his pigs, but now and then carried off one of his calves, notwithstanding the many attempts he had made to shoot it. The Painter, as he sometimes called it, had on several occasions robbed him of a dead deer; and to these exploits the squatter added several remarkable feats of audacity which it had performed, to give me an idea of the formidable character of the beast. Delighted by his description, I offered to assist him in destroying the enemy, at which he was highly pleased, but assured me that unless some of his neighbors should join us with their dogs and his own, the attempt would prove fruitless. Soon after, mounting a horse, he went off to his neighbors, several of whom lived at a distance of some miles, and appointed a day of meeting.

The hunters, accordingly, made their appearance, one fine morning, at the door of the cabin, just as the sun was emerging from beneath the horizon. They were five in number, and fully equipped for the chase, being mounted on horses, which in some parts of Europe might appear sorry nags, but which in strength, speed, and bottom, are better fitted for pursuing a cougar or a bear through woods and morasses than any in that country. A pack of large ugly curs were already engaged in making acquaintance with those of the squatter. He and myself mounted his two best horses, whilst his sons were bestriding others of inferior quality.

Few words were uttered by the party until we had

reached the edge of the Swamp, where it was agreed that all should disperse and seek for the fresh track of the Painter, it being previously settled that the discoverer should blow his horn, and remain on the spot until the rest should join him. In less than an hour, the sound of the horn was clearly heard, and, sticking close to the squatter, off we went through the thick woods, guided only by the now and then repeated call of the distant huntsman. We soon reached the spot, and in a short time the rest of the party came up. The best dog was sent forward to track the Cougar, and in a few moments the whole pack were observed diligently trailing, and bearing in their course for the interior of the Swamp. The rifles were immediately put in trim, and the party followed the dogs, at separate distances, but in sight of each other, determined to shoot at no other game than the Panther.

The dogs soon began to mouth, and suddenly quickened their pace. My companion concluded that the beast was on the ground, and putting our horses to a gentle gallop, we followed the curs, guided by their voices. The noise of the dogs increased, when all of a sudden their mode of barking became altered, and the squatter, urging me to push on, told me that the beast was *treed*, by which he meant that it had got upon some low branch of a large tree to rest for a few moments, and that should we not succeed in shooting him when thus situated, we might expect a long chase of it. As we approached the spot, we all by degrees united into a body, but on seeing the dogs at the foot of a large tree, separated again and galloped off to surround it.

Each hunter now moved with caution, holding his gun ready, and allowing the bridle to dangle on the neck of his horse, as it advanced slowly towards the dogs. A shot from one of the party was heard, on which the Cougar was seen to leap to the ground, and bound off with such velocity as to show that he was very unwilling to stand our fire longer. The dogs set off in pursuit with great eagerness and a deafening cry. The hunter who had fired came up and said that his ball had hit the monster, and had probably broken one of his fore-legs near the shoulder, the only place at which he could aim. A slight trail of blood was discovered on the ground, but the curs proceeded at such a rate that we merely noticed this, and put spurs to our horses, which galloped on towards the centre of the Swamp. One bayou was crossed, then another still larger and more muddy; but the dogs were brushing forward, and as the horses began to pant at a furious rate, we judged it expedient to leave them and advance on foot. These determined hunters knew that the Cougar being wounded, would shortly ascend another tree, where in all probability he would remain for a considerable time, and that it would be easy to follow the track of the dogs. We dismounted, took off the saddles and bridles, set the bells attached to the horses' necks at liberty to jingle, hoppled the animals, and left them to shift for themselves.

Now, reader, follow the group marching through the swamp, crossing muddy pools, and making the best of their way over fallen trees and amongst the tangled rushes that now and then covered acres of ground. If you are a hunter yourself, all this will appear nothing to you; but if crowded assemblies of "beauty and fashion," or the quiet enjoyment of your "pleasure-grounds," alone delight you, I must mend my pen before I attempt to give you an idea of the pleasure felt on such an expedition.

After marching for a couple of hours, we again heard the dogs. Each of us pressed forward, elated at the thought of terminating the career of the Cougar. Some of the dogs were heard whining, although the greater number barked vehemently. We felt assured that the Cougar was treed, and that he would rest for some time to recover from his fatigue. As we came up to the dogs, we discovered the ferocious animal lying across a large branch, close to the trunk of a cotton-wood tree. His broad breast lay towards us; his eyes were at one time bent on us and again on the dogs beneath and around him; one of his fore legs hung loosely by his side, and he lay crouched, with his ears lowered close to his head, as if he thought he might remain undiscovered. Three balls were fired at him, at a given signal, on which he sprang a few feet from the branch, and tumbled headlong to the ground. Attacked on all sides by the enraged curs, the infuriated Cougar fought with desperate valor; (See *Frontispiece*;) but the squatter advancing in front of the party, and almost in the midst of the dogs, shot him immediately behind and beneath the left shoulder. The Cougar writhed for a moment in agony, and in another lay dead.

The sun was now sinking in the west. Two of the hunters separated from the rest, to procure venison, whilst the squatter's sons were ordered to make the best of their way home, to be ready to feed the hogs in the morning. The rest of the party agreed to camp on the spot. The Cougar was despoiled of its skin, and its carcass left to the hungry dogs. Whilst engaged in preparing our camp, we heard the report of a gun, and soon after one of our hunters returned with a small deer. A fire was lighted, and each hunter displayed his *pone* of bread, along with a flask of whisky. The deer was skinned in a trice, and slices placed on sticks before the fire. These materials afforded us an excellent meal, and as the night grew darker, stories and songs went round, until my companions, fatigued, laid themselves down, close under the smoke of the fire, and soon fell asleep.

I walked for some minutes round the camp, to contemplate the beauties of that nature, from which I have certainly derived my greatest pleasures. I thought of the occurrences of the day, and glancing my eye around, remarked the singular effects produced by the phosphorescent qualities of the large decayed trunks which lay in all directions around me. How easy, I thought, would it be for the confused and agitated mind of a person bewildered in a swamp like this, to image in each of these luminous masses some wondrous and fearful being, the very sight of which might make their hair stand erect on his head! The thought of being myself placed in such a predicament burst over my mind, and I hastened to join my companions, beside whom I laid me down and slept, assured that no enemy could approach us without first rousing the dogs, which were growling in fierce dispute over the remains of the Cougar.

At daybreak we left our camp, the squatter bearing on his shoulder the skin of the late destroyer of his stock,

THE TRAVELLER AND THE POLECAT.

and retraced our step until we found our horses, which had not strayed far from the place where we had left them. These we soon saddled, and jogging along, in a direct course, guided by the sun, congratulating each other on the destruction of so formidable a neighbor as the Panther had been, we soon arrived at my host's cabin. The five neighbors partook of such refreshment as the house could afford, and dispersing, returned to their homes, leaving me to follow my favorite pursuits.

## THE TRAVELER AND THE POLE-CAT.

On a journey from Louisville to Henderson, in Kentucky, says Mr. Audubon,* performed during very severe winter weather, in company with a foreigner, the initials of whose name are D. T., my companion spying a beautiful animal, marked with black and pale yellow, and having a long and bushy tail, exclaimed, "Mr. Audubon, is not that a beautiful squirrel?" "Yes," I answered, "and of a kind that will suffer you to approach it, and lay hold of it, if you are well gloved." Mr. D. T. dismounting, took up a dry stick, and advanced toward the pretty animal, with his large cloak floating in the breeze. I think I see him approach, and laying the stick gently across the body of the animal, try to secure it; and I can yet laugh almost as heartily as I then did, when I plainly saw the discomfiture of the traveler. The Pole-

* Ornithological Biography.

cat,* (for a true Pole-cat it was, the *Mephitis Americana* of zoologists,) raised its fine bushy tail, and showered such a discharge of the fluid given him by nature as a defence, that my friend, dismayed and infuriated, began to belabour the poor animal. The swiftness and good management of the Pole-cat, however, saved its bones, and as it made its retreat towards its hole, it kept up at every step a continued ejectment, which fully convinced the gentleman that the pursuit of such squirrels as these was at the best an unprofitable employment.

This was not all, however. I could not suffer his approach, nor could my horse; it was with difficulty he mounted his own; and we were forced to continue our journey far asunder, and he much to leeward. Nor did the matter end here. We could not proceed much farther that night; as, in the first place, it was nearly dark when we saw the Pole-cat, and as, in the second place, a heavy snow-storm began, and almost impeded our progress. We were forced to make for the first cabin we saw. Having asked and obtained permission to rest for the night, we dismounted and found ourselves amongst a crowd of men and women who had met for the purpose of *corn-shucking*.

To a European who has not visited the western part of the United States, an explanation of this corn-shucking may not be unacceptable. Corn (or you may prefer calling it maize) is gathered in the husk, that is, by breaking each large ear from the stem. These ears are first thrown into heaps in the field, and afterwards carried in carts to the barn, or, as in this instance, and in

* In most parts of the country, this animal is called *Skunk*.

such portions of Kentucky, to a shed made of the blades or long leaves that hang in graceful curves from the stalk, and which, when plucked and dried, are used instead of hay, as food for horses and cattle. The husk consists of several thick leaves rather longer than the corn-ear itself, and which secure it from the weather. It is quite a labor to detach these leaves from the ear, when thousands of bushels of the corn are gathered and heaped together. For this purpose, however, and in the western country more especially, several neighboring families join alternately at each other's plantations, and assist in clearing away the husks, thus preparing the maize for the market or for domestic use.

The good people whom we met with at this hospitable house, were on the point of going to the barn, (the farmer here being in rather good condition,) to work until towards the middle of the night. When we had stood the few stares to which strangers must accustom themselves, no matter where, even in a drawing-room, we approached the fire. . What a shock for the whole party! The scent of the Pole-cat, that had been almost stifled on my companion's vestments by the cold of the evening air, now recovered its primitive strength. The cloak was put out of the house, but its owner could not be well used in the same way. The company, however, took to their heels, and there only remained a single black servant, who waited on us until supper was served.

I felt vexed at myself, as I saw the traveler displeased. But he had so much good breeding as to treat this important affair with great forbearance, and merely said he was sorry for his want of knowledge in zoology. The good gentleman, however, was not only deficient in zoological lore, but, fresh as he was from Europe, felt more than uneasy in this out-of-the-way dwelling, and would have proceeded towards my own house that night, had I not at length succeeded in persuading him that he was in perfect security.

We were shown to bed. As I was almost a stranger to him, and he to me, he thought it a very awkward thing to be obliged to lie in the same bed with me, but afterwards spoke of it as a happy circumstance, and requested that I should suffer him to be placed next the logs, thinking, no doubt, that there he should run no risk.

We started by break of day, taking with us the frozen cloak, and after passing a pleasant night in my own house, we parted. Some years after, I met my Kentucky companion in a far distant land, when he assured me, that whenever the sun shone on his cloak, or it was brought near a fire, the scent of the Pole-cat became so perceptible, that he at last gave it to a poor monk in Italy.

The animal commonly known in America by the name of Pole-cat, is about a foot and a half in length, with a large bushy tail, nearly as long as the body. The color is generally brownish-black, with a large white patch on the back of the head; but there are many varieties of coloring, in some of which the broad white bands of the back are very conspicuous. The Pole-cat burrows, or forms a subterranean habitation among the roots of trees, or in rocky places. It feeds on birds, young hares, rats, mice, and other animals, and commits great

MR. AUDUBON HUNTING.

depredations on poultry. The most remarkable peculiarity of this animal is the power, alluded to above, of squirting for its defence a most nauseously scented fluid contained in a receptacle situated under the tail, which it can do to the distance of several yards. It does not, however, for this purpose, sprinkle its tail with the fluid, as some allege, unless when extremely harassed by its enemies. The Pole-cat is frequently domesticated. The removal of the glands prevents the secretion of the nauseous fluid, and when thus improved, the animal becomes a great favorite, and performs the offices of the common cat with great dexterity.

## DEER HUNTING.

THE different modes of destroying Deer, says Mr. Audubon,* are probably too well understood, and too successfully practiced in the United States; for, notwithstanding the almost incredible abundance of these beautiful animals in our forests and prairies, such havoc is carried on amongst them, that in a few centuries, they will probably be as scarce in America, as the Great Bustard now is in Britain.

We have three modes of hunting deer, each varying in some slight degree, in the different States and Districts. The first is termed *Still Hunting*, and is by far the most destructive. The second is called *Fire-light Hunting*,

* Ornithological Biography.

and is next in its exterminating effects. The third, which may be looked upon as a mere amusement, is named *Driving*. Although many deer are destroyed by this latter method, it is not by any means so pernicious as the others. These methods I shall describe separately.

*Still Hunting* is followed as a kind of trade, by most of our frontier men. To be practiced with success, it requires great activity, an expert management of the rifle, and a thorough knowledge of the forest, together with an intimate acquaintance with the habits of the deer, not only at different seasons of the year, but also at every hour of the day, as the hunter must be aware of the situations which the game prefers, and in which it is most likely to be found, at any particular time. I might here present you with a full account of the habits of our deer, were it not my intention to lay before you, at some future period, in the form of a distinct work, the observations which I have made on the various quadrupeds of our extensive territories.

Illustrations of any kind require to be presented in the best possible light. We will therefore suppose that we are about to follow the *true hunter*, as the Still Hunter is also called, through the interior of the tangled woods, across morasses, ravines, and such places where the game may prove more or less plentiful, even should none be found there in the first instance. We will allow our hunter all the agility, patience, and care, which his occupation requires, and will march in his rear, as if we were spies, watching all his motions.

His dress, you observe, consists of a leather hunting-shirt, and a pair of trowsers of the same material. His feet are well moccasoned: he wears a belt round his waist, his heavy rifle is resting on his brawny shoulder; on one side hangs his ball-pouch, surmounted by the horn of an ancient buffalo, once the terror of the herd, but now containing a pound of the best gunpowder; his butcher-knife is scabbarded in the same strap, and behind is a tomahawk, the handle of which has been thrust through his girdle. He walks with so rapid a step, that probably few men could follow him, unless for a short distance, in their anxiety to witness his ruthless deeds. He stops, looks at the flint of his gun, its priming, and the leather cover of the lock, then glances his eye towards the sky, to judge of the course most likely to lead him to the game.

The heavens are clear, the red glare of the morning sun gleams through the lower branches of the lofty trees, the dew hangs in pearly drops at the top of every leaf. Already has the emerald hue of the foliage been converted into the more glowing tints of our autumnal months. A slight frost appears on the fence-rails of his little cornfield. As he proceeds, he looks to the dead foliage under his feet, in search of the well known traces of a buck's hoof. Now he bends toward the ground, on which something has attracted his attention. See! he alters his course, increases his speed, and will soon reach the opposite hill. Now he moves with caution, stops at almost every tree, and peeps forward as if already within shooting distance of the game. He advances again, but how very slowly! He has reached the declivity, upon which the sun shines in all its growing splendor; but mark him! he takes the gun from his shoulder, has already thrown aside the leathered cover of the lock, and is wiping the edge of his flint with his tongue. Now he stands like a monumental figure, perhaps measuring the distance that lies between him and the game which he has in view. His rifle is slowly raised, the report follows, and he runs. Let us run also. Shall I speak to him, and ask him the result of his first essay? Assuredly, reader, for I know him well.

"Pray, friend, what have you killed?" for to say, "What have you shot at?" might imply the possibility of his having missed, and so might hurt his feelings. "Nothing but a buck." "And where is it?" "Oh, it has taken a jump or so, but I settled it, and will soon be with it. My ball struck, and must have gone through his heart." We arrive at the spot where the animal had laid itself down among the grass, in a thicket of grape vines, sumachs, and spruce bushes, where it intended to repose during the middle of the day. The place is covered with blood, the hoofs of the deer have left deep prints in the ground, as it bounced in the agonies produced by its wound; but the blood that has gushed from its side, discloses the course which it has taken. We soon reach the spot. There lies the buck, its tongue out, its eye dim, its breath exhausted: it is dead. The hunter draws his knife, cuts the buck's throat almost asunder, and prepares to skin it. For this purpose he hangs it upon the branch of a tree. When the skin is removed, he cuts off the hams, and abandoning the rest of the carcass to the wolves and vultures, reloads his gun, flings the venison, enclosed by the skin, upon his back, secures it with a strap, and walks off in search of more game, well knowing that in the immediate neighborhood, another at least is to be found.

Had the weather been warmer, the hunter would have sought for the buck along the *shadowy* side of the hills. Had it been the spring season, he would have led us through some thick cane-brake, to the margin of some remote lake, where you would have seen the deer immersed to his head in the water, to save his body from the tormenting attacks of moschettoes. Had winter overspread the earth with a covering of snow, he would have searched the low damp woods, where the mosses and lichens, on which at that period the deer feeds, abound, the trees being generally crusted with them for several feet from the ground. At one time, he might have marked the places where the deer clears the velvet from his horns by rubbing them against the low stems of bushes, and where he frequently *scrapes* the earth with his forehoofs; at another, he would have betaken himself to places where persimons and crab-apples abound, as beneath these trees the deer frequently stops to munch their fruits. During early spring, our hunter would imitate the bleating of the doe, and thus frequently obtain both her and the fawn; or, like some tribes of Indians, he would prepare a deer's head, placed on a stick, and creeping with it amongst the tall grass of the prairies, would decoy the deer within reach of his rifle. But we have seen enough of the *still hunter*. Let it suffice for me to add, that by the mode pursued by him, thousands of deer are annually killed, many individuals shooting these animals merely for the skin, not caring for even the most valuable portions of the flesh, unless hunger, or a near market, induces them to carry off the hams.

The mode of destroying deer by *fire-light*, or, as it is named in some parts of the country, *forest-light*, never fails to produce a very singular feeling in him who witnesses it for the first time. There is something in it which at times appears awfully grand. At other times, a certain degree of fear creeps over the mind, and even affects the physical powers, of him who follows the hunter through the thick undergrowth of our woods, having to leap his horse over hundreds of huge fallen trunks, at one time impeded by a straggling grape-vine crossing his path, at another squeezed between two stubborn saplings, whilst their twigs come smack in his face, as his companion has forced his way through them. Again, he every now and then runs the risk of breaking his neck, by being suddenly pitched headlong on the ground, as his horse sinks into a hole covered over with moss. But I must proceed in a more regular manner, and leave my reader to judge whether such a mode of hunting would suit his taste or not.

The hunter has returned to his camp or his house, has rested and eaten of his game. He waits impatiently for the return of night. He has procured a quantity of pine-knots filled with resinous matter, and has an old frying-pan, that, for aught I know to the country, may have been used by his great-grandmother, in which the pine-knots are to be placed when lighted. The horses stand saddled at the door. The hunter comes forth, his rifle slung on his shoulder, and springs upon one of them, while his son, or a servant, mounts the other, with the frying-pan and the pine-knots. Thus accoutred, they proceed towards the interior of the forest. When they have arrived at the spot where the hunt is to begin, they strike fire with a flint and steel, and kindle the resinous wood. The person who carries the fire moves in the direction judged to be the best. The blaze illuminates the near objects, but the distant parts seem involved in deepest obscurity. The hunter who bears the gun keeps immediately in front, and after a while discovers before him two feeble lights, which are procured by the reflection of the pine fire from the eyes of an animal of the deer or wolf kind. The animal stands quite still. To one unacquainted with this strange mode of hunting, the glare from its eyes might bring to his imagination some lost hobgoblin that had strayed from its usual haunts. The hunter, however, nowise intimidated, approaches the object, sometimes so near as to discern its form, when raising the rifle to his shoulder, he fires and kills it on the spot. He then dismounts, secures the skin and such portions of the flesh as he may want, in the manner already described, and continues his search through the greater part of the night, sometimes until the dawn of day, shooting from five to ten deer, should these animals be plentiful. This kind of hunting proves fatal, not to the deer alone, but also sometimes to wolves, and now and then to a horse or a cow, which may have straggled far into the woods.

Now, reader, prepare to mount a generous, full blood Virginian Hunter. See that your gun is in complete order, for, hark to the sound of the bugle and horn, and the mingled clamor of a pack of harriers! Your friends are waiting you, under the shade of the wood, and we must together go *driving* the light-footed deer. The distance over which one has to travel is seldom felt, when pleasure is anticipated as the result: so, galloping we go pell-mell through the woods, to some well-known place, where many a fine buck has drooped its antlers under the ball of the hunter's rifle. The servants, who are called the *drivers*, have already begun their search. Their voices are heard exciting the hounds, and unless we put spurs to our steeds, we may be too late at our stand, and thus lose the first opportunity of shooting the fleeting game as it passes by. Hark again! the dogs are in chase, the horn sounds louder and more clearly. Hurry, hurry on, or we shall be sadly behind!

Here we are at last! Dismount, fasten your horse to this tree, place yourself by the side of that large yellow poplar, and mind you do not shoot me! The deer is fast approaching; I will to my own stand, and he who shoots him dead wins the prize.

The deer is heard coming. It has inadvertently cracked a dead stick with its hoof, and the dogs are now so near it that it will pass in a moment. There it comes. How beautifully it bounds over the ground! What a splendid head of horns! How easy its attitudes, depending, as it seems to do, on its own swiftness for safety! All is in vain, however: a gun is fired, the animal plunges and doubles with incomparable speed. There he goes! He passes another stand, from which a second shot, better directed than the first, brings him to the ground. The dogs, the servants, the sportsmen are now rushing forward to the spot. The hunter who has shot it is congratulated on his skill or good luck, and the chase begins again in some other part of the woods.

A few lines of explanation may be required to convey a clear idea of this mode of hunting. Deer are fond of following and retracing the paths which they have formerly pursued, and continue to do so even after they have been shot at more than once. These tracks are discovered by persons on horseback in the woods, or a deer is observed crossing a road, a field, or a small stream. When this has been noticed twice, the deer may be shot from the places called *stands* by the sportsman, who is stationed there, and waits for it, a line of stands being generally formed so as to cross the path which the game will follow. The person who ascertains the usual pass of the game, or discovers the parts where the animal feeds or lies down during the day, gives intimation to his friends, who then prepare for the chase. The servants start the deer with the hounds, and by good management, generally succeed in making it run the course that will soonest bring it to its death. But, should the deer be cautious, and take another course, the hunters, mounted on swift horses, gallop through the woods to intercept it, guided by the sound of the horns and the cry of the dogs, and frequently succeed in shooting it. This is extremely agreeable, and proves successful on almost every occasion.

Hoping that this account will be sufficient to induce you, kind reader, to go *driving* in our western and southern woods, I now conclude my chapter on Deer Hunting by informing you, that the species referred to above is the Virginian Deer, *Cervus Virginianus;* and that, until I be able to present you with a full account of its habits and history, you may consult for information respecting it the excellent *Fauna Americana* of my esteemed friend Dr. Harlan, of Philadelphia.

## SCIPIO AND THE BEAR.

The Black Bear, (*Ursus Americanus*,) says Mr. Audubon,* however clumsy in appearance, is active, vigilant, and persevering; possesses great strength, courage, and address; and undergoes with little injury the greatest fatigues and hardships in avoiding the pursuit of the hunter. Like the deer, it changes its haunts with the seasons, and for the same reason, namely, the desire of obtaining suitable food, or of retiring to the more inaccessible parts, where it can pass the time in security, unobserved by man, the most dangerous of its enemies. During the spring months, it searches for food in the low, rich, alluvial lands that border the rivers, or by the margins of such inland lakes as, on account of their small size, are called by us ponds. There it procures abundance of succulent roots, and of the tender juicy stems of plants, upon which it chiefly feeds at that season. During the summer heat, it enters the gloomy swamps, passes much of its time in wallowing in the

* Ornithological Biography.

mud, like a hog, and contents itself with crayfish, roots, and nettles, now and then, when hard pressed by hunger, seizing on a young pig, or perhaps a sow, or even a calf. As soon as the different kinds of berries which grow on the mountains begin to ripen, the Bears betake themselves to the high grounds, followed by their cubs. In such retired parts of the country where there are no hilly grounds, it pays visits to the maize fields, which it ravages for awhile. After this, the various species of nuts, acorns, grapes, and other forest fruits, that form what in the western country is called *mast*, attract its attention. The Bear is then seen rambling singly through the woods to gather this harvest, not forgetting meanwhile to rob every *bee-tree* it meets with, Bears being, as you well know, expert at this operation. You also know that they are good climbers, and may have been told, or at least may now be told, that the Black Bear now and then *houses* itself in the hollow trunks of the larger trees for weeks together, when it is said to suck its paws. You are probably not aware of a habit in which it indulges, and which, being curious, must be interesting to you.

At one season, the Black Bear may be seen examining the lower part of the trunk of a tree for several minutes with much attention, at the same time looking around, and snuffing the air, to assure itself that no enemy is near. It then raises itself on its hind legs, approaches the trunk, embraces it with its fore legs, and scratches the bark with its teeth and claws for several minutes in continuance. Its jaws clash against each other, until a mass of foam runs down on both sides of the mouth. After this it continues its rambles.

In various portions of our country, many of our woodsmen and hunters who have seen the Bear performing this singular operation just described, imagine that it does so for the purpose of leaving behind it an indication of its size and power. They measure the height at which the scratches are made, and in this manner can, in fact, form an estimate of the magnitude of the individual. My own opinion, however, is different. It seems to me that the Bear scratches the trees, not for the purpose of showing its size or its strength, but merely for that of sharpening its teeth and claws, to enable it better to encounter a rival of its own species during the amatory season. The Wild Boar of Europe clashes its tusks and scrapes the earth with its feet, and the Deer rubs its antlers against the lower part of the stems of young trees or bushes, for the same purpose.

Being one night sleeping in the house of a friend, I was awakened by a negro servant bearing a light, who gave me a note, which he said his master had just received. I ran my eye over the paper, and found it to be a communication from a neighbor, requesting my friend and myself to join him as soon as possible, and assist in killing some bears, at that moment engaged in destroying his corn. I was not long in dressing, you may be assured, and on entering the parlor, found my friend equipped, and only waiting for some bullets, which a negro was employed in casting. The overseer's horn was heard calling up the negroes from their different cabins. Some were already engaged in saddling our horses, whilst others were gathering all the cur-dogs of the plantation. All was bustle. Before half an hour had elapsed, four stout negro men, armed with axes and knives, and mounted on strong nags of their own, (for you must know, kind reader, that many of our slaves rear horses, cattle, pigs, and poultry, which are exclusively their own property,) were following us at a round gallop through the woods, as we made directly for the neighbor's plantation, a little more than five miles off.

The night was none of the most favorable, a drizzling rain rendering the atmosphere thick and rather sultry; but as we were well acquainted with the course, we soon reached the house, where the owner was awaiting our arrival. There were now three of us armed with guns, half a dozen servants, and a good pack of dogs of all kinds. We jogged on towards the detached field in which the bears were at work. The owner told us that for some days several of these animals had visited his corn, and that a negro who was sent every afternoon to see at what part of the enclosure they entered, had assured him there were at least five in the field that night. A plan of attack was formed: the bars at the usual gap of the fence were to be put down without noise; the men and dogs were to divide, and afterwards proceed so as to surround the bears, when, at the sounding of our horns, every one was to charge towards the centre of the field, and shout as loudly as possible, which it was judged would so intimidate the animals, as to induce them to seek refuge upon the dead trees with which the field was still partially covered.

The plan succeeded. The horns sounded, the horses galloped forward, the men shouted, the dogs barked and howled. The shrieks of the negroes were enough to frighten a legion of bears, and those in the field took to flight, so that by the time we reached the centre, they were heard hurrying towards the tops of the trees. Fires were immediately lighted by the negroes. The drizzling rain had ceased, the sky cleared, and the glare of the crackling fires proved of great assistance to us. The bears had been so terrified, that we now saw several of them crouched at the junction of the larger boughs with the trunks. Two were immediately shot down. They were cubs of no great size, and being already half dead, we left them to the dogs, which quickly despatched them.

We were anxious to procure as much sport as possible, and having observed one of the bears, which, from its size, we conjectured to be the mother, ordered the negroes to cut down the tree on which it was perched, when it was intended the dogs should have a tug with it, while we should support them, and assist in preventing the bear from escaping, by wounding it in one of the hind legs. The surrounding woods now echoed to the blows of the axemen. The tree was large and tough, having been girded more than two years, and the operation of felling it seemed extremely tedious. However, it began to vibrate at each stroke; a few inches alone now supported it; and in a short time it came crashing to the ground, in so awful a manner, that bruin must doubtless have felt the shock as severely as if we should feel a shake of the globe, produced by the sudden collision of a comet.

The dogs rushed to the charge, and harassed the bear on all sides. We had remounted, and now surrounded the poor animal. As its life depended upon its courage and strength, it exercised both in the most energetic manner. Now and then it seized a dog, and killed him by a single stroke. At another time, a well administered blow of one of its fore-legs, sent an assailant off yelping so piteously, that he might be looked upon as *hors de combat*. A cur had daringly ventured to seize the bear by the snout, and was seen hanging to it, covered with blood, whilst a dozen or more scrambled over its back. Now and then the infuriated animal was seen to cast a revengeful glance at some of the party, and we had already determined to despatch it, when, to our astonishment, it suddenly shook off all the dogs, and before we could fire, charged upon one of the negroes, who was mounted on a pied horse. The bear seized the steed with teeth and claws, and clung to its breast. The terrified horse snorted and plunged. The rider, an athletic young man, and a capital horseman, kept his seat, although only saddled on a sheep's skin tightly girthed, and requested his master not to fire at the bear. Notwithstanding his coolness and courage, our anxiety for his safety was raised to the highest pitch, especially when in a moment we saw rider and horse come to the ground together; but we were instantly relieved, on witnessing the masterly manner in which Scipio despatched his adversary, by laying open his skull with a single well-directed blow of his axe, when a deep growl announced the death of the bear, and the valorous negro sprung to his feet unhurt.

Day dawned, and we renewed our search. Two of the remaining bears were soon discovered, lodged in a tree about a hundred yards from the spot where the last one had been overpowered. On approaching them in a circle, we found that they manifested no desire to come down, and we resolved to try *smoking.* We surrounded the tree with a pile of brushwood and large branches. The flames ascended and caught hold of the dry bark. At length the tree assumed the appearance of a pillar of flame. The bears mounted to the top branches. When they had reached the uppermost, they were seen to totter, and soon after, the branch cracking and snapping across, they came to the ground, bringing with them a mass of broken twigs. They were cubs, and the dogs soon worried them to death.

The party returned to the house in triumph. Scipio's horse being severely wounded, was let loose in the field, to repair his strength by eating the corn. A cart was afterwards sent for the game. But before we had left the field, the horses, dogs, and bears, together with the fires, had destroyed more corn within a few hours, than the poor bear and her cubs had, during the whole of their visits.

## HUNTING THE GRIZZLY BEAR.

The following is an account of two grizzly bears taken by General Pike, in the Rocky Mountains, and afterwards exhibited at the Philadelphia Museum:

These bears were taken in rather a southern latitude, among the Rocky Mountains; and they are said to have been littered about the 1st of March, 1807, which, by the way, shows that this species produces later in the year than the Brown Bear. They were so young that they could take only milk, and in that state they were carried a long distance. Pike's account of their conduct on the march, shows both how they might have been tamed, and how they were not:—" I had a cage," says he, "prepared for both, which was carried on a mule, lashed between two packs; but I always ordered them to be let out the moment we halted, and not shut up again till we were prepared to march. By this treatment, they became exceedingly docile *when at liberty*, following my men like dogs through our camps, and the small villages and forts where we halted. When well supplied with sustenance, they would play like young puppies with each other and the soldiers; but the instant they were shut up, and placed on the mule, they became cross, as the jolting of the animal knocked them against each other, and they were sometimes left exposed to the scorching heat of a vertical sun for a day, without food or a drop of water, in which case, they would worry and tear each other, till nature was exhausted, and they could neither fight nor bawl any longer."

The following is the account of their conduct in the museum:—" When first received, they were quite small, but speedily gave indications of that ferocity for which this species is so remarkable. As they increased in size, they became exceedingly dangerous, seizing and tearing to pieces every animal they could lay hold of, and expressing extreme eagerness to get at those accidentally brought within sight of their cage, by grasping the iron bars with their paws, and shaking them violently, to the great terror of spectators, who felt insecure while witnessing such displays of their strength. In instance, an unfortunate monkey was walking over the top of the cage, when the end of the chain which hung from his waist, dropped through within reach of the bears; they immediately seized it, dragged the screaming animal through the narrow aperture, tore him limb from limb, and devoured his mangled carcass almost instantaneously. At another time, a small monkey thrust his arm through an opening in the bear cage, to reach after some object, one of them immediately seized him, and, with a sudden jerk, tore the whole arm and shoulder blade from the body, and devoured it before any one could interfere. They were still cubs, and very little more than half grown, when their ferocity became so alarming as to excite continual apprehension lest they should escape, and they were killed in order to prevent such an event."

Upon comparing the account of the soldier, who had no "story" to tell, but simply the truth, with that of the museum describer, in regard to these, the same animals, it cannot fail to strike the reader that there is a wonderful coincidence between these and the accounts of similar parties respecting the common hyæna. Every one who knows anything about domestic economy in the Dukhun, must be aware that the domestication of the hyæna as a substitute for the dog, is a very common occurrence there; and the memory which the hyæna at the Zoological Gardens retained of the kindness of colonel

Sykes, after the lapse of two years, and the apparent joy with which it welcomed him, though he gave it nothing, are interesting traits in the animal economy. Yet this same hyæna has, "time out of mind," been the "ferocious and untameable"—the very ultimate example of unrelenting cruelty.

Some of the habits of the bears and the hyæna are similar: for instance, they both consume dead carcasses; but otherwise, the hyæna is by much the more carnivorous animal of the two, especially in the structure of its teeth, and therefore the accounts of the untameable disposition of the one animal are no more deserving of rational credence, than those of the other.

We have no intentions of pleading specially for the grizzly bear, or for any animal whatever; but, though it is nearly exploded among all who *study* natural history, there is a great deal of the ridiculous exaggeration introduced by the showmen, still current in the country, and in so far perpetuated by compilers; and this remaining delusion, it becomes our duty, writing as we do for the public, by every means in our power to dispel. It is also our duty to mention, for the sake of those who have not the opportunity of seeing animals in a state of nature, or in that semi-freedom which they enjoy in zoological gardens, that, in the pigeon-holes of a traveling caravan, they see only the dwarfed or emaciated forms of the animals, and nothing whatever of their natural dispositions. Indeed, if the gentlest mouthpiece of the menagerie that ever told the terrors of a tiger to the wondering rustics at a fair, were to get only twelve months of the tenement and treatment of his beast, he would be the more ferocious animal, and therefore the better spectacle of the two.

But while we must not judge of the character of the powerful bear, under notice from the museum account, as little can we do it from the accounts of the hunters; for if the one shows us an animal soured and irritated by captivity, the other displays it with all its formidable energies aroused in defence of its life. Of these accounts by the hunters, we shall, however, give the substance of one instance from the expedition of Lewis and Clark, on the Missouri. One evening, the men in one of the hindmost of the canoes, perceived a grizzly bear lying on the open ground, about three hundred paces from the river; and six of them, good hunters, went to attack it. They got within forty paces unperceived, when four fired, all hitting, and two balls passing directly through the lungs. The bear sprang up and ran furiously at them with open mouth, upon which the two hunters who had reserved their fire, gave it, both hitting, and one breaking his shoulder blade, which somewhat retarded his motions. But before they could reload, he came so close upon them, that they were obliged to make directly for the river, and before they reached it, the bear was almost within paw's length. Two jumped into the canoe, and the other four concealing themselves among the willows, fired as fast as they could load. They struck him several times, but that only made him proceed more furiously in the direction whence the wound came. At last they were obliged to throw down their guns and pouches, and jump from a bank twenty feet high, into the river. But bruin is more expert both at jumping and swimming,

HUNTING THE GRIZZLY BEAR.

than even a backwoods' rifleman, so he plunged in after them, and was almost in the act of seizing the hindmost man, when one of those on shore shot him through the head, and he expired. When they dragged him on shore, they found that eight balls had passed through his body in different directions.

## HUNTING THE GRIZZLY BEAR IN HIS DEN.

THE every-day sports of the wild woods include many feats of daring that never find a pen of record. Constantly in the haunts of the savage, are enacting scenes of thrilling interest, the very details of which would make the denizen of enlightened life turn away with instinctive dread. Every Indian tribe has its heroes, celebrated respectively for their courage in different ways exhibited. Some for their acuteness in pursuing the enemy on the war-path, and others for the destruction they have accomplished among the wild beasts of the forest. A great hunter among the Indians is a marked personage. It is a title that distinguishes its possessor among his people as a prince; while the exploits in which he has been engaged hang about his person as brilliantly as the decorations of so many orders. The country in which the Osage finds a home, possesses abundantly the Grizzly Bear, an animal formidable beyond any other inhabitant of the North American forests: an animal seemingly insensible to pain, uncertain in its habits, and by its mighty strength able to overcome any living obstacle that comes within its reach, as an enemy. The Indian warrior, of any tribe, among the haunts of the Grizzly Bear, finds no necklace so honorable to be worn as the claws of this gigantic animal, if he fell by his own prowess; and if he can add an eagle's plume to his scalp-lock, plucked from a bird shot while on the wing, he is honorable indeed. The Indian's "smoke," like the fire-side of the white man, is often the place where groups of people assemble to relate whatever may most pleasantly while away the hours of a long evening, or destroy the monotony of a dull and idle day. On such occasions, the old "brave" will sometimes relax from his natural gravity, and grow loquacious over his chequered life. But no recital commands such undivided attention as the adventures with the Grizzly Bear; and the death of an enemy on the war-path hardly vies with it in interest.

We have listened to these soul-stirring adventures over the urn, or while lounging on the sofa; and the recital of the risks run, the hardships endured, have made us think them almost impossible, when compared with the conventional self-indulgence of enlightened life. But they were the tales of a truthful man; a hunter, who had strayed away from the scenes once necessary for his life, and who loved, like the worn-out soldier, to "fight his battles over," in which he was once engaged. It may be, and is the province of the sportsman to exaggerate; but the "hunter," surrounded by the magnificence and sublimity of an American forest, earning his bread by the hardy adventures of the chase, meets with too much reality to find room for coloring—too much of the sublime and terrible in the scenes with which he is associated, to be boastful of himself. Apart from the favorable effects of civilization, he is also separated from its contaminations; and boasting and exaggeration are "settlements" weaknesses, and not the products of the wild woods.

The hunter, whether Indian or white, presents one of the most extraordinary exhibitions of the singular capacity of the human senses to be improved by cultivation. The unfortunate deaf, dumb, and blind girl, in one of our public institutions,* selects her food, her clothing, and her friends, by the touch alone—so delicate has it become from the mind's being directed to that sense alone. The forest hunter uses the sight most extraordinarily well, and experience at last renders it so keen, that the slightest touch of a passing object on the leaves, trees, or earth, seems to leave deep and visible impressions, that to the common eye are unseen as the path of the bird through the air. This knowledge governs the chase and the war-path; this knowledge is what, when excelled in, makes the master-spirit among the rude inhabitants of the woods; and that man is the greatest chief who follows the coldest trail, and leaves none behind by his own footsteps. The hunter in pursuit of the Grizzly Bear is governed by this instinct of sight. It directs him with more certainty than the hound is directed by his nose. The impressions of the bear's footsteps upon the leaves, its marks on the trees, its resting-places, are all known long before the bear is

. * Hartford Asylum for the Deaf and Dumb.

really seen; and the hunter, while thus following "the trail," calculates the very sex, weight, and age with certainty. Thus it is that he will neglect or choose a trail; one because it is poor, and another because it is small, another because it is with cubs, and another because it is fat, identifying the very trail as the bear itself; and herein, perhaps, lies the distinction between the sportsman and the huntsman. The hunter follows his object by his own knowledge and instinct, while the sportsman employs the instinct of domesticated animals to assist his pursuits.

The different methods to destroy the Grizzly Bear, by those who hunt them, are as numerous as the bears that are killed. They are not animals which permit of a system in hunting them; and it is for this reason they are so dangerous and difficult to destroy. The experience of one hunt may cost a limb or a life in the next one, if used as a criterion; and fatal, indeed, is the mistake, if it comes to grappling with an animal whose gigantic strength enables him to lift a horse in his huge arms, and bear it away as a prize. There is one terrible exception to this rule; one habit of the animal may be certainly calculated on, but a daring heart only can take advantage of it.

The Grizzly Bear, like the tiger and lion, have their caves in which they live; but they use them principally as a safe lodging-place when the cold of winter renders them torpid and disposed to sleep. To these caves they retire late in the fall, and they seldom venture out until the warmth of spring. Sometimes two occupy one cave, but this is not often the case, as the unsociability of the animal is proverbial, they preferring to be solitary and alone. A knowledge of the forests, and an occasional trailing for bear, inform the hunter of these caves, and the only habit of the Grizzly Bear that can with certainty be taken advantage of, is that of his being in his cave alive, if at a proper season. And the hunter has the terrible liberty of entering his cave single-handed, and there destroying him. Of this only method of hunting the Grizzly Bear we would attempt a description.

The thought of entering a cave, inhabited by one of the most powerful beasts of prey, is calculated to try the strength of the best nerves; and when it is considered that the least trepidation, the slightest mistake, may cause, and probably will result in the instant death of the hunter, it certainly exhibits the highest demonstration of physical courage to pursue such a method of hunting. Yet there are many persons in the forests of North America who engage in such perilous adventures with no other object in view than the "sport" or hearty meal. The hunter's preparations to "beard the lion in his den," commence with examining the mouth of the cave he is about to enter. Upon the signs there exhibited he decides whether the bear is alone; for if there are two, the cave is never entered. The size of the bear is also thus known, and the time since he was last in search of food. The way this knowledge is obtained, from indications so slight, or unseen to an ordinary eye, is one of the greatest mysteries of the woods. Placing ourselves at the mouth of a cave containing a Grizzly Bear, to our untutored senses there would be nothing to distinguish it from one that was empty; but if some

Diana of the forest would touch our eyes, and give us the instinct of sight possessed by the hunter, we would argue thus: "From all the marks about the mouth of the cave, the occupant has not been out for a great length of time, for the grass and the earth have not been lately disturbed. The bear is in the cave, for the last tracks made are with the toe marks towards the cave. There is but one bear, because the tracks are regular and of the same size. He is a large bear; the length of the step and the size of the paw indicate this; and he is a fat one, because his *hind feet do not step in the impressions made by the fore ones*, as is always the case with a lean bear." Such are the signs and arguments that present themselves to the hunter; and mysterious as they seem, when not understood, when explained they strike the imagination at once as being founded on the unerring simplicity and the certainty of nature. It may be asked, How is it that the Grizzly Bear is so formidable to numbers, when met in the forest, and when in a cave can be assailed successfully by a single man? In answer to this, we must recollect that the bear is only attacked in his cave when he is in total darkness, and suffering from surprise and the torpidity of the season. These three things are in this method of hunting taken advantage of; and but for these advantages, no quickness of eye, no steadiness of nerve or forest experience, would protect for an instant the intruder to the cave of the Grizzly Bear. The hunter, having satisfied himself about the cave, prepares a candle, which he makes out of the wax taken from the comb of wild bees, softened by the grease of the bear. This candle has a large wick, and emits a brilliant flame. Nothing else is needed but the rifle. The knife and the belt are useless; for if a struggle should ensue that would make it available, the foe is too powerful to mind its thrusts before the hand using it would be dead. Bearing the candle before him, with the rifle in a convenient position, the hunter fearlessly enters the cave. He is soon surrounded by darkness, and is totally unconscious where his enemy will reveal himself. Having fixed the candle in the ground in firm position, with an apparatus provided, he lights it, and its brilliant flame soon penetrates into the recesses of the cavern—its size of course rendering the illumination more or less complete. The hunter now places himself on his belly, having the candle between the back part of the cave where the bear is, and himself; in this position, with the muzzle of the rifle protruding out in front of him, he patiently waits for his victim. A short time only elapses before Bruin is aroused by the light. The noise made by his starting from sleep attracts the hunter, and he soon distinguishes the black mass, moving, stretching, and yawning, like a person awaked from a deep sleep. The hunter moves not, but prepares his rifle; the bear, finally roused, turns his head towards the candle, and, with slow and wading steps, approaches it.

Now is the time that tries the nerves of the hunter. Too late to retreat, his life hangs upon his certain aim and the goodness of his powder. The slightest variation in the bullet, or a flashing pan, and he is a doomed man. So tenacious of life is the common black bear, that it is frequently wounded in its most vital parts, and will still escape or give terrible battle. But the Grizzly Bear seems to possess an infinitely greater tenacity of life. His skin, covered by matted hair, and the huge bones of his body, protect the heart, as if incased in a wall; while the brain is buried in a skull, compared to which adamant is not harder. A bullet, striking the bear's forehead, would flatten, if it struck squarely on the solid bone, as if fired against a rock; and dangerous indeed would it be to take the chance of reaching the animal's heart. With these fearful odds against the hunter, the bear approaches the candle, growing every moment more sensible of some uncommon intrusion. He reaches the blaze, and either raises his paw to strike it, or lifts his nose to scent it, either of which will extinguish it, and leave the hunter and the bear in total darkness. This dreadful moment is taken advantage of. The loud report of the rifle fills the cave with stunning noise, and as the light disappears, the ball, if successfully fired, penetrates the eye of the huge animal—the only place where it would find a passage to the brain—and this not only gives the wound, but instantly paralyzes, that no temporary resistance may be made. On such chances the American hunter perils his life, and often thoughtlessly courts the danger.

# CURIOUS METHOD OF HUNTING THE DEER.

In the great plains between Oakinagan and Spokan, says Mr. Ross Cox, there are at particular seasons numbers of small deer. The editor of Lewis and Clarke classes them as antelopes; but how much soever they may resemble those animals in swiftness and shape, their horns, as described by naturalists, are totally different. Their flesh is sweet and delicate, and they generally go in small herds. Towards the latter end of the summer they are in prime condition, and at that season we had some excellent sport in hunting them. The Indians, however, are not satisfied with our method of taking them in detail. On ascertaining the direction the deer have chosen, part of their hunters take a circuit in order to arrive in front of the herd, while those behind set fire to the long grass, the flames of which spread with great rapidity. In their flight from the devouring element they are intercepted by the hunters, and, while they hesitate between these dangers, great numbers fall by the arrows of the Indians.

The wolves almost rival the Indians in their manner of attacking the deer. When impelled by hunger, they proceed in a band to the plains in quest of food. Having traced the direction which a herd have taken, they form themselves into a horse-shoe line, the extreme points of which they keep open on the grand ravine. After some cautious manœuvring they succeed in turning the progress of the deer in that direction. This object effected, they begin to concentrate their ranks, and ultimately hem in their victims in such a manner as to leave them no choice but that of being dashed to pieces down the steep and rocky sides of the ravine, or falling a prey to the fangs of their merciless pursuers.

## BEAR HUNTING ADVENTURE OF ICHABOD MERRITT.

In December, 1820, there being a light snow, Merritt, with two other companions, (one of whom had been a sailor,) while upon a hunting excursion, came upon the track of a full grown bear, which, after following for a time, they found had ascended a huge white-wood (or poplar) tree. This had been broken off some seventy feet from the ground, and it was supposed that the bear must have secreted itself within its hollow at the top. Unwilling to lose their game, and ready for any daring enterprise, they looked about for ways and means to accomplish their object. They first proposed cutting the tree down. But this at the root was sound and not less than eighteen feet in circumference. This with only one axe, and that a dull one, they could not accomplish that day, and if left over night the bear would escape. The sailor proposed that if a smaller tree could be felled and lodged against the large one, he would climb it to the top and shoot the bear. A beech tree was then cut and lodged agreeable to their wishes. The sailor, who had often ascended the waving mast, had now a chance to show his intrepidity upon a forest tree. He prepared himself for the enterprise, and now he began to think should he succeed in gaining the top and miss his first shot, his situation would be dangerous in the extreme. The enraged bear would undoubtedly claim the premises, especially should it be a she-one with her cubs, she would doubtless claim her right and title to that elevated position, and a battle would ensue. In this case all would agree that the bear would have its choice of location and the advantage of position. In the struggle, too, the beech might be dislodged from the white-wood, and he would either fall with it to the ground or be left at the top of the tree. The first would be certain death, and the other would be no enviable situation. These were solemn thoughts for the sailor, and they probably weakened his nerves so much that it was found when he attempted to climb, that he could not ascend, after repeatedly trying, one inch beyond the assistance of his companions.

This so vexed Merritt that he told him to come down and he would try what he could do towards climbing the tree. He then slung his rifle to his hunting belt with the muzzle downwards and began to ascend the tree. This he succeeded in doing, and of getting from the topmost branches of the beech upon the limbs of the white-wood just high enough to look over in the hollow. It was dark, and all he could see was a pair of eyes several feet below him. After informing his companions and charging them to shoot the bear the moment it came out of the tree, and that he should depend upon them for protection if he missed, he fired into the tree, and then retreated back into the top of the beech and immediately reloaded. While doing this the bear with two cubs came out of the hollow of the tree. At this moment one of those below fired, but being so much agitated, he missed. The cubs took to a limb while the old bear made towards Merritt. She was in a menacing attitude and but a few feet above him when he made a second fire. This proved fatal and the bear fell. In falling she just brushed against him. Another hunter now coming up shot one of the cubs, and Merritt at his leisure reloaded and shot the other. He then succeeded in getting safely to the ground.

## UGLY ADVENTURE WITH A BEAR.

About the middle of May, 1803, a man living seven or eight miles east of Youngstown, had business that called him to that place. He started in the morning on foot, and, having accomplished his business, was on his return home. When within a mile and a half of his home, he was attacked by a large bear. Being unarmed and unable to outrun the bear, he sprang to climb a small tree. Before he got out of reach the bear caught him by the foot; but having got hold of a limb sufficiently strong, he held on until he drew his foot from her jaws and got out of reach. But the bear still kept at the root of the tree. This was about two o'clock, P. M. The man hallooed for help, and was heard by two men who were splitting rails about half a mile distant. They thought it was the noise of some wild animal and paid no further attention to it, until they returned to their cabin in the evening; but, as the noise continued, and attending to it more particularly they, concluding it was the voice of a person in distress, took each one his axe and ran in the direction of the voice, and answered the call. As soon as they got near enough to understand him, he told them he was badly wounded by a bear then at the root of the tree, and not to venture up unless they were armed; but they rushed on, and the bear ran off. They carried the man to his home, where he was confined the most of the summer.

## ADVENTURES IN THE BACKWOODS.

In the autumn of the year, says an old traveler, I was on a journey to the frontier portion of the States, but had a vast track of the "Backwoods" to travel through. I was in company with a gentleman, a friend of mine, his wife and sister; also a maid-servant, who was in the capacity of nurse, formed one of the party. My friend, who was city bred, had foolishly enough brought a close carriage with him, to the back settlements, when he first located himself there. At the time of our journey, he had resided about five years in the woods, during which his city-built chariot had never been used. The roads, in fact, rendered it quite unsafe to use a carriage of that description; but now that they were about to visit their city friends, he was anxious to do so in the style they knew he had formerly been accustomed to. I, also, had a carriage;

but mine was a true backwoods' affair, a regular yankee Dearborn wagon, with wooden springs, and a variety of flaming daubs of paint, laid on with true backwoods' taste, that is, with no taste at all. There was one thing about it which amused me exceedingly, and that was, a flaring device, or coat of arms, on the most conspicuous panel of the machine. The artist had undoubtedly intended it for the British lion and unicorn, but for what purpose I could not devise, as the wagon was not built "to order," but for whoever might wish to purchase it; and as all kings, princes, and potentates are considerably below *par* in Yankee land, I was puzzled to account for this strange whim of the wagon-maker. He had attempted no motto; but over the cipher were two "bending plumes," but the third of the prince of Wales' feathers was omitted, for there was, in fact, no room for it. The unicorn looked more like an enormous ram, with a single horn stuck on the top of his head, than the beast it was intended to represent; while the lion was in a recumbent position, looking over his right shoulder at his neighbor, with a look which seemed to say, "What strange company brother Jonathan has introduced me to!" But although the wagon had been somewhat disfigured with this painting, yet it had been made of the best white oak and hickory, and was really a tough and useful conveyance. With my friend's close carriage, and my own open wagon, we set forward on our journey; but the roads were so exceedingly deep, that the chariot stuck fast in the mud just as night came on; and although I took the whole party into my vehicle, in order to lighten it, my friend's horses were unable to draw it out. A considerble delay took place in our vain endeavors; but finding it could not be moved, we at last proceeded to the next house, about four miles, leaving the baggage in the chariot. We had now to get assistance, that is, we prevailed upon the person, at whose house we had arrived, to send off two pair of oxen, (horses he had none,) and two of his sons, to bring forward the deserted carriage, and about midnight they returned, "all safe and clever."

The following morning we set out pretty early, and in about two hours reached the place where we proposed taking breakfast. When we drove up to the house we had no obsequious landlord running out to welcome us; for on alighting and inquiring for him, Mrs. Le Barre (the landlady) told us he was not at home. "Who," I inquired, "will take care of our horses?"

To which, she very tartly replied, "Yourselves, I guess; for," continued she, "I shall likely have enough to do indoors."

Having acted my part of ostler, I repaired "indoors" to give directions about breakfast, as it had been arranged that I was to manage such matters. "Mrs. Le Barre," said I, "we shall want breakfast; what could you let us have?"

"I guess you can have tea if you wish; but I must first get baby quieted."

Now it so happened that my friend, who had been indisposed, was obliged to breakfast on tea, while the young lady breakfasted on coffee; and to sum up the matter, my friend's wife never drank either tea or coffee, but always chocolate! After baby was quieted, and tea fairly under way, I ventured to hint, that we should also require a little coffee, although I announced it with fear and trembling. But the greatest difficulty yet remained; and it was not until after many attempts that I got Mrs. Le B. informed, "that we should also want a little chocolate."

"Tea, coffee, and chocolate!" exclaimed the astonished woman; and lest some disagreeable salutation should be offered me, I hastened to the other room, taking shelter amongst my friends. I never shall forget the look mine hostess gave me, when I had announced chocolate in addition to tea and coffee; nor do I suspect that she will ever forget the party that had the unreasonableness to ask for such an unheard of variety. Since that time I have found it necessary to call on Mrs. Le B., but never dared to hint that we were old acquaintances.

The North American wolf is naturally shy, and if we may place confidence in those stories we hear, of the ravages committed by the wolves inhabiting some of the mountainous regions of Europe, he is, by comparison with his brethren of the Old World, a very harmless sort of creature. This great mildness of disposition is not, however, owing to any physical deficiency; for, although certainly less voracious than the European wolf, he is somewhat larger and stronger. In America they are rarely known to attack human beings; for, during a long residence in a district where they were rather numerous, I never was able to make out a clear case where a person had been attacked by them. I have indeed heard of persons being pursued, or *hunted*, as the Americans call it, by a number of wolves, but in all such cases the individuals were on horseback; and therefore the probability is, that the wolves pursued the horses, and not the men. However, from the facts I am about to relate, it would seem otherwise.

A medical gentleman, residing not far from the Chemung river, a tributary of the noble Susquehanna, had, one night in the middle of winter, been visiting a sick person at a distance of eight or ten miles from his own house. The country in that vicinity was then quite new, and but very few settlers had encroached on the aborinal forests. The doctor had been accustomed for some years, to travel through those wild regions at all seasons, and at all hours, by day and by night, but never had been in any way molested; nor had he ever had the slightest apprehension of danger from the wolves that were known occasionally to inhabit the surrounding woods. On the night in question, he set off homeward at a late hour, as he frequently had been wont to do; but before he had proceeded far, he became aware of his being pursued by a gang of wolves. The night was exceedingly frosty, but clear and star-light. For awhile they were only heard at a distance, but by-and-by the doctor could clearly distinguish five or six of them in full chase within less than twenty rods of him. The snow being pretty deep at the time, he found it was impossible to leave them, so he made up his mind to quit his horse, and ascend the first tree which appeared favorable for such a purpose. It was not long before such a one offered, and, permitting his horse to go at large, he was amongst the branches in a few seconds, and quite out of the reach of his hungry pursuers. He never doubted but they would continue in pursuit of his horse, which he flattered himself, would be able, now that he was relieved from his load, to make his escape. But to his surprise, he beheld no fewer than eight large wolves come round the tree on which he had taken shelter, and, instead of pursuing his horse, quietly awaited his coming down. Although he had no wish to descend under such circumstances, he was fully aware of the fate that awaited him should he find it expedient to remain until morning in his present situation. To escape from the effects of the keen frost he knew was impossible, and therefore he determined to maintain his position, in spite of the occasional serenading of the party below. What his feelings were during the night, or how the wolves contrived to amuse themselves for so many hours, I cannot precisely state; but about day-dawn they united in a farewell howl, and left the poor benumbed doctor at liberty to descend. With great difficulty he succeeded in reaching the ground, and with still more, he managed to reach the nearest dwelling, distant about three miles, from whence he was conveyed to his own house in a sleigh. Had his family been aware that the horse had returned without his rider, they undoubtedly would have gone in search of the doctor, and most probably have relieved him from his imprisonment at a much earlier hour. But although the horse had no doubt galloped straight to its stable door, the family knew nothing of its arrival until daylight returned.

. The doctor did not escape without experiencing the

ill effects of roosting for half a dozen hours in a leafless tree, in a severe North American January's frost; for a mortification ensuing in both his feet, the only chance of saving his life, was by amputating both his legs. However, the doctor yet lives to narrate his adventure, or as he terms it, "his wolf scrape;" and is one of the few instances on record in his part of the world of having been in real danger of becoming a supper for a few of those hungry animals.

The winter was more than usually severe among the mountains on the north waters of the Susquehanna. The snow fell pretty early in the month of December, so that winter might be said to have set in pretty decidedly some time before Christmas. I had been on a visit for a few weeks in the vicinity of S—— L——; but had accepted of an invitation to meet a party of my own countrypeople, at the residence of my kind friends, Mr. and Mrs. T——, on the last day in December, with an understanding that we were "to dance in the new year;" for even in the back settlements of America, we could at times meet and dance, and enjoy whatever the country afforded, forgetting for a time the gayer and more splendid scenes we had once been familiar with in our dear native country. The distance I had to travel was but six miles; yet the road—if a dim track through the woods might be so called—was at all seasons bad, now the snow was so deep that it was rendered still worse, so that it took a considerable time to get through it. At that season of the year, the wolves occasionally infest the neighborhood; and although at all seasons depredations are liable to be committed upon the small flocks of sheep in the vicinity, yet it is in winter, when they *pack* and hunt together, that the greatest danger is to be apprehended. The day previous to my proposed visit, a party of thirteen (for their numbers were easily ascertained by their tracks in the snow) had issued from their haunts in the adjoining forest, and destroyed nearly fifty sheep belonging to the gentleman with whom I was sojourning. Although they had probably sucked the blood of the chief part of the sheep they had killed, they of course had not been able to devour the carcasses of more than a fourth part; it looked as if they had slaughtered them through sheer wantonness. My invitation to my friends was to dine, at two o'clock; for it is not customary to keep to the extremes of fashion in the backwoods. I, however, for some reason or other, saw fit to defer going until evening, when, as my road lay close along the edge of the swamp the wolves were known to inhabit, I stood a good chance of being serenaded by their wild and melancholy howlings, and probably might arouse some of them from their lairs. My friends pressed me to travel by daylight, but I kept my determination; and just as the shades of evening were closing in, I desired my horse to be got ready; and when the boy brought him saddled to the door, he called my attention to the howling of the wolves, which could be distinctly heard in the exact direction of the road I had to travel, although the noise seemed to proceed from a swamp at a couple of miles distance. Being prepared with a stout cudgel in lieu of a riding-whip, I mounted my horse, and set forward, already beginning to repent of having delayed my journey until so late an hour. By the time I had passed the scene of carnage of the preceding day, and was about to enter the dark and almost trackless woods, daylight had totally disappeared, and nothing remained for me but to pursue my way, and make the best of it.

I had not proceeded far, ere I came to a steep descent, where the water, from an adjoining spring, had overflowed the snow, which was consequently formed into a continued sheet of ice, all the way down the declivity. My horse being smooth-shod, I deemed it safer to walk; therefore, dismounting and taking the bridle in my hand, I endeavored to lead the way down the slippery path. Before, however, I had got half way to the bottom, away slid both my feet, and down I came. My horse was so started at the suddenness of my fall, that he made a spring to one side of the track, lost his footing, and came down close beside me. But in the spring he made when I fell, from my hand being fast in the bridle, I was jerked back some distance up the hill with such force, that, when I recovered a little from the shock, I felt fully persuaded that my shoulder was dislocated. We both, however, gathered ourselves up as well as we were able; and there we stood, in no condition to protect ourselves from the wolves, should they see fit to attack us; for from the way in which my horse stood, I was afraid that he had suffered still more damage than myself. When the pain of my shoulder had somewhat subsided, I examined it more minutely, and convinced myself that it was not dislocated; but the severe wrench had injured it so much, that I had no hope of making use of that arm during the remainder of my ride. And as regarded my horse, I was pleased to find that he still possessed the use of his four legs, although one of them moved with less ease than it had done before. Having contrived to get to the bottom of the descent, I again mounted, with extreme difficulty—for I could only use my left hand—in which I had to grasp both the bridle and my war-club. Had the wolves attacked us we should have been in considerable danger; for I found, on proceeding, that one of my horse's fore-legs was severely sprained: but either they were not aware of our condition, or they were in no need of a supper; for on getting beyond the confines of the swamp, I aroused several of them from their quiet hiding-places; and instead of stopping to scrutinise me and my horse, away they ran through the thick underwood, while I hallooed with all my might, giving every tree within the reach of my club, a good left-handed blow or two. In this manner, I continued along the dim and unbroken track, feigning to be a very hero,—although I candidly confess that I only recollect one or two instances in my whole life when I felt so thoroughly intimidated. Afterwards, I could not help thinking that I had only received the reward of my folly,—for I had sprained my own shoulder severely,—injured my horse's leg,—disappointed myself of the pleasant society of my friends for a few hours,—and all this for the credit of being able to boast of having dared to ride past the "wolf swamp" after night-fall, when it was known that thirteen ravenous wolves were inhabiting it.

## HUNTING A BLACK BEAR IN HIS DEN.

On a cold and cloudy day in January, 1804, I surveyed a tract of one thousand acres of land on the Little Miami, which included the Old Chillicothe town, about three miles north of this place, assisted by William and John Stevenson, or Stinson, as they were commonly called, as Chainmen, both of whom were old hunters.

In running the back line of the survey, which was mostly through a large thicket, I was about one hundred yards in advance of the chainmen and marker. Having halted to set the compass, my attention was attracted by a pile of fresh earth at the root of a large white-oak about twenty yards distant, which had fallen several years before; the trunk of which gradually rose from the root till about twenty-five feet back, it was elevated several feet from the ground. A small dog which accompanied us ran to the place and commenced barking quite fiercely. I hastened to see what the dog had discovered, and, springing upon the fallen tree, and looking over it, I discovered a large bear snugly ensconsed in his den within six feet of where I stood, staring at me with no very pleasant countenance, which induced me to retreat in double-quick time; but finding I was not pursued, I halted when I reached the compass that I had left standing.

The chainmen and marker hastened up, and inquired what was the cause of my running so fast? Upon informing that I had found a bear, they accompanied me back to the log, which we all mounted and had a fair view of him in his den, while he calmly returned our gaze, without showing any sign of either fear or hostility; supposing, no doubt, that his den was impregnable, as the tree in falling had raised several cart-loads of earth on its roots, which time had settled in the shape of a regular mound; under which he had excavated a cavern several feet in depth, sufficiently large to turn round in and to lodge comfortably.

A council of *war* was held forthwith to devise a plan for attacking Bruin. One, proposed by John Stinson, was with the marker's tomahawk and my steel-pointed jacob staff; but William Stinson, the oldest and most experienced hunter of the party, objected, saying, that from his great size and strength, if the bear was insulted with such puny weapons, he would certainly be the death of some of us; and this plan was abandoned by common consent. What then was to be done? To leave him undisturbed in his nest was not to be thought of by old hunters. After further hurried consultation, it was agreed that John should go home for his gun and dogs, while the rest remained to keep watch over Bruin's movements.

Accordingly, John set off at a long trot, while we who remained kindled a fire and patiently waited for his return. In about an hour he gave notice of his approach by a shout, which we promptly answered. He was accompanied by William McFarland, a near neighbor, both on horseback, armed with their trusty rifles, and followed by some half dozen of dogs of known *pluck* and eager for a *row*. Our armed heroes, on joining us, hastily dismounted and were rejoiced to hear that Cuffey still remained in his den. John claimed as his right the honor of leading the attack and giving the first shot, and instantly mounted the log, while I at the same moment followed his example and stood close behind him. Unfortunately, his nerves had become so much disturbed by his long race and the excitement of the moment, that when he raised "Betty," as he called his rifle, to his shoulder, he could not hold her steady, but shook and *wabbled* so much that he hesitated for some seconds to shoot. Seeing the tremor which had seized him, I entreated him to give me the gun; but this he refused. I then told him to make a sure shot, and "give it to him" above the eyes; he instantly fired, and the ball only glanced the side of his mouth, although the muzzle of his gun was not more than three feet from the bear's head. "Quick as wink" he gave a "tremendous" snort and sprang at John, who at the same moment jumped off the log and fell at full length on the ground. We all thought his hour was come, as the bear, with open mouth, flew on him, but fortunately, McFarland, on seeing John's trepidation before he fired, had cocked his gun and, before Bruin could seize his prostrate foe, put the muzzle against his side and shot him through the lungs, while the dogs seized him at the same instant and saved John's life. After a brief scuffle with the dogs, whom he knocked about as if they had been mere puppies, while the blood flew in streams from his side, mouth, and nose, he entered his cavern and soon breathed his last. On dressing him, he was found to be in prime order, and weighed near four hundred pounds.

## ADVENTURES OF AN ENGLISH SPORTSMAN ON THE PRAIRIES.

WE found tolerable accommodations in the Charleston Tavern, and the landlord was civil after a manner—which means no manners at all. Our advent created some little sensation, no *little* questioning, and a monstrous deal of incredulity as to our motives of travel. Strange, that in this new world, they won't allow a poor idle Briton to go gaping about, doing *gobe mouche*, as he does in the old! We found the little western hamlet not entirely destitute of amusement on the evening of our arrival; for in the next house to our inn, on one side, a most absurd legal cause was in process of trial before a justice,—a case of "Fiddlers" *versus* "Dancers," wherein the former claimed compensation from the latter for professional labors at a certain house-warming; and wherein, after much noisy and nasal balderdash from a couple of rival attorneys, the steward of the ball was compelled to pay the piper. And, on the other hand, the neighboring house was brilliantly lighted up for a phrenological lecture, which was numerously attended. It is somewhat singular that a practical people like the Americans should affect so intangible a science, yet they certainly do so in an extraordinary degree. Most things are good in their way, and in their place; and I will confess that the ingenious theories of Gall and Spurzheim have had their charms for me; but to be followed up, and pelted with skulls and crossbones, is the height of boredom; and such was the craniological uproar from morn till night in the Charleston Tavern, as to be perfectly "assommant."

The enthusiastic lecturer, followed by a train of disciples, carried about with him, whether in bar, bed-room, or reading-room, a couple of thick skulls—besides his own; and had each been furnished with a tongue, a more unceasing gabble of "organs," "developments," "propensities," could not have been sustained. If we entered his presence, a dead silence ensued—a score of eyes perused our craniums—and I verily believe, the singularly ample brow of one of our party would hardly have escaped forcible manipulation, had we not ordered our wagon, and changed the scene and subject for a most refreshing drive.

Most beautiful was the course we took down the river, and through the small village of Geneva,—nowise like its ancient namesake, unless in its republicanism! Having feasted our eyes upon all the scenic perfections possessed by a slow silver stream, gliding between high and woody banks, ruddy with Autumn's tints, and dotted with lovely islands, we again returned to Charleston, having during our drive marked our shooting-ground for the morrow.

The following day, keeping to the woods, we had some tolerable sport, quail-shooting—not heightened by a thorough wetting,—bagging about seventy head of game, chiefly those birds; but finding, on inquiry, that there was no farmer on the neighboring prairie whose dwelling could accommodate three strangers,—and further, the weather changing for the worse, and thereby warning us to change our front to the eastward, we resolved to return with our friend Barns to Elk Grove, and thus secure a mode of retreat to Chicago at a moment's notice. On regaining our hotel, after a long and wet day's work, I looked forward with some complacency to a good night's rest. Vain hope!—our ruthless man of skulls had converted the bar-room, separated by a thin deal floor from my chamber, into his Golgotha, and harangued a half-drunken audience till long after midnight, to the utter expulsion of the balmy god. I did not pray for him that night! Even the hardy Barns never closed an eye. Had a dozen whooping "Redskins" of the prairie rushed upon the nocturnal orgies of the Professor, and commenced their own peculiar experiments upon his cranium, I would not have pulled a trigger in his defence!

On the 8th of October, we left Fox River, and, by a fresh route across the plains, commenced our retreat. Crossing the "Nine-mile Prairie," there was scarcely a stick of timber, a hut, or other object, within the range of vision. Now and then our driver would draw our attention to an almost invisible atom on the "billowy plain," which proved to be a single horseman hunting for his cattle, turned out to graze on the fenceless pastures. Anon, we descried afar off, a heavy canvass-topped wagon, crawling slowly westward, like a huge white maggot—its interior filled with the *personnel* and *materiel* of a migrating family. On approaching us, eager faces were protruded from the rude vehicle; and earnest inquiries regarding distances, the "chills and fever" (ague,) or other equally urgent matters, were shouted out. Many a weary mile had these adventurous people traveled from their late home towards the setting sun; and they were now, perhaps, drawing nigh the bourne of their pilgrimage!

The next object on the boundless waste that attracted our gaze was a group of tall cranes, or herons—prairie turkeys, the squatters call them—looming gigantic in their solitude, and at intervals dancing, with absurd gravity, a kind of minuet—no! mazourka is the word. The bowing and pirouetting of these solemn-looking bipeds made us all laugh heartily. I fancied them so many Principals of Colleges, *unbending* after their academic labors. Our borderer assured us that the prairie turkeys seldom meet on the green without getting up a dance. My attempt to treat them to a ball of another description proved a failure, for before I arrived within range, they broke up their party, and swooped heavily away. How I longed at that moment for my fleet Arab and my long-winged Bheiree!* Never saw I a country so perfectly adapted to Falconry,—and there flew the quarry famed for the finest of flights! The ardent sportsman might spur his steed for miles over these plains without once removing his eyes from their ærial chase; and it must be his fault if he lose his hawk for want of riding,—unless, indeed, it should chance to get *spitted* by its sharp-billed foe, no uncommon incident in heron-flights. But "hold hard" Pen! or I shall soon be in the thick of a hawking digression. Besides, in a few days I shall have enough of this ever-prevailing pastime on board a Yankee steamboat!

Our second approach to Elk Grove was greeted warmly by the ladies of that sylvan retreat; for we brought back the Padrone with us. During the two fol-

* The bird used in India for long flights.

lowing days we enjoyed a very good grouse-shooting, beating fresh ground on the rolling prairie, about three miles from our temporary home, and sacking fifty-six brace of prairie hens, and a few quail. The weather was cool and breezy—the birds plentiful, though wild—and the undulating form of the ground proved much more favourable to marking than the uniform flat prairie was found to be.

A great drawback to prairie grouse shooting, is the unavoidable waste of game. Four or five brace of these heavy birds are quite load enough for the shooter to carry, and will fill to the throat any ordinary game-bag. Nor do these distant plains afford the vigilant "cad" of the English country village, or the "slip of a b'y" of the Irish hut, in aid of the sportsman's shoulders. Not to us was the pleasing importance of the British grouse shooter, as he packs, directs, and despatches his valued hamper to some expecting friend! *We* had no southron patron, no parliamentary voter, to propitiate through the palate!—no cormorant tradesman to whose monetary impatience a sop might be thrown from a distant moor! Occasionally, therefore, when we were not fortunate enough to fall in with the cottage of some settler, who was willing to exchange a draught of milk for a brace or two of birds, we found ourselves obliged to abandon part of our game to the kite and the prairie wolf. What else was to be done? Humanity and the member for Galway would exclaim, "Kill no more than you and your friends can eat!" Not more fruitless is the usual injunction of the careful mamma to the Indian cadet, to "wear flannel, and save money!"

yet both are most right, most reasonable, most impossible to obey! Our only consolation lay in the delight shown by the farmers at the havoc we made among the enemies of their grain crops.

In more than one lonely log hut, when driven thereto for food or shelter, we found young and strikingly pretty women, spinning or cooking, whilst the good man worked in the fields; and although they seemed sometimes a little startled by the unwonted appearance of a "gentleman sportsman," their cheese, milk, and buckwheat bread, were always most liberally offered; nor could they be persuaded to receive payment. Marryat, in awarding to the American fair the title of the "*prettiest* women in the world," (the epithet guardedly chosen, no doubt) does not, so far as I have had occasion of judging, give them more than their due. On these savage prairies, even, I noted more than one "western flower," that, transplanted to more civilized regions, would not have disgraced the choicest parterre.

I have named the waste of game as a serious drawback to the prairie shooter; but in the opposite scale, I must throw the delightful sense of independence and freedom with which he treads the springy sod of the prairie, and inhales its healthful breezes. He shoots without leave or "license." He feels himself lord of Nature's manor, the sporting inheritance of the "younger son." He flatters no muir-owning laird, he fees no peculative keeper, and should he see a couple of strapping young fellows, marching straight upon his position, he expects no rough warning to quit the property; on the contrary, one of them (so it happened to me) perhaps civilly asks to be allowed to look on at the sport, as he had never seen "shooting on the wing:" whilst the other, with a bow that would have been creditable to a Stanhope, a Cavendish, or a Paget, invites you to beat the coverts round his domicile on the morrow, and to dine at "his poor cottage," at two o'clock, an invitation which the former urges you to accept, with the whispered hint that his friend's "sisters are the finest *gurls* in the section, and his pork first rate!"

It was with no little regret, that on the 11th of October, forced away by bad weather, we bade adieu to Elk Grove; and, turning our backs upon the Far West, were driven by our faithful friend Barns, through a perfect hurricane of wet to Chicago. Under such meteorological auspices, I cannot say that the prairie wore a pleasing aspect. Our horses could hardly be brought to face the pitiless storm—a mouse could not have found shelter in a dozen miles, and the poor prairie hens, battered by the storm, and flying about in despair, had no leisure to rejoice over the retreat of their worst enemies, ourselves. What must be a mid-winter journey on these plains? the sleigh-borne traveler steering by compass across a trackless sea of snow, and through a fog of sleet!

In our return down the lakes, we were most fortunate in our vessel—the Illinois being a splendid, well-formed, and extremely fast boat, and the captain precisely the character fitted to rule the crowds of wild customers who frequent his decks. Huge in person, and rough and resolute in manner, though attentive in all essentials to his passengers; I don't know that anything could be more characteristic of his style, than the significant simplicity of the single word "Blake," in gold letters over his cabin door, instead of the invariable " Captain's Cabin." It reminded us of all the awful notices, " Spring-guns set here," or "Beware the dog," of the old country. I thought of our own old Blake, too, and of his famous apophthegm, "Sailors must not mind politics, but only keep foreigners from fooling us."

At Mackinaw, that gem of the Lakes, so warmly and deservedly lauded by Mrs. Jamieson, we enjoyed a stroll of two hours on shore, visiting the fort, now held by a small garrison of United States' Artillery, and the ruined redoubt of the British, on the very pinnacle of the island, from which a most striking prospect, embracing an extensive archipelago of wooded isles, lies spread beneath the spectator. The beauty of this island is more remarkable from its possessing so happy a *foil* in the hideous and dismal shores of neighboring Michigan.

Running at the rate of twelve knots down Lake Huron, and darting like a kingfisher along the rapid stream of Detroit river, our swift vessel reached the city of that name, on the evening of the 15th; a passage of about sixty-seven hours from Chicago. From Detroit, I was tempted to accompany my brother-sportsman of the 34th, to Amherstburgh, the present station of that regiment; whilst my regimental friend, whose home was more attractive than mine, pursued his course to the Falls. The annual races were going on at Amherstburg, on my arrival,[*] and the quail shooting was at its height, so that I

[*] I had, by my arrival at this place, the great satisfaction of accomplishing an object which I had long set my heart upon, namely, the
20

was fortunate as to season, and passed some very pleasant days there. The races took place on an excellent course, formed by the 34th, on the glacis of Fort Malden; and on the very ground rendered famous by bloody conflicts, maintained during the last and former wars by the British, French, Canadians, Americans, and Indians, a vast concourse of these several people were now met in amity to enjoy the sports. The Indians stood somewhat aloof from the crowd, and did not seem much inspired by the equestrian exploits; but the French and Yankees joined zealously in the amusements. Among the "Red skins," I noted not a few erect and actively-made fellows, painted, feathered, and tinselled, and looking as proud as peacocks. In the evening I met one of the objects of my admiration staggering homeward from the race-course, uproariously drunk! Where was now the proud gait and dignified reserve of the descendant of Tecumseh? Where, indeed! A drunken Indian is, in my eyes, almost as loathsome a sight as a drunken woman; and of the disgust with which the spectacle impresses me, not a little may be placed to the account of the civilized Briton who first taught the "noble savage" the brutalizing use of the fire-water. I will hereupon give the United States government, in two words, a hint for their conduct of the Florida war. Let them lay whiskey on the "war-path" of their Indian foes—a more potent agent than less "villainous saltpetre," or the West Indian bloodhound, proposed, to be employed

visiting of this Ultima Thule of Her Majesty's Western dominions, as I had done, eleven years before, that of her Eastern, the passes of the Himalaya Mountains.

against them. Poisoning wells would, to be sure, be hardly a more unrighteous mode of warfare; but what feature of this most unwarantable, and hitherto unsuccessful conflict, is otherwise than unrighteous?

The sport most novel to me, at the Malden races, was a trotting match on horseback, à la Yankee—three horses, and heats of three miles—merciless work, ridiculous and ungraceful as a spectacle, and destructive of all the romance, if there be any, of horsemanship. The English regulation of backing the wheels in harness, and turning the horse in riding, should the trot be broken, is not observed, nor indeed, necessary in this country; for an American trotter loses speed by galloping.

Amherstburg is an excellent shooting quarter; snipe and wild fowl are in swarms, woodcock and quail abundant, the latter, the finest of the species I have ever seen; and wild turkeys and deer are to be had by a little labor. Among the officers of the 34th, there are many keen sportsmen, and good shots, and the destruction of game must be considerable. My best day's sport at this place, amounted to fourteen brace and a half of quails, a couple of ducks, a woodcock, and, though last not least, as my shoulders can testify, a wild turkey. On the following day, I got another of this noble kind of feathered game; and on each occasion was much favored by luck, for I shot them both in fields of Indian corn—my charge an ounce of quail-shot—instead of hunting for them in the woods, to the abandonment of smaller game, and using ball or slugs, as is usually necessary. A very uncommon opportunity of killing, right and left, wild turkeys on the wing, was given to me on the second day, and had my second barrel been loaded with an Ely's cartridge, some of which I had with me, it is probable that, giving myself credit for ability to hit a haystack at thirty yards, the gigantic gobbler (the cock bird is so called by the natives) would, as in life, so in death, have been united with his feathered, and I may add, fat and fair partner. The addition to my shooting-book of the wild turkey, is so far satisfactory, that I believe I may now boast of having bagged, in their natural state, and in their native clime and covert, each kind of the "feathered tribes domestic," that strut or flutter in the English farm-yard, from the royal peacock, now seldom seen on festive board, to the diminutive and pie-frequenting pigeon.

The country and soil around Amherstburg, are such as would please the eye of the tourist, the sportsman, and the settler. The banks of the river are picturesque, game is most abundant, the land extremely rich, the crops plentiful, and the timber, among which, I must beg to include the *mahogany* of the 34th mess!—unexceptionable.

On the 24th of October, at eight P. M. precisely, withdrawing my legs from under the above-named hospitable board, I drained a glass of Pickwick's favorite liquor, (need I particularize " cold punch ?") to the health of that gallant regiment, at whose mess I was not suffered to feel, like the worthy philosopher above mentioned, when in the pound, that I "hadn't got no friends," and was rowed, in the dark, by the garrison crew, alongside the Buffalo steamer, up whose lofty side I was hauled, hand over hand, by the passengers, as she backed her paddles, though still going six or eight knots, to pick me up.

## BEAR HUNTING IN ARKANSAS.

The following incidents occurred to Mr. Gerstaecher, (whose narrative we have already quoted,) while he was hunting and traveling in Arkansas.

Arkansas was overrun at this time with a number of bad characters, gamblers, drunkards, thieves, murderers, who all thought that the simple-minded backwoodsmen were easier to be cheated than the wary settlers in the older states. This circumstance had given so bad a name to Arkansas, that many thought all its inhabitants went about armed to the teeth with pistols and bowie-knives; but I have traversed the State in all directions, and met with as honest and upright people as are to be found in any other part of the Union.

On the 24th of October, two heavily laden carts arrived, each drawn by one horse: they contained all sorts of things useful for settlers. Their owners are called peddlers, and they ask high prices for their goods, and are said to make a good thing of it. S. bought only a few trifles.

S., having sold most of his cattle, decided on parting with this farm, and removing to Oiltrove bottom. Our contract having been dissolved by Uhl's departure and my frequent sickness, was no longer to be thought of.

Preparations were made for moving; S. had been already to White river and made his purchase. When about to start, we found that two more oxen were necessary: we had four, but the load was too heavy with such soft boggy roads. So we rode into the woods, and drove a couple of wild bulls into the inclosure, threw nooses over their horns, and fastened them to trees. They made tremendous efforts to free themselves, jerking the leather thongs with all their force; and when they found all their struggles were in vain, they threw themselves on the ground and bellowed with rage. Thus they remained all the day and night, during which we gave them nothing but a little water to quench their thirst. About nine o'clock next morning they were yoked each with a steady old hand; the whips cracked, voices shouted, and partly from the shower of blows that fell on them, partly dragged along by their stout companions, after four or five hours' useless opposition, they went as well as if they had done nothing all their lives but draw a cart.

The heavy wagon made slow progress along the muddy tracts, softened by the autumnal rains. We arrived at White river on the morning of the 4th of November, and had to wait on the bank till evening, as it was blowing a storm, and it would have been dangerous to trust the heavy wagon to the ferry-boat in such weather.

White river is beyond all dispute the most beautiful river of Arkansas. Its clear waves form a striking contrast to those of the Mississippi and Red rivers; only towards its mouth the banks are low, and the land swampy; higher up it is enclosed by picturesque hills. It rises in the Ozark mountains, in the northwest angle of the State, where there is game in abundance; it divides into two arms, one of which falls into the Mississippi, and the other into the Arkansas.

As the wind fell, the dry cold air changed into a damp fog, which soon turned to rain, and we were glad to find shelter under the roof of a free negro, who kept a sort of tavern. Merry peals of laughter resounded from the well-lighted room, where a bright fire was blazing, and very comfortable did its warmth appear to us after our exposure to the weather. Three jovial looking fellows were sitting round it, telling stories, and roaring with laughter. Three long American rifles, with their shot-belts hanging on them, leaning in a corner, showed that the party, if not regular woodsmen, were at least out on a shooting excursion. A half empty whiskey-bottle stood on the table, and after a short conversation, I learnt that the little fat man, with sparkling eyes and ruby nose, sitting enjoying himself in the corner, and making constant love to the whiskey-bottle, was Magnus the distiller, who, with a couple of friends, was on his way to the swamps, from whence we came, for the sake of buffalo hunting. The little man drank my health, and amused me very much with his drolleries. He could think of nothing but buffaloes, swore only by buffaloes, made bets in buffalo-skins, estimated every thing by their value, and tormented the small modicum of understanding which the whiskey had left in his brains, to devise how he should be able to transport at the greatest advantage the skins of all the buffaloes he meant to kill.

- It was all in vain that I attempted to give him an idea of the almost impenetrable swamps, of the difficulty of finding the few buffaloes which were there, and of the almost impossibility when found of bringing their skins or any other part away; his countenance bore the same joyous, amicable expression as before. When I had finished my remarks, he handed me the bottle, which I put to my lips without drinking. In a voice trembling with emotion, he assured me that he was prepared to venture every thing, even life itself, for the sake of killing a buffalo, and when life was at stake, who could take into consideration a few insignificant swamp-holes or thorns! And then, as it struck him that he was a father of a family, his voice became weaker and more tremulous, his emotion increased, a flood of tears gushed from his eyes, and before I was aware, the little round figure was hanging to my neck. The heavy weight forced from me a sigh, which he took for sympathy, and he began to squeeze so hard that I was afraid I should be suffocated, when his two friends, who had been more moderate with the bottle, sprang to my rescue. But this was no easy matter, and as he clung to me he cried out, "Let me alone! he's my friend—he, he will save me!" I escaped from him by a sudden wrench, and his companions carried him off to bed, he all the while throwing about his little fat arms and legs, and called them good-for-nothing buffalo dogs. Then he again began to whine and cry, the sounds changing gradually, first into a groan and then into a snore.

We arrived at the new farm about noon next day, and found the former proprietors loading their wagon. They took their leave in the afternoon, and left us a memorial, an incredible quantity of dirt. As soon as our wagon was cleared, and the things under cover, S. returned with the two drivers for another load, leaving me in the house alone. It was in the midst of a thick forest, with a field of about seven acres, surrounded by the largest trees. But I had not much time to contemplate the beauties of nature, for, in unloading and stowing away, the hours had flown on the wings of the wind. The sun had set before I had collected wood from the forest to keep up a fire for the night, or had had time to prepare my supper; the latter duty did not take long, for my whole store of provisions consisted of maize flour, dried venison, and wild honey.

Darkness, thick darkness, lay upon the slumbering earth: yielding up my imagination to the memorials of old times, I drew the solitary chair to the blazing fire, took out my zither, and with soft mournful tones, soothed the home-sickness which in loneliness forces itself on the heart. After a time, overcome by fatigue, I extended myself on my buffalo skin before the fire, and soon a succession of fantastic dreams flitted across my brain. The little fat distiller sat with me and mine in a garden at Leipzig, relating all the hardships and dangers which he had undergone at the buffalo hunt, while my dear mother listened to him with astonishment; many other loved forms were sitting round a large table, each with their coffee before them, when we were all disturbed by a loud knocking at the gate, and started up to see what was the matter, except the little distiller, who laughingly told us it was only a tame buffalo that he had tied up at the gate. The knocking growing louder and louder, I jumped up in alarm: the fire was burnt out, thick darkness surrounded me, but the repeated loud knocking shook off the remains of sleep, and I hastened to the door.

One of the drivers who had left the day before, stepped into the room, his teeth chattering with ague. I made haste to light the fire, which soon burnt up brightly, and then looked to my patient, who had sunk down on a chair, telling me with a weak voice that his last hour was come. Luckily, I had some coffee at hand, and made him drink a couple of cups, as hot as possible, sweetened with honey. He then threw himself on the skin and was soon asleep. Next day he was somewhat better, and we passed the time as well as we could, till S. should come with his second load. I employed myself in collecting wood for the fire, and in shooting turkeys, to make our provisions last. After a week, during the last days of which, we had lived on turkeys and pumpkins, taking the latter which were very sweet and delicate, from the field of a neighbor at no great distance, S. arrived with the rest of his property, cows, horses, pigs, geese, cats, chickens, and dogs. Then there was all the bustle of arranging and settling, and then another attack of ague, which seemed regularly to have fixed itself on me in this unhealthy country. I bore up against it, but was not well enough to mount a horse till the 20th of November, when I took a ride of four or five miles with my rifle, for a breath of fresh air.

These swamps and morasses partly realize the idea which Europeans entertain of the primitive forest, but in which they are frequently deceived, for the simple reason, that on the higher dry grounds, which are covered with dry leaves and wood, fires are often made, not only by shooting parties, but by the settlers, for the sake of the grass, which comes up all the sooner, when all these enormous quantities of leaves, &c., have been burnt; and the fire does not consume the young plants only, but considerably checks the growth of the older trees, excepting in the marshes, where the ground even in summer is moist; and there the trees grow to a colossal grandeur, I have seen some measuring seven, eight, and even nine feet in diameter.

Towards evening I saw a young buck, walking quietly and circumspectively through the wood; I dismounted and left the horse to graze at leisure, while I crept nearer. He stopped when he saw the horse pawing the ground, raised his handsome head, and snuffed the air; my ball whistled through his ribs, and he fell lifeless to to the ground. Weak as I was, it was some time before I could lift the not very large animal on to the horse, when I rode slowly homewards. Just before dark, I shot a turkey with the other barrel, and did not load again, not expecting to get another shot so late in the evening. The full moon set its soft silvery light among the dark shadows of the trees, to point out my path. I might have ridden for about an hour and a half through the thick forest, on my heavily laden horse, and had gained a cattle track, which led to the house; the stillness of the night was broken by the cow-bells, the baying of the dogs, and the neigh of my horse, in expectation of a good supper, when there was a sudden rustling among the bushes on my right. I pulled up, and a herd of swine rushed in wild haste across the path, just in front of me. I was about to ride on when I heard further rustling amongst the dry leaves, and then one of largest bears of the swamps stood in the path, not above six paces from my horse's nose. He did not seem to to know what to make of the figure looming through the glade of the forest, by the light of the moon, and began to snuff the air. My rifle was not loaded, and the thought flashed upon me that I should have to fight it out with my knife; but I resolved first to try and send him a bit of lead. I placed the butt of my gun on my left toe, and succeeded in loading; but as I was about to place the copper cap, the horse, who had hitherto stood quite still, seemed inclined to examine the object before him a little closer, and giving a snort made a step forward. Master bruin, however, did not seem to like this, and with one bound he was in the jungle. Having finished my loading, I slipped off my horse, and crept into the bushes to get a shot if possible. I may have gone about twenty paces over the dry leaves, when I stood still to listen. Not the slightest sound was to be heard; though I was firmly convinced that the bear could not be above ten paces off, for the leaves were so dry that if he had gone further I must have heard it. I raised my foot gently to make another step forward, when the bear who had been standing so motionless before me, that I took him for the root of a fallen tree, almost brushed my face, and took himself off with a growl; before I could recover from my surprise, he had disappeared.

I returned, quite disappointed, to my horse, who remained quietly grazing, and rode away with two good resolutions in my head,—first, never to go a step with my gun unloaded; secondly, to seek a nearer acquaintance with Bruin on the morrow, if possible.

On the 22nd of November, I was early afoot, and although the weather was cold and disagreeable, I set off with a neighbor and eleven dogs, full of joyous hopes.

Bear-shooting in America differs according to the time of the year, and the habits of the animal. It was now late in the autumn, almost winter, so that they could be hunted with dogs. Well mounted, with not less than from four to about eight or ten dogs, the hunters seek in the thickest and most unfrequented parts of the forest the favorite haunts of the bear. The men ride slowly through the thorns and creepers, the dogs seeking in all directions till they find a fresh trail, or a bear breaks cover, when they follow up in full cry. If the bear is fat he seldom runs far, but takes to a tree, or shows fight; if there are not dogs enough to master him, he knocks them over and continues his flight. If he takes to a tree, his fate is soon sealed by the rifle.

We had ridden along quietly for about an hour, when the dogs gave tongue, and started off, we after them as well as we could. My horse was an old hand at it, and I had nothing to do but to sit fast as he leaped the fallen trees, and try to avoid the creepers, which however often checked, and sometimes threw us.

Keeping up with the dogs was out of the question. I had long lost sight of my companion; I listened, and it appeared that the bear had turned to the left, towards the river; could he reach it, he was safe,—it was too cold for the dogs—besides, they would hardly venture to swim, and we also must have remained on the bank.

I changed my course to cut him off, and luckily hit upon one of the cattle tracks that cross the wood in all directions. Once clear of the thorns, we went at a good pace, and soon heard the pack approaching. Suddenly the horse swerved to one side with a snort, and the bear burst out of the thicket. The moment he saw the horse, he stopped short and gave a deep growl. I had sprung off, and the bear had hardly stopped, when my ball was in his shoulder. The pack was close upon him, and he summoned all his strength to escape from the dogs; but the wounded shoulder checked his pace, the dogs attacked him, and he rose on his hind legs to oppose them. I could not venture a second shot for fear of injuring some of them, so charged him with my knife, and plunged it from behind the shoulder into his heart; this, with the furious bites of the dogs, soon ended his life.

My companion arrived at this moment, tired to death, all torn with the thorns, and his horse covered with foam. He was not a little vexed at coming too late; however, he helped to break up the bear, and strip off his skin,—and as each of us had a bag under the saddle, we divided the prize, and rode slowly home. The carcase is always equally divided amongst the hunters; the skin belongs to the first shot.

## COLONEL DAVID CROCKETT'S ENCOUNTER WITH A BEAR.

IN his autobiography * the Colonel gives the following story. His dogs had once attracted his attention to a tree where there was no game. He thus proceeds:

When they saw me coming, away they went again; and, after a little time, began to bark as before. When I got near them, I found they were barking up the wrong tree again, as there was no game there. They served me in this way three or four times, until I was so infernal mad, that I determined, if I could get near enough, to shoot the old hound at least. With this intention I pushed on the harder, till I came to the edge of an open prairie, and looking on before my dogs, I saw in and about the biggest bear that ever was seen in America. He looked, at the distance he was from me, like a large black bull. My dogs were afraid to attack him, and that was the reason they had stopped so often, that I might overtake them. They were now almost up with him, and I took my gobblers from my back and hung them up in a sapling, and broke like a quarter horse after my bear, for the sight of him had put new springs in me. I soon got near to them, but they were just getting into a roaring thicket, and so I couldn't run through it, but had to pick my way along, and had close work even at that.

In a little time I saw the bear climbing up a large black oak tree, and I crawled on until I got within about eighty yards of him. He was sitting with his breast to

---

* Life of Colonel David Crockett, published by G. G. Evans, Philadelphia, 1859.

me; and so I put fresh priming in my gun, and fired at him. At this he raised one of his paws and snorted loudly. I loaded again as quick as I could, and fired as near the same place in his breast, as possible. At the crack of my gun here he came, tumbling down; and the moment he touched the ground, I heard one of my best dogs cry out. I took my tomahawk in one hand, and my big butcher-knife in the other, and run up within four or five paces of him, at which he let my dog go, and fixed his eyes on me. I got back in all sorts of a hurry, for I know'd if he got hold of me, he would hug me altogether too close for comfort. I went to my gun and hastily loaded her again, and shot him the third time, which killed him good.

I now started for home, and got my brother-in-law, and my young man, and four horses, and went back. We got there just before dark, and struck up a fire, and commenced butchering my bear. It was some time in the night before we finished it; and I can assert, on my honor, that I believe he would have weighed six hundred pounds. It was the second largest I ever saw. I killed one, a few years after, that weighed six hundred and seventeen pounds. We got our meat home, and I had the pleasure to know that we now had plenty, and that of the best; and I continued through the winter to supply my family abundantly with bear-meat and venison from the woods.

www.ingramcontent.com/pod-product-compliance
Lightning Source LLC
Chambersburg PA
CBHW031901220426
43663CB00006B/719